Catholic Social Teaching

Catholic Social Teaching
*As I Have Lived, Loathed,
and Loved It*

Philip S. Land, S.J.
Foreword by James Hug, S.J.

Loyola University Press
Chicago

© 1994 Center of Concern
All rights reserved
Printed in the United States of America

Loyola University Press
3441 North Ashland Avenue
Chicago, Illinois 60657

Center of Concern
3700 13th Street, N.E.
Washington, D.C. 20017

Cover design by Tammi Longsjo
Interior design by Jill Salyards

Library of Congress Cataloging-in-Publication Data
Land, Philip S.
Catholic social teaching: as I have lived, loathed, and loved it:
how one Catholic—and others—think about social teaching and the
ministry of social doing / by Philip S. Land.
    p.   cm.
    Includes bibliographical references and index.
    ISBN 0-8294-0808-8 (alk. paper)
    1. Sociology, Christian (Catholic) 2. Land, Philip S. 3. Church
    and social problems—Catholic Church. 4. Catholic Church
    —Doctrines. I. Title.
BX1753.L34   1995
261.8'0822—dc20   94-13207
                                                        CIP

To the Thirty-fourth General Congregation of the Society of Jesus, 1995.

Jesuits the world over, facing what the future holds, are as never before preparing as a body for that event. With faith in the Spirit and in one another, the preparations will prove a generous response to God's call in a true kairos *moment.*

Contents

✠ Foreword

F ather Land was justly proud of many accomplishments during his years with the Pontifical Commission Justice and Peace from the mid-sixties, when it was founded—at the end of Vatican II—to the mid-seventies, when he was forced to leave Rome for his dissent against *Humanae Vitae* (Condemnation of artificial birth control). I will highlight just three of them.

In recent years, some of Father Land's fondest memories were of the key role he played in the foundation of the Society for Development and Peace (SODEPAX), a joint commission of the Vatican and the World Council of Churches to address issues of society, development, and peace. Father Land had helped conceptualize and organize the commission at an outdoor restaurant in Trastevere in Rome. He identified and secured George Dunne, S.J., to be its first director. He helped to prepare a number of international conferences to launch the commission. When the work of those conferences was criticized by Latin Americans for failing to embrace the liberation agenda, Father Land helped organize more conferences to explore the liberation perspective. Later, Gustavo Gutierrez sent him an autographed copy of his classic *Theology of Liberation,* thanking him for the invitation to discuss these ideas at one of those meetings, "thus providing the occasion for me to write this book."

Then in 1970, the staff of the Pontifical Commission Justice and Peace was asked to prepare the preliminary document for the upcoming synod of bishops. Father Land served as the principal drafter of the document *Justitia in Mundo* (Justice in the World).

Father Land was the obvious choice when someone was needed to present the draft to the commission of cardinals and bishops responsible for the synod. When he reached the passage arguing that the Church should not speak about injustice unless it was willing to recognize its own injustice, one of the cardinals objected, "The Church does not have any injustices." The room fell silent. Finally, Father Land spoke up: "Your Eminence, I really believe if we cannot say that the Church has injustices, we should not have a document." The ice was broken. Father Land won the day. The passage remains in the final document from the synod, a lasting inspiration for those working for justice to this day.

Once accepted, the preliminary document was forwarded with a study guide and questions to every diocese in the world. Father Land helped to prepare those materials and six background pamphlets to go with them. He made sure all six came from the perspective of the peoples of the Southern Hemisphere and included among them one containing the highlights of the Medellin Conference of Bishops held in 1968 in Colombia. For the first time, the foundational liberation themes were made available to the worldwide Church.

As replies to the study guide and questions flowed back to the Vatican, Father Land was again selected to sift and digest them. He prepared the final document and wrote the keynote address for the synod, which was delivered by the presiding cardinal. Though the cardinal of Genoa said to him, "You are destroying the Church!" the synod document passed with 94 percent of the vote. Father Land then was instrumental in developing six commentaries on the document to help guarantee that its impact would be broad and deep worldwide, as indeed it has been.

Then he and the rest of the staff at the Pontifical Commission Justice and Peace went back to working for the establishment of justice and peace commissions in every nation, building thereby a strong infrastructure to guarantee that Catholic social teaching like that of the synod would fall upon fertile ground and lead to social action.

During these years, Father Land was frequently part of Vatican delegations to international meetings. Vatican delegates were instructed to remain unobtrusive, but that was not possible for him. On one occasion, in a working group, he introduced language for the United Nations charter on the Rights and Duties of States that one delegate dismissed as the foggiest motion she had ever heard. However, at the urging of an African delegate, Father Land defended his suggestion, resulting in nearly unanimous support for his position. His proposal is perhaps more crucial today than it was twenty years ago, namely, that the UN charter should (and now does) contain language about the "obligation of the nation or nations toward the international good under the guidance of international social justice."

While Father Land's life held far more than a normal share of dramatic moments, policy battles, and escapades, most people who knew him in recent years will testify that the greatest of his world-class achievements was his profound humanity. That humanity was the result of many a fierce and painful fray as he attempted to respond to the challenges of the twentieth century as an intellectually honest and loyal person of faith in the Church.

Father Land's life spanned a substantial part of the twentieth century, from before the 1917 codification of canon law through Vatican II's attempt to shift the Church's focus from the law to the Spirit, and to recent efforts to regain some central ground in that movement. Standing with the Church, Father Land engaged each of the forceful winds that blew through the open windows of *aggiornamento*—winds of modern psychological, sociological, and historical thinking; of civil rights and liberation movements; of feminism and ecology; of ecumenism and the emergence of the age of the laity in the Catholic Church. He embraced and was personally transformed by the truth and beauty he found in each development. Nor did he fail to challenge them when he felt it necessary.

Two keys help explain Father Land's remarkable spirit. The first key appeared shortly after he joined the Jesuits in 1929. After the stock market crash in October 1929, when poor and homeless people began to show up at the novitiate seeking help, and Phil and other young novices talked with them, the experience ignited in him a commitment to the poor and marginalized that governed the choice of his life's work and inspired his daily choices thereafter.

The second key relates to Teresa of Avila, whom he called "my great saint of prudence." In his studies, Father Land came across a story on how Teresa had struggled with deciding whether to close a particular monastery. After agonizing over the issues and consulting with many, she came to the moment of decision. She said, "I know, whichever way I decide, having so carefully tried to work out its morality, that it will be good before God, even though a week later I may regret it." Reflecting on her remarks, Phil exclaimed, "Ah, that's a magnificent moral system. Can you imagine what a relief it was for Teresa? I run into so many people who are so tortured about God's will. It's a huge opening—a moral system in which you are privileged to make mistakes!"

Father Land died on January 20, 1994, as this volume was being prepared for publication.

James Hug, S.J.
Executive Director
Center of Concern
Washington, D.C.

✠ Preface

B efore explaining the title and subtitle, I have several remarks to make. First, and perhaps most important of all, I treat much more the methodology than the content of Catholic social teaching. In addition, there are a few chapters—those on the reign of God in society, on structural change, and on political theology—which thrust toward the ministry of promoting social justice, acting, and intervening.

This is a book about one person's journey, a journey of change and growth to hew out fundamental ideas about social doing, and about practical political wisdom. Most of that change has gone on in my approach, in my method, rather than in content. I now believe that to have a method of reflecting on Catholic social teaching is more important than to have a body of fixed truths.

Second, because of its theological orientation, method impinges on content in this book. This will be puzzling to those who, like myself, grew up with a largely philosophical Catholic social teaching. Actually, while people like myself were moving toward theology, theologians were exploring the more philosophical themes of Catholic social teaching.

John Coleman (1982b, 67) notes this double movement in a 1978 essay on political theology. He observes that "many systematic theologians have explicitly turned their attention to the ethical and political as necessary ingredients in a valid hermeneutic of biblical and doctrinal symbols." He cites as examples Avery Dulles, David Tracy, Langdon Gilkey, and Gregory Baum. He further characterizes this "turn to ethical and political consequences of doctrinal statements as a necessary feature of theology." All of this, Coleman adds, was inspired by political theology. Having noted this movement from theology to philosophy, Coleman notes a reverse movement as well: "Catholics have begun to transform traditional Church's social teaching, largely, if not entirely philosophical, into a genuine theology based on the Bible" (ibid., 68). I maintain that especially in his encyclical *Centesimus Annus* (Hundredth anniversary of *Rerum Novarum*) John Paul II is most explicit about his social teaching being in this genre.

I plainly stand in that second current. From my earlier excessively philosophical understanding of Catholic social teaching, I have proceeded to a theological understanding of Catholic social teaching. My movement was inspired mainly by Vatican II, but not exclusively by it. Hence, the reader will encounter the gospel call to love of neighbor, social grace, the unity of the orders of creation and redemption, the reign of God, reading signs of the times to find out God's call, and the eschatological aspects of the political order.

This new impetus to work out Catholic social teaching more in theological than philosophical terms brought me into a perplexing situation in the late seventies. Shortly after my return to the States from my twenty-year sojourn in the Eternal City, I was invited to give summer courses of a couple weeks on Catholic social teaching at two Jesuit universities. I gave the students a large dose of the theological themes noted above. It proved too large for the organizers of the course who had invited me. They were distinctly displeased. Though presumably of the new school of contextual and historical theology, they nevertheless expected that such methodology (assuming that it was my approach) would be applied to more traditional normative statements of Catholic social teaching.

On the philosophical side in this book are some chapters mainly devoted to another dialogue going on within my understanding of Catholic social teaching, the channeling of the normative component of nature through the freedom and historicity of the subject.

Third, for a variety of reasons, a fairly large number of Catholics have dismissed Catholic social teaching. Some consider it too abstract. Others believe it demands acceptance when the proposition set forth lacks compelling intellectual justification. For others Catholic social teaching is based excessively on reason, inadequately founding itself on the Bible. For still others, Catholic social teaching fails to address the real sufferers of their society.

Reflecting on all these complaints, I encountered Protestant sources that affirmed Catholic social teaching. The World Council of Churches' *Ecumenical Review* devoted an entire issue to the hundredth anniversary of *Rerum Novarum* (The Condition of Labor). The secretary-general of WCC, Emilio Castro (1991), in an editorial introduction says of *Rerum Novarum:* "This encyclical, a landmark in Roman Catholic social thought, has had an influence far beyond the inner circles of the Roman Catholic Church." In the opening article, Latin America's illustrious Protestant theologian, Jose Miguez Bonino (1991), says: "In the last hundred years the Catholic magisterium has developed a significant body of teaching on social questions. . . ." In another article, Dr. John S. Pobee, associate director of the WCC's Programme on Ecumenical Theological Education in Bossey, Switzerland, adds: "I am happy for the landmarking social statements by the church of Rome" (Pobee 1991).

This is a book about the retrieval of Catholic social teaching, celebrated by a growing number of Protestants, condemned by a large (now smaller) number of Catholic thinkers. That retrieval ends (see the concluding chapter) by reintroducing the thirteenth-century Dominican theologian Thomas Aquinas. In his moral treatises, Aquinas embraces the whole spectrum of theological and moral virtues. I have singled out Thomas's approach to making moral judgments in the political field. Although I use a number of lengthy quotations from Aquinas, some are a bit abstruse. I hope that will not dissuade readers from exploring my retrieval of the immense contribution Aquinas has made to Catholic social teaching.

Fourth, Saint Ignatius of Loyola says in his *Spiritual Exercises* that love shows itself, not in words, but in deeds. The 1971 synod (which produced *Justitia in Mundo*) takes the same position. After declaring that "while the Church is bound to give witness to justice, she recognizes that anyone who ventures to speak to people about justice must first be just in their eyes"; the synod goes further to affirm that "unless the Christian message of love and justice shows its effectiveness through action . . . it will only with difficulty gain credibility with the men of our times" (*JM* 35; Gremillion 1976). John Paul II echoes that sentiment in his encyclical celebrating

Rerum Novarum: "Today more than ever, the church is aware that her social message will gain credibility more immediately from the witness of action than as a result of its internal logic and consistency" (*CA* 57). This book has little more to say about the credibility of the Church's witness, but I recognize that we had better not call others to the reforms we are not prepared to undertake in our own conduct.

Fifth, I am deeply concerned to avoid sexist language. In an earlier draft I resolutely inserted *sic* in quotations whenever exclusively masculine language occurred. However, this practice resulted in an annoying and disfigured text. A quotation of six lines required seven *sic*s. So, in spite of some misgivings, I have decided to let the exclusively masculine language stand.[1]

The fundamental question I addressed in this essay asks, could some others be moved by my discovery that embracing the historical and experiential in social teaching does not require abandoning what is right and necessary at the core of natural law? Might they not be helped as I was to see that they need not throw the baby out with the bathwater as they shift from rigid neo-scholastic natural law to historicism and biblical and theological themes?

Sixth, the pages that follow record much ambivalence, if not downright ambiguity at times. Where this is true, what light am I providing? I have thought that over and come to the conclusion that I am not different from most people in this matter. It is only a question of the content of one's ambiguities. All, or almost all, have their ambiguities, mainly because we are all caught up in choices between values that are hard to weigh up. Uncertainty is the very stuff of ambiguity. So it may well be that, as I have learned from another's wrestling with values in conflict, others may learn from my grappling with mine.

Next, is what I have produced in these chapters indisputably Catholic social teaching? When I note with satisfaction that the response of Catholic social teaching to conservative positions is founded solidly on indisputable philosophy (or, at least, on my idiosyncratic interpretation of indisputable philosophy), is this Catholic social teaching? For example, are the philosophical norms brought together in chapter 11 objective or universal? Or are they just the plain ideology of popes or of myself? These are surely legitimate questions.

Finally, for whom am I writing this book? Certainly not for professional theologians in social ethics. Some of these may here or there find an enlightening elaboration of themes long familiar to them. But I have neither the competence to address such theologians nor the desire to do so. The audience I aspire to reach is rather that of social practitioners, perhaps some *praxis*-oriented theologians, certainly people desiring to explore the theological dimension of Catholic social teaching and to debate methodological issues.

The title I owe to my colleague, James Hug, S.J.[2] Before I examine some aspects of the title, I must make some remarks to help you understand the structure of the book.

I have two comments to make about the title. First, it is Catholic social teaching, not Catholic social thought. For half a century I have lectured on Catholic social teaching. I am now persuaded that *thought* is too fixed, too determined, too eternal. It suggests "fixed in cement." It is already there, already thought out, the Church's possession; its doctrine, firmly set and binding, only needing to be taught. This attitude reminds one of *Les Pensèes du Pascal.*

Catholic social teaching, I now believe, consists largely of truths for social action fabricated through reading signs of the times. Alternatively, Catholic social teaching may very well evolve from a people who, suffering some particular situation, work out their social and political truth by allowing their suffering to guide their analysis and their theologizing. I say more about this below. But why not Catholic social *thinking?* Is this not still more dynamic, more forward-thrusting? Perhaps so. But teaching has for me precisely that thrust forward, while it tenaciously clings to its moorings.

Second, the title links ministry of social action to teaching. That is because, as I explain more amply in the last chapter, Catholic social teaching is for me a practical wisdom. It is a *practikon*. It is *praxis*. Thus, it is forged in doing. Doing will force rethinking, refurbishing of a truth that may have lost some of its tenability.

And why the quixotic subtitle? It reflects my half century of teaching, writing the Church's social teaching, and living with it in other ways. Sometimes I found it unresponsive to reality or idealistic in the sense of being purely ideational and unhistoric. In addition, the subtitle conveys my satisfaction and joy in finding that Catholic social teaching—I limit myself here to its more philosophical side—often hit the nail on the head, where other systems of social teaching failed.

"Catholic social teaching I have lived" refers to the subject matter of the first two chapters, "One Catholic Social Teaching Journey." The last part of the subtitle, "Catholic social teaching I have loathed," refers to all the tortured wrestling with the uncertainties of the analyses I essayed as groundwork for my social thinking. Did I have my economic facts and analysis correct? If that was correct, were my ethical analyses on target? How much of what I affirmed as Catholic social teaching would not, on closer inspection, turn out to be my ideology? Much of my moral teaching in the social field came out of neo-scholasticism, which implanted in my head a set of "eternal verities." As I came to acknowledge that many of them were not eternal truths at all, I loathed (a milder verb would be more appropriate here) the educational system that had taught them as verities and I loathed my own complicity in passing them on to others.

Elitism! Many critics, mostly liberation theologians, condemned the papal encyclicals of Catholic social teaching for their elitism. They expected the rich and the powerful, the employer class, to change unjust structures. Until very recently, the appeal for workers to change the unjust structures of their societies was not heard. Rather, workers must not heed those who were calling for class struggle, for the popes conceived of society as a harmony of ordered relations. Classes would abide in all-encompassing love and peace. But the injustice would go on eternally, because the popes assured the oppressors there would be no class struggle!

I came to loathe the very word *order* as it is used in papal writing. I do not doubt that social relationships must have order, but official Catholic social teaching meant much more by that term, recalling the Latin *ordo,* a set of relationships directly willed by God. Since the Creator knows what ordered relationships of human society should be, they must be implemented in society as eternally fixed social systems.

For the ecclesiastical mind the term *order* suggested that disorderliness was out of order. Disorder evoked stress, uncertainty, the peril of uncharted waters. It was wholly unimaginable that disorder could be a necessary condition for bringing forth the new. "The old order changeth yielding place to the new, and God fulfills himself in many ways." Such a belief was foreign to the training I received. Disorder and its uncertainties were viewed as calls for authority to restore order.

In recent decades, I learned to loathe Church teaching about women. Here, if any place, a patriarchal ideology paraded as social teaching. Following his position on natural law, Leo XIII's *Rerum Novarum*, as the writings of his successors had, proclaimed that "it is according to women's nature to be in the home. Home keeping is their natural vocation." Curiously, nowhere does a papal encyclical speak of "men's natural vocation." But papal teachings insist that women do have a vocation accorded them by nature to be homemakers. Just why men do not share that homemaking nature by nurturing, cooking, or housekeeping has not been made clear. Presumably, nature frees them for work outside the home.

Why must women be almost completely excluded from careers outside the home? This demurrer should not be taken to mean that I do not celebrate women's nurturing characteristics. Nor do I fail to recognize that many mothers, forced by sheer economic necessity to take a job, would much prefer to be home with their children. Nor should this be interpreted as unconcern for the future of the family.

There was much more I loathed, as the reader encounters in the first chapter.

In the subtitle, "Catholic social teaching I have loved" refers to the new beginnings after the death of neo-scholasticism. I loved the emerging ideas, the more historical approach to the normative, the new processes and methodology, all the biblical and theological themes unfolding in the years before Vatican II, both in the council and in the theology that grew out of it. I loved the social and political dimensions that the Scriptures were bringing to Catholic social teaching.

To confine myself here to my love of the noetically normative,[3] that is, to what proved authentic in the more philosophical norms of Catholic social teaching, I note that until Vatican II philosophical metaphors dominated cultural metaphors and theological symbols. I loved and indeed delighted in my repeated experiences of the ability of Catholic social teaching to critique and illuminate contradictions in our contemporary culture and society. Once Catholic social teaching embraced more of culture and theology, its critical function gained hugely. This is the burden of chapter 7 (Moral Making in the Social Order) and chapter 8 (The Reign of God over Social Structures), but it is also noted in chapter 5 (Catholic Social Teaching 1).

In Moscow in the early seventies, two peace institutes of Vienna, one Catholic, one Soviet, invited some twenty European religious peaceniks to meet in Moscow with the Soviet's Peace Committee to promote detente. I was the only non-European then in the Pontifical Commission Justice and Peace (more about this later.) To my astonishment the secretary of state sanctioned my going, albeit unofficially. In the Soviet capital I was asked to speak to the assembly, including prominent Soviets, about Catholic social thinking. At the end of my presentation one of the more eminent Soviets took the floor to declare that if Karl Marx had heard what they had, he could never have asserted that religion is the opiate of the people. Later, over coffee, a Communist economist from Czechoslovakia told me that the eminent Soviet would never have dared make that statement in public if he did not really mean it. He had heard a body of truth that wholly captivated him. My Communist friend viewed Catholic social teaching (or, at least, my rendering of it) more kindly than did Cardinal Santos, archbishop of Manila, who forbade his seminarians to attend my lectures at the Jesuit Ateneo de Manila. (Although Western officials later dismissed détente as a trap, I wonder if some of the Soviet overtures in that epoch, such as the one I participated in, were not genuine enough, even if commingled with the harsh reality of the Cold War.)

I experienced joy and satisfaction repeatedly as I worked on my *Shaping the Welfare Consensus: The U.S. Catholic Bishops' Contribution* (1988). Therein I became convinced that Catholic social teaching decisively drove a *via media* between conservatives and liberals in the raging and still ongoing debate. It did so, not by chipping a little off both of the opposed philosophies, but rather by inserting between them its own original understanding of the social dimension of human persons. When the conservatives would trust welfare virtually exclusively to market forces and individual effort and when the liberals would entrust the bulk of welfare to government, Catholic social teaching affirms the principle of subsidiarity. Unlike the liberal or conservative positions, this principle is bipolar: individuals and small social units do as much as they can do for themselves; larger organizations do what the individual and small organizations cannot do for themselves.

Catholic social teaching offered its own solution on another issue in the welfare debate. Conservatives considered welfare a giveaway. Saying that taxpayers demand a quid pro quo, they wanted to force mothers with small children who received government payments to work. Liberals, swayed by the force of this argument, but still seeking a decent welfare program, were prepared to support the work requirement provided that Medicaid and child care were added to the conservative program. Catholic social teaching interposed a different principle. It began with the premise that the whole of society benefits from mothers (or fathers) staying home to raise children. The *quid* in a quid pro quo, if one insists on that language, is the contribution made by parents to society as a whole. The *quo,* the return society makes, is the welfare payment. Catholic social teaching would approve a voluntary program of employment for welfare recipients, but remains opposed to compulsory work.

An analogous point gave me further satisfaction: Catholic social teaching paired rights and responsibilities. In the debate over welfare, liberals pushed for rights (entitlements) while conservatives demanded full responsibility from welfare recipients. Liberals gave only slight attention, if any, to responsibilities. Conservatives harped insistently on responsible work attitudes and resoluteness in seeking job training.

As I read Catholic social teaching, it spoke equally of rights and responsibilities, but it was conscious of the danger in pushing responsibility and assuming that enough jobs paying enough to lift workers out of poverty were available. (Three years after I did that study, I read in the news that a group of Republican members of Congress were shocked that a two-year study they sponsored reported that thousands of jobs fail to pay enough to lift the employee out of poverty.) I carefully examined the claim that most welfare recipients were women who preferred a handout from government to earning their way, but I was keenly aware that some liberals blindly responded to any and every call for new entitlements, a response that could not be countenanced by Catholic social teaching. And conservatives, naturally, viewed as socialist the bishops' stand in "Economic Justice for All" that rights are not just the political rights to free speech, representation, and freedom of enterprise, but also include access to gainful employment, gratifying and useful human work, and a voice in the economic as in the political order.

An item in the *Washington Post* (November 4, 1990) enhances my satisfaction with the capacity of Catholic social teaching to correct absurd social views. Mr. Herbert Stein, former member of a presidential economic council, writes about proportionate taxation in this vein: "The feeling that fairness requires taxing richer people a larger proportion of their income than less rich people is a perfectly legitimate feeling. That feeling is a sufficient justification for progressive taxation." I agreed with this point. Stein, however, goes on: "But there is no requirement for anyone to have that feeling. . . . There is no objective argument to convert someone who does not have it."

Thus, in Stein's philosophy of feelings as guide to policy, there can be no commonly accepted policies. In contrast the beauty of Catholic social teaching and other social philosophies is that they provide a foundation built on our common human nature. Consequently there is a common good to which all contribute according to their abilities and from which all share according to their needs.[4]

Surely one of the most powerful and most consistently unchallengeable contributions of Catholic social teaching has been its function as critic of culture and society. Indeed, for some this is the only legitimate function of Catholic social teaching. In other words, for them Catholic social teaching can help us to detect untruth, but it has nothing positive to say about what the contours of society ought to look like.

For instance, that Catholic social teaching condemns some facets of capitalism has proven unsatisfactory to those who believe that capitalism merits outright rejection by Christian theology. For example, when Count Della Torre was editor of the official Vatican daily *Osservatore Romano,* in the latter days of World War II, it condemned capitalism as atheistic on its front page. Although official Catholic social teaching did not totally reject capitalism, it has persistently, accurately, and ever more comprehensively critiqued its failures.

The U.S. Catholic bishops strongly criticized capitalism in *Economic Justice for All,* their economic pastoral of 1986, even while acknowledging that the U.S. economic system had been highly productive in goods, jobs, and economic well-being. The Canadian bishops were much more negative in their earlier economic pastoral. In their earlier drafts, the U.S. bishops sounded more like their Canadian cousins, but yielded to the criticism that they had pushed critiques of capitalism too far. Some U.S. Catholics would have preferred the earlier, more critical drafts.

John Paul II, for his part, has many of us puzzled. He had been a severe critic of capitalism up to the 1991 celebration of the hundredth anniversary of *Rerum Novarum.* Indeed, his 1981 encyclical, *Laborem Exercens* (Human Work) inverted the traditional relationship which places capital over labor. One prominent theologian (Baum 1987) declared that the pope now stood on the side of socialism. That position cannot easily be sustained after John Paul II's encyclical *Centesimus Annus,* which celebrates *Rerum Novarum.* There, on the contrary, many have found strong praise of capitalism or, at least, of the business makers and their market economy.

While capitalism predated the Enlightenment of the eighteenth century, capitalism is justifiably regarded as a major fruit of that philosophy's concentration on the individual and science as the tools of progress. The Catholic church has come to recognize, especially since Vatican II, what was right and good in the Enlightenment. In particular it has moved toward recognizing the legitimate autonomy of the secular. But there were fundamentally corrosive elements in that movement. My book, *Shaping the Welfare Consensus,* extensively explored its conservative and liberal roots in the Enlightenment. Much of my socioeconomic critique was based on the principal documents of Catholic social teaching. I analyzed the fruits of individualism in the profit motive and in the theory of unfettered economic markets. Both analyses relied on the scientific spirit of the Enlightenment and its rejection of all transcendental morality.

There was much more that would prove destructive in the Enlightenment. It was aggressively anthropocentric, with disastrous results for the environment. It was committed to patriarchalism. Hence, because the Enlightenment was a man's world, women were confined to the home to nurture children and provide the morality that was not required in the world of men's affairs. Women were excluded from science, which, like business and commerce, was the exclusive domain of men.

According to the economic theory of the Enlightment, male aggressivity, competition, and getting ahead by climbing over the bodies of others characterized the world of commerce. A crude calculus of individual profit making would determine all economic decisions. Industrialism was molded in the male matrix of individualism.[5]

Experiences of both loathing and loving occupy these pages. I am moved to recount them because people who have heard me explore them have repeatedly urged me to share with others in writing. Over the past four decades I have written fairly extensively on Catholic social teaching. I have also taught in the classsrooms of St. Louis University, the Pontifical Gregorian University in Rome, and numerous others. I have spoken on Catholic social teaching in a dozen different countries on five continents. From all that, I have repeatedly been exhorted to "write that up."

Writing that up turns out to be writing up the half-century learning process of one Phil Land. Only the first chapters are *nominatim* biographical, but, in effect, so are the remaining chapters. I do not know whether all theology is biographical, but I do know that the life of Jesus was finally fixed in the New Testament and it is in that life that we Christians discover the elements of our faith and ethics. No one fails to recognize the amount of autobiography contained within the pages of Saint Augustine, and much contemporary theology is narrative. Frequently it narrates the story of one's own experience or that of another. Alongside the traditional norms of ethics, some moralists insist that others—holy people—can teach the norms that Jesus lived.

Here is one aspect of the narrative about Christ that affects my moral making: it is narrated that Jesus proclaimed the universally salvific will of the Father. By this I understand that I and all others are anthropologically eschatological, that I am not totally defined anthropologicaly by averring that I have mind and body or that I am a spirit incorporated. Neither do freedom and responsibility (with rights and duties) define me. For besides these two tremendous gifts of nature, God has given to us human beings the gift of living into and beyond the last days, the *eschata*. I can reject that gift, and, if I do, being with God for all eternity will not be verified of me. That promise, that salvation, has been given to me to either reject or accept.

The Jesus story, which becomes a part of my story, adds several dimensions to my living the moral life, as Vatican II confirms. The council laid stress on Jesus' gift of his Spirit to dwell with the Church all its days, providing light to understand what is moral and strength to live by that light. I do not claim that Christian norms are superior to those of non-Christians, but the Jesus story conveys attitudes that would not easily be available in other traditions. Other chapters explore how the story of Jesus affects Catholic social teaching and life.

I would like to note here two concepts which I have learned from the German theologian Karl Rahner, and which I develop in this book: that the ground of all moral making is the fundamental option for God as ground of our being and that love of neighbor is strengthened by realizing its inseparability from love of God. I also like Rahner's way of linking the reign of God in creation and in redemption. That linking, we shall see, has fundamental meaning for a good society.

Another concept with social meaning is God's call to us. There may be little or none at all of the thematic or the normative in God's call to us. But many of the attitudes that readers encounter here demonstrate that I view Catholic social teaching and Catholic social doing as based on far more than norms and themes. These chapters show my strong emphasis on Jesus living, doing, and calling us to the reign of God. Jesus guarantees us that faithful discipleship will move toward the reign on earth and the reign that lies beyond.

These paragraphs on the normative lead me to make one further comment. The last chapter is entitled "Practical Reason, Practical Wisdom, and the Retrieval of Thomas Aquinas." Writers about morals often question the term *practical reason*. For them, it precludes the experiential, the historic, and the individual with individual experience. They emphasize the role of Jesus in making us conscious of the reign of God. Theologians since Vatican II are right in raising such questions about the role of reason in moral theology, but, as I say in the text, they do not condemn practical reason as the moral agent developed by Aquinas but as the neo-scholastics distorted it.

This, too, I address. I believe that my last chapter reveals Thomas as a forerunner of the post–Vatican II theologians. Obviously, over the centuries new and vital insights in theology have come to bear on moral making. Indeed, Vatican II heralds these. I do not suggest that the great Dominican theologian had already thought of all these. But in my reading of him, Aquinas's methodology in moral science is reflected in recent moral theology, albeit in different terminology.

The same is true of practical wisdom, as I choose to translate Aquinas's virtue of prudence. It contains much of the historical and the singular. It draws upon experience, looking at the totality of an act and not only at the thing done. Therefore Aquinas says that the person making a moral judgment is an artist.

I write as a social economist who, in the years of Vatican II and since the council, gave as much time to theology as to economics. But I do not write as a professional theologian, although my themes and methodological explorations carry me deeply into theological ground. I several times sensed that I was in over my head. Yet I had to be there and struggle to swim, avoiding shoals of more perilous waters. There are murky spots in these pages. But then I am not writing for professional theologians. I am trying only to throw light on issues of Catholic social teaching for practitioners in social teaching and doing.

✠ Acknowledgments

T his book was produced by fits and starts as other tasks
intervened. One result is that it has been in the hands of
a series of editors—all very capable—before encountering the
final and definitive editors of Loyola University Press.

Ruth Coyne, then on the staff of the Center of Concern,
edited the earliest manuscript. A very radically altered version
then fell under the scrutiny of Mary Elsbernd, O.S.F., recently
returned from completing her doctorate at Louvain in the field
of this book's subject matter, Catholic social teaching. Elsbernd
is now in the theology department at Loyola University of
Chicago.

Several months later, after my reworking of the manuscript
to incorporate that editor's suggestions, the future book was
assigned to two young interns working with Center of
Concern in the summer of 1992: Suzanne de Crane, finishing
her doctorate in social ethics at the University of Toronto, and
Brian Berry, S.J., doctoral candidate in Catholic social teaching
at Boston University. With tremendous enthusiasm these two
plunged into what was for them a work of love. Their force-
fulness and drive energized me for my final tasks.

More Readers

Then three Jesuit companions generously undertook a further
reading, from which followed more suggestions that sent me
back to the grindstone. These readers were Patrick Burns, president of the Jesuit National Conference and a Rahner scholar;
Paul Harmon, secretary of the same conference for Jesuit formation and student of the theology that grounds this present study;
and finally Drew Christiansen, director of the International
Division of the U.S. Catholic Bishops' Conference. Christiansen,
a widely published social ethician, taught theology for years at

Santa Clara University, Jesuit School of Theology, Berkeley, and the University of Notre Dame.

Center of Concern Staff

Though not a member of this center, Msgr. Joseph Gremillion, a well-known writer in this field, did at one time associate himself with us on a project. In the book, I express my admiration for his earlier leadership in bringing the Pontifical Commission Justice and Peace into existence, forwarding it through highly innovative initiatives (some troubling for the conservatives of the Vatican—did someone say, Are there any other types there?) and future-looking ecumenical enterprises. In our years of working together, Gremillion gave me most generous support.

The book notes my equal debt to William Ryan, S.J. (like Joe Gremillion a onetime student of mine), who invited me to the center seventeen years ago. Because the book recounts my debts to research colleagues of the center I need not repeat that here, except that James Hug, S.J., present director of Center of Concern and former professor of ethics at one of our Jesuit theologates, helped me to think through the world of newly minted social ethics that he had mastered.

And I must also acknowledge the great help and encouragement I have always had from our staff: people like Terri Herschfeld, who looks for financing for our work (and who is one of that battalion of young masters of the computer who pulled me back from the brink of disaster), and Jane Deren, who finalized the editing and publishing process with Loyola University Press.

[At the time of his unexpected death on January 20, 1994, Rev. Philip S. Land, S.J., was well along with the process of preparing this manuscript for press. The editors have, however, had to face the challenge of verifying quotations, translations, and references for numerous sources on which the author had based his book, sometimes with only ambiguous or incomplete information. Thus, although we have not succeeded in every case, we have endeavored to approach the high standard of scholarship that this study deserves.]

✠ Abbreviations

A fter the first full reference to the works below, abbreviations are used in both text and notes; Arabic numerals are those of sections or paragraphs. Encyclicals, documents of Councils and Synods, and works of Saint Thomas Aquinas are listed by short Latin title and usually identified by subject (in parentheses in English), author, and date. Works of Aquinas are in a separate list.

CA   *Centesimus Annus* (Hundredth anniversary of *Rerum Novarum*), John Paul II, 1991.

DH   *Dignitatis Humanae* (Religious Freedom), Vatican II, 1965.

DR   *Divini Redemptoris* (Atheistic Communism), Pius XI, 1937.

DV   *Dei Verbum* (Divine Revelation), Vatican II, 1965.

EJA   *Economic Justice for All: Catholic Social Teaching and the U.S. Economy*, U.S. National Conference of Catholic Bishops, 1986.

EN   *Evangelii Nutiandi* (Evangelization in the Modern World), Paul VI, 1975.

GS   *Gaudium et Spes* (The Church in the Modern World), Vatican II, 1965.

JM   *Justitia in Mundo* (Justice in the World), Synod of Bishops' Second General Assembly, 1971.

LE   *Laborem Exercens* (Human Work), John Paul II, 1981.

MM   *Mater et Magistra* (Christianity and Social Progress), John XXIII, 1961.

OA   *Octogesima Adveniens* (Eightieth anniversary of *Rerum Novarum*), Paul VI, 1971.

PP	*Populorum Progressio* (Development of Peoples), Paul VI, 1967.
PT	*Pacem in Terris* (Peace on Earth), John XXIII, 1963.
QA	*Quadragesimo Anno* (Fortieth anniversary of *Rerum Novarum*), Pius XI, 1931.
RN	*Rerum Novarum* (The Condition of Labor), Leo XIII, 1891.

Selected Works of Saint Thomas Aquinas (1225–74)

CG	*Summa contra Gentiles* (Truth of the Catholic Faith).
DV	*Quaestiones Disputatae de Veritate* (Debated questions: Truth).
Eth	*Ethicorum* expositio *[ad Eudemus Rhodensus]* (Aristotle's *Eudemian Ethics*).
Log	*Analyticorum espositio* (Aristotle's *Logic*).
NE	*Ethicorum expositio* (Aristotle's *Nicomachean Ethics*).
Pol	*Politicorum expositio* (Aristotle's *Politics*).
ST	*Summa Theologiae.*
SL	*IV libros Sententiarm Petri Lombardi* (Peter Lombard).

One Catholic Social Teaching Journey: Early Decades

Early Jesuit Years

I got into social problems before I had any acquaintance with Catholic social teaching. Over sixty years ago, in my last week at Jesuit-run Bellarmine High, in Tacoma, Washington, I decided to enter the Jesuit novitiate. There were no clouds, as yet, on the economic horizon. In the first days of August 1929, I took the Greyhound bus to Los Gatos, California, where the novitiate of the California Province was located. Still no economic clouds. But two months later the bottom had fallen out of our world. The Great Depression had settled in.

Unbelievably, we novices at Los Gatos lived tranquil lives in almost total oblivion of the raw reality of the depression. We were shielded from the sufferings of our suddenly impoverished countrymen. We never left the sacred precincts of our sheltered oasis of normality. The only manifest poverty that came under our purview was the regular line of well-dressed males begging a handout at our kitchen door. We novices heard that some were businesspeople and bankers of San Francisco, some sixty miles to the north, who had been wiped out by the stock market crash.

We never saw a newspaper. That was secular and presumably an interference with the progress of our spirituality and our liberal arts education. We did learn to read the Latin poet Ovid. I still remember from him one phrase: *stratus sub arbore* (lounging under a tree). We had no course in the social sciences in the four years at Los Gatos, not even in the two-year collegiate program that followed the novitiate, nor did we in the three years of philosophy that followed at Mount St. Michael's, in Spokane, Washington. Nor were there supplementary lectures on any social problems at either institution. Only the poor life we lived at Mount St. Michael's helped us share something of the poverty of the era.

If I censure here, it is the system which I am criticizing, not the good people who taught us. They themselves were equally victims of the system, though I am not sure that any of these teachers felt himself victimized. That this system was condemnable is shown by the quite opposite idea Jesuits have today about where and what a novitiate ought to be.

Then came the miracle. Leo Robinson, S.J., fresh from a doctorate in sociology, entered the life of our house of philosophical studies. Robinson offered an elective introductory course on social issues which I eagerly attended with a handful of others. We exchanged ideas and information. I became an enthusiastic follower of Franklin Delano Roosevelt. I continue that enthusiasm, for Roosevelt's National Recovery Act and his Blue Eagle broke into what I had experienced as rather sterile philosophical studies.

The opportunity to deliver a special lecture to my fellow "philosophers" on "The American Founding Fathers and Catholic Philosophy" provided the occasion to spend months of reading and reflection on the origins of the Founders' philosophy. I also read eminent thinkers on the public good, like Grotius, Pufendorf, Suarez, Bellarmine, and Soto. I devoted considerable time to reading the *Federalist Papers,* an enriching and exciting study. My admiration for the Founding Fathers' philosophy of public order at a later stage of my formation was attenuated only as I fell under the influence of theologians pressing for a major role for Scripture and theology in laying the foundations of social living.

In those times we young Jesuits interrupted our Scholastic training after seven years for three years of teaching in one of our high schools before we continued with our final four years of theology. This interruption brought me back to Bellarmine, where I had graduated seven years earlier.

Tacoma was a lumber town and the terminal for three transcontinental railroads. Since there was little building anywhere during those depression years, the demand for lumber and for railroading was minimal or nonexistent. I saw what seemed to be millions of board feet of finished lumber rotting on the docks of Tacoma's harbor. Unemployment in Tacoma was horrendous. The Jesuit faculty lived meagerly off two cows tethered in our yard (milked by the rector) and occasional canned food collections organized by the school's Mothers club. My brother-in-law was a railroader. Visits to my sister's home showed me an even starker reality than we were living in our Jesuit community.

I read and I listened regularly on radio to the firebrand lecturer, Fr. Charles Coughlin of Detroit. Through careful alternative reading I discovered the atrocious unfairness of his attack on Jews as manipulators of our financial markets. I still owe him, however, a debt of gratitude for helping me understand our ever-deepening depression and the economic forces behind that colossal failure of the economic system.

Shapers of My Social Formation: Institute of Social Order

During the following four years of theology, I managed to keep up on the desperate world beyond our oasis of tranquillity, despite a smorgasbord of largely sterile and largely outdated neo-scholastic theology. My provincial superior during those years was the same Leo Robinson who had fed my ravishing appetite with an introduction to social sciences at the mount. In my final year of theology, he informed me that he was thinking of sending me to study at the St. Michael Institute of Toronto in preparation for teaching philosophy at the Mount.

I suggested an alternative I had been mulling over for some time. Robinson came to believe it held more promise for me and for the province. This was to start a Labor School at our province's Seattle University. Labor Schools emerged on the

Northeast Coast during the late thirties. Great diocesan priests, along with Jesuits, were the leaders in creating this new social force. Jesuits used their existing educational institutions, opening them to union people for night courses. The program was dedicated to preparing union leaders for more effective leadership of poor workers. Classes and seminars were offered in economics, introductory sociology, labor history, public speaking, writing skills, and contract negotiation. All of the programs included a large dose of Catholic social teaching.

While encouraging me in my project, my provincial urged me to prepare for that work with a solid grounding. That for him implied a Ph.D. in economics. I would have settled for the same informal preparation as had other founders of Labor Schools, all of whom relied on well-prepared volunteers able to provide a solid roster of courses. Having been satisfied with the program in sociology he had followed at St. Louis University, Father Robinson urged that institution on me for economics.

This turned out to be a fateful choice. The U.S. Jesuits were just then forming a new social apostolate to be housed at St. Louis University. One component was a faculty capable of giving the Jesuits studying there a rounded and integral approach to their respective disciplines. One endeavor of the Institute of Social Order was a review, *Social Order.* After a few years of mixed success—although *Social Order* was an unqualified success—the Institute of Social Order collapsed. It was put to death by the U.S. provincials. The history of the Institute of Social Order and its demise after only ten years of promise has yet to be written. I will not attempt that here, but rather will explain the role it played in my development.

One component of the Institute of Social Order was its teaching unit, the Institute of Social Sciences (ISS). While availing itself of the faculties of St. Louis University, the Institute of Social Sciences added special courses provided by visiting specialists. I eagerly sought out those in Catholic social teaching. Those courses, together with the fine offerings of St. Louis University economics and business faculties, gave me a rich introduction to Catholic social teaching.

I had the good fortune to have Bernard Dempsey, S.J., Director of the School of Business, as the moderator of my program. For his own doctoral dissertation at Harvard, Dempsey had written and published a treatise on three seventeenth-century forerunners of Adam Smith in economics. The three were all Jesuits of northern Europe. Together they offered a remarkable treatment of markets, but—unlike Adam Smith's—socially regulated markets.

Under Dempsey's guidance I read copiously in these and similar authors. I also read Adam Smith, including the final volume. This to my surprise attributed to government a role not unlike that Franklin Roosevelt proposed in his New Deal. At the opposite pole I read Karl Marx. I did not find his economics as interesting as his study of capitalistic alienation of the fruit of the worker's labor. Then, as now, I believed there was a good deal to his theory, but not as much as many liberation theologians find in it.

Dempsey set me on course for another fateful development in my pursuit of Catholic social teaching when he suggested that I take for my dissertation topic a central theme of Pius XI's 1931 social encyclical, *Quadragesimo Anno* (Fortieth anniversary of *Rerum Novarum*). Its central theme was the social reorganization of the economy rooted in the medieval guild system. In this system, the reciprocal contributions of the crafts, industries, or services assured the well-being of all the crafts and industries in the society. This system was known rather generally in English-speaking countries as Industries and Professions. In Germany and other European countries it was known as *Berufstand,* which translates literally into English as the Vocational Order. This social organization united employees, workers, and others of a community through their socially productive function rather than promoting the market's separation of employers into givers and takers of work. *Vocational* referred to the crafts, industries, and services, while *order* referred to *ordering* society. The Vocational Order also became known as corporatism because of its social, organic centering. Unfortunately this term became confused with Mussolini's state corporatism.

My study examined the question of the viability of the Vocational Order as an economic system for the United States. That investigation proved a never-ending frustration for me until finally I abandoned it. I gradually came to perceive that, despite its inspiring vision, the Vocational Order could never be viable in the United States. Our economy was too complex. For example, would one assign a Greyhound Corporation to the transportation, food, or communications order?

During the defense of my dissertation, one of the examiners, Professor Boris Ischboldin, an exile who enriched several U.S. universities during World War II, delicately and without insisting pointed out a fundamental contradiction in the thesis when I left theory and came to practice. I had discovered that contradiction early on and, since I was unable to resolve it, I had hoped that it might slide by unnoticed.

Despite my misgivings, ten years later in Rome I was instrumental in an effort to uphold the Vocational Order in an encyclical marking the anniversary of *Quadragesimo Anno*.

Even if I gained little from my study insofar as applying Vocational Order to the United States, I learned immensely from the solidarist social teaching that undergirded the idea. That solidarism stemmed largely from the German Jesuit Heinrich Pesch. Over the decades solidarism has remained a main root of Catholic social teaching. The same can be said for the concept of social framing of markets, which fully acknowledges the good of the free market, but recognizes the equal good of social framing of its economic productivity.

Other Shapers of My Catholic Social Teaching

My dissertation on the Vocational Order successfully defended, I began to deepen and generalize my studies of Catholic social teaching and—initially—of the Vocational Order. I must here recognize other contributors to Catholic social teaching and to Catholic social action. It was this ongoing conversation with so many that shaped and continued to shape me.

Many persons contributed to me personally and through their contributions to the interpretation of Catholic social teaching. Many of these contributions were seeds of new thinking, a kind of trailblazing. I came to realize that official teaching normally does not break new ground. Rather, it brings official teaching in line with the achieved or at least substantial and growing consensus among theologians.

Trailblazing is done by the theologians, whose new thinking is often rejected by Rome in its initial presentation; finally it becomes endorsed by the official Church by acclamation of the faithful and thus becomes Catholic teaching.

For example, the vocational or corporative order which was the centerpiece of *Quadragesimo Anno* came out of the tradition of the German Jesuit Heinrich Pesch and the Study Circle of Koenigswinter on the Rhine. A few decades later, however, the growing consensus of theologians and political leaders within Catholic social ethics circles lost confidence in the potential of this centerpiece for social reform. It subsequently disappeared also from the official teaching of the Church.

Another example comes from Vatican II, the constitution *Gaudium et Spes* (The Church in the Modern World). Its decidedly forward-looking ideas stem from the theological explorations in a half-dozen centers. Gustav Thils of Louvain was developing a new theology of work, *La thèologie du Travail.* Karl Rahner was breaking new ground with his works on the person, the orders of creation and of redemption, the nature of the Church, and Christology "from below." The two French Dominicans, Yves Congar and Marie-Dominique Chenu, were writing on the Church and social teaching. Congar had been breaking new ground in the theology of the laity. In the United States John Courtney Murray was an innovative thinker, especially on religious liberty. One way or another all these thinkers entered the mainstream of Catholic social teaching, either in its official presentation or in its unofficial but authentic stream of *doctrina recepta,* that is, what the believing community recognizes as truly Catholic social teaching.

Lying somewhere between official (Vatican or papal) positions and contributions of individual theologians or schools of theology is the growing phenomenon of hierarchical pastorals. Notable here are the hemisphere-wide Latin American conferences in Medellin (1968) and in Puebla (1979). The 1983 pastoral of the Canadian Catholic Conference, "Ethical Reflections on the Economic Crisis,"[1] is another such statement. The U.S. Catholic hierarchy has also issued important statements on social conditions as early as the 1919 statement of the old Catholic Welfare Council. Two of the most recent statements are "The Challenge of Peace: God's Call and Our

Response" (1983) and "Economic Justice for All: Catholic
Social Teaching and the U.S. Economy" (1986).

The roster of contributors to the body of official teaching
and to my formation, however, must be lengthened much further. Later chapters will amply illustrate the eminence of
Thomas Aquinas. I have already noted my discovery of seventeenth-century Jesuits. But there have been scores of others
over the centuries. G. K. Chesterton was noteworthy for his
distributism. Dorothy Day quietly crusaded for nonviolence
when it was unpopular in Catholic circles in the United States.
Now a good deal of her advanced thinking appears in hierarchical and even papal reflections.

Both Goetz Briefs, then of Georgetown University, and
Franz Mueller, emeritus of St. Thomas College in Minneapolis,
advanced Catholic social teaching here and abroad. Jacques
Maritain, who taught for years at the University of Chicago
Divinity School, was an immense influence on me personally.
Most recently John Cort (1989) has given us an admirable
account of Christian socialism.

On the other side of the Atlantic, one of my favorite sources
of new thinking was the largely lay voice of the famous French
Semaine Sociale. This annual social week had its imitators in
Italy, Spain, and Germany. I followed carefully the Semaine's
studies and the reports of the German Katholikentagen.

While speaking of Germany we must mention the famous
Study Circle of Koenigswinter on the Rhine. The roster of
names associated with that Catholic social study body is
impressive: Briefs, who at that time taught in Berlin; Mueller,
who later taught at Cologne; Oswald von Nell-Breuning of the
Jesuit theologate in Frankfurt (actively writing up to his death
in 1991 at age 101); and Gustav Gundlach, then of Berlin
(later my colleague at the Gregorian University in Rome).[2]
Nell-Breuning and Gundlach, while deriving their social philosophy from the solidarist fountainhead of Heinrich Pesch, at
times diverged violently in application.[3]

I must also pay my respects to the German Catholics of the
Midwest who had brought me abreast of developments in
Germany and other European countries. The Central Verein's
Central Blatt, now called *Social Justice Review* and published
in St. Louis, influenced me the most. It introduced me to

Pesch through the Jesuit essayist W. Engelen. I later read Pesch's seven-volume *Lehrbuch* in its entirety. Other prestigious names who published in that review I met at the dinner table of St. Louis University: Albert Munsch, S.J., and Joseph Husslein, S.J. Husslein later became the general editor of Bruce Publishing Company's Science and Culture series as well as contributing volumes of his own. Munsch introduced me to the *Central Blatt,* which by this time was published mostly in English with only a small German section. Somehow the predominant figure of the Central Verein, Frederick Kenkel, never came to my attention.

The Central Verein and the *Central Blatt* tie me to another eminent figure in Catholic social teaching in the United States who had immense influence on me and a generation of practitioners in the social field. John A. Ryan and his doctoral dissertation, *A Living Wage: Its Ethical and Economic Aspects* (1908), exerted strong influence on Catholic social teaching for decades in the United States. Ryan's book, *A Better Economic Order* (1935), also had lasting influence. Yet another outstanding classic was surely the Program of Social Reconstruction from the Administrative Board of the National Catholic War Council, which incorporated many of of John Ryan's ideas.

In the forties, another flurry of Catholic involvement in social action began. This was the heyday of the Labor Schools and the Young Catholic Worker Movement. Although efforts to introduce Catholic unions and a Catholic employers' association failed, a couple of Catholic union guilds were attempted. Neither Msgr. George Higgins, this country's best-known labor priest, nor my colleague, Fr. Ben Masse, S.J., believed in separate Catholic unions, employers' associations, or, for that matter, such professional associations as Catholic lawyer guilds. Masse used the columns of the Jesuit review *America* to push the New Deal, unions, and other social causes. While on the staff of *America* (briefly, between the Institute of Social Order and the call to Rome), I tended to resist Masse's more progressive social stands. Later I was much more supportive.

Two other staff members at *America* must be noted, John LaFarge, S.J., and Robert Hartnett, S.J. LaFarge (Uncle John to us) had behind him a long career of quietly fighting for causes. He championed African-American causes, demanding an end to discrimination, even by his own Maryland Province Jesuits. LaFarge created the Catholic League against Racism and Segregation. Later his vision brought forth four or five other movements that fostered newness in Catholic life.

Hartnett was editor in chief of *America* when I came on board. I admired him immensely. Hartnett reserved to himself weekly two editorial columns. He did not care what else went into the magazine. In my time his editorials were very often directed to exposing Senator Joseph McCarthy. This was an extraordinarily courageous venture. One editorial alone cost us nearly a thousand cancellations. Jesuits, who especially in the Midwest were generally pro-McCarthy, demanded that the provincial superiors of the U.S. Jesuits oust Hartnett. They finally succeeded. During that period I was invited to talk at Marquette University in Milwaukee, McCarthy's backyard. On the morning after the talk, the Jesuit community honed in on me. By midmorning, I remember, I was thinking that I was like the martyr Saint Lawrence, who, after he had been roasted on one side, was turned over to be roasted on the other. Their attack on me, as a representative of *America,* did not let up for hours.

Under the influence of Archbishop Edwin O'Hara and with the driving, imaginative force of Msgr. Luigi Ligutti, the National Catholic Rural Life Conference was born. I had a close working relationship with Ligutti during his long stay in Rome as Permanent Observer of the Holy See to the Food and Agricultural Organization of the United Nations. Ligutti had an instinct for very many of the progressive ideas of Vatican II. But he also had a simple philosophy which expressed itself in homey aphorisms. He recounted one to a class I taught at the Gregorian: "a lot of little people doing a lot of little things in a lot of different places can change the world." Ligutti believed in little people in little places.

What we called the Chicago crowd was mainly priests with some important laypeople who created powerful instruments for social development. From the hierarchy, Bishop Bernard Sheil inspired them with his courageous leadership. The diocesan priest Dan Cantwell was well known for his social leadership. Ed Marciniak, creator of the influential periodical

Work, remains active today with his studies in urban planning. He is president of the Institute of Urban Life at Loyola University of Chicago.

Out of that movement came such great figures as Msgr. John Egan,[4] of whom it was frequently said "his life would make a great book," and Msgr. George Higgins, whose remarkable career as labor priest, consultor to the U.S. Catholic Bishops' Conference, and columnist on social issues had been chronicled earlier (Costello 1984).

About this time, the Catholic Sociological Society and the Catholic Economic Society were born. Their periodicals influenced my thinking. The Catholic Economic Society began *The Review of Social Economy,* now published under the auspices of its successor, the Association for Social Economics. From its first issue the review provided a forum for views about Christian ethics and economics. The Jesuits Thomas Devine and Bernard Dempsey molded the early review. A third review, *Christ's Blueprint of the South,* was begun by another Jesuit, Louis B. Twomey, director of the Industrial Relations Institute at Loyola University of New Orleans. Begun in the fifties, the journal continued after Twomey's death. It has changed title but remains a very useful essay in social analysis and advocacy. Twomey did economics with me in the Institute of Social Sciences, as did other Jesuits who shared so much with me. Among them, Jim Goodwin devoted his life to teaching sociology and counselling for long years at Seattle University. Joe Becker, still active in his research center at Xavier University, Cincinnati, has recently been honored for his publications, especially those about unemployment, in a special issue of *The Review of Social Economy.* Mort Gavin went on to an eminent career forming labor leaders—my early ambition. Twomey, my most intimate associate as we exchanged ideas over the years, was a living inspiration with his deep commitment to the labor union movement, the cause of the poor, and social justice. One other Jesuit, whose name comes up later in this book, George Dunne, had been withdrawn from teaching in the Institute of Social Sciences at the request of the president of St. Louis University. Dunne relates the incident, one redounding to his honor, in his recent autobiography (1990).

My memory travels back gratefully to Dom Virgil Michel, editor of the Benedictine liturgical review *Orate Fratres,* now known as *Worship.* Michel showed us the social side of the mystical body of Christ. Indeed, for him society—U.S. society in particular—could not be founded exclusively on either the Catholic concept of the natural law or its civic virtues. On this point he was in sharp contrast to John Courtney Murray, whose norms for society (so it seemed to me) were wholly philosophical. Michel's thought on this issue was a forerunner of Vatican II's. As the council unfolded, I reflected on the vision of society Virgil Michel had expounded—so in contrast to our Church historians' vision, which conceded to civic virtues in the United States the exclusive custody of public order.

Martin Hellriegel's ideas were close to the ideas of Michel. *The Catholic Worker* and its saint, Dorothy Day, as well as the imaginative Peter Maurin, influenced me enormously. Dorothy and Peter joined Virgil Michel in asserting a role, a very prominent role, for theology in shaping society. They also taught me that living with the poor and contact with the sufferers of society were new sources of Catholic social teaching.

The Jesuit Institute of Social Order to which I belonged attested to this flow of energy into the social order. Its review, *Social Order,* was begun with fanfare and great enthusiasm. Both the Institute of Social Order and *Social Order,* however, were allowed by superiors, as I have already noted, to drizzle out to a miserable end. Many prominent people in social movements have told me how they regretted the demise of *Social Order.* It had established itself in its short life as unique in its field.

Another towering figure among the pioneers was John Courtney Murray, S.J.[5] Among his prodigious writings probably the most eminent is his *We Hold These Truths* (1960). That book, as much of Murray's other writings, made Catholics conscious of the "American Proposition" and helped them relate their Catholicism to such issues as civic virtue, rights, and separation of church and state. Shortly after, in Vatican II, Murray became a principal figure in shaping one of the council's greatest successes, its declaration on religious freedom.

Still Other Shapers: the Commentators

Catholic social teaching and I also owe a debt to commentators on the whole body of official Church documents. Thanks to Bernard Dempsey, S.J., Oswald von Nell-Breuning's commentary (1936) on *Quadragesimo Anno* was made available in English. Jean-Yves Calvez and Jacques Perrin's commentary, *The Church's Social Thought from Leo XIII to Pius XII* (1961) in translation from the French, remains one of the best overviews ever produced. Although untranslated, the commentary by Jean Villain, *L'Enseignement Sociale de l'Eglise Introduction, Capitalisme, Socialisme* (1953), influenced me significantly. Another classic in translation was Johannes Messner's *Social Ethics* (1949).[6] Another appreciated commentary was John Cronin's *Social Principles and Economic Life* (1959).

Donal Dorr's *Option for the Poor: 100 Years of Vatican Social Thought* (1983) is yet another excellent commentary. Still a constantly consulted source is Msgr. Joseph Gremillion's collection of official social statements, *The Gospel of Peace and Justice: Catholic Social Thought Since Pope John* (1976). Unfortunately Gremillion's carefully reflective introduction to the documents is often overlooked.

This sampling is by no means an exhaustive list of the contributions made by the commentators.

More Pioneers

I have confined this historical note to those pioneers who influenced me in my more formative years. One other must be recorded here, Joe Fitzpatrick, S.J. Long before ordination, Fitzpatrick began one of the first Labor Schools, housed at Xavier High School in downtown New York City in the late thirties. Fitzpatrick, long identified with the sociology department of Fordham University, actively promoted the inculturation center begun by Ivan Illich in Cuernavaca, Mexico. He is also one of the most important figures in the Catholic Hispanic movement.

A host of younger contemporaries have succeeded these pioneers. From their studies, often in other than Catholic theological centers, they have introduced the thinking of their teachers into Catholic social teaching. They have also advanced analysis and reflection on many issues. It would take more acquaintance with them than I have had to do justice to all of them. Some do figure in these pages, but an adequate notice of them is quite beyond me.

It was not until after my graduate studies that I truly discovered Thomas Aquinas, the thirteenth-century theologian. Even though Aquinas had been the bread and butter of my courses in philosophy and theology, I had never been introduced to the works that now gripped me. The first was on ethical method, specifically his *ratio practica,* practical reason as opposed to speculative reasoning. The second was his remarkable treatise on the virtue of prudence. For Aquinas *prudentia* was a power of the Spirit thrusting into responsible action; it did not connote the English sense of prudence, as expressed in the phrase "don't rock the boat" or "be cautious."

By this time I had become enamored of natural law, although with ambivalence. It therefore astonished me to find that Aquinas in his moral system devoted only one question (with several articles) to natural law, whereas he dedicated an abundance of questions (each with several articles) to the ultimate practical moral judgment under the guidance of prudence. I found myself reflecting as well on the fact that Thomas preferred the term *ius gentium* to that of natural law. *Ius gentium* reduced the absoluteness, the utter universality of natural law statements, to a less imposing generalization of what people normally do everywhere (*ut in pluribus*—as people do generally).

A word, however, about my ambivalence about natural law. Despite believing that private ownership of productive property was of natural law, I was capable in practice of accepting common ownership as equally valid. I first took this position when a student from southern India told me in class at St. Louis that private ownership was against the culture of the people with whom he worked. I responded that whatever he and his people after due reflection see as fitting their culture would be moral. That was nearly two decades before Vatican II.

Later I would have misgivings about that solution because it was at variance with tradition. My continuing ambivalence about moral absolutes and organicism of Catholic social teaching as opposed to historicity led me to waver, but I leaned more frequently toward natural law, even after Vatican II had begun.

One Catholic Social Teaching Journey: Middle Decades, Both Banks of the Tiber

Rome on a Rebuke

I n the fall of 1955, when I served a brief stint on the staff of the Jesuit review *America,* unbeknownst to me, I was being looked over as a possible editor in chief. I was rejected in favor of Thurston Davis, S.J., who was there with me for the same testing. I am quite sure that the staff and board of *America* were unanimous in their choice. I had nothing of Davis's extraordinary writing ability or the promotional ability he soon displayed. The one contribution I might have made would have been to keep the magazine from slipping into the more conservative tone of his preference, in contrast to that of his predecessor, Robert Hartnett, S.J., who had been dumped by the board as too liberal, or at least, for many Jesuits, as too aggressively anti-Joe McCarthy.

Back I went to my job with the Institute of Social Order in St. Louis. For a short while I seemed firmly rooted in that enterprise and content. But after only months, the Gregorian University, through a request from Jesuit headquarters, invited me to present myself in Rome. Understandably, the head of the ISO was as reluctant as I to have me separated so soon after reinstatement. So we dragged our heels.

We dragged our heels so long that I received just about the severest admonishment a Jesuit can get, a telegram in Latin from the acting general of the order (the general was ill). *"Miramur ad vestram resistentiam ad acceptandam vocationem ad Cathedram Gregorianam."* We are astounded at your resistance to accepting the call to the Chair of the Gregorian.

I do not now know whether it was all that latinity or the shock of recognizing my very nonprompt obedience, but short days thereafter I was flying to Paris in a Boeing four-engine, arriving on the Feast of the Immaculate Conception 1955.

Centuries-Old Jesuit University

The Gregorian was home for the next twenty years. At my arrival, we Jesuits were celebrating well over four hundred years of existence as an order. My new post was in the world's largest priest factory. At that time, the Greg had 1,700 seminarians, a large graduate faculty in the sacred sciences, and 700 graduate students. The faculty of social sciences had been added to the sacred sciences about the end of World War II.

In those days the language of instruction, including instruction in the social sciences, was Latin. I taught economics in the language of the Caesars. This proved only that it could be done, not that it should be. Finding words for abstract theory was easy enough. "Theory of marginal productivity" is three Latin words, requiring only proper endings. The time, however, I put in trying to find words for institutional situations was enormous. How to say "strike," for example. I once even tried "yellow-dog contract," which, as I remember it, is a contract of employment in which the employee agrees never to seek unionization. Jokingly, I translated "yellow-dog contract" literally as *contractus canis flavi*. You can imagine the bewilderment of the students. Fortunately after a couple of years our faculty was able to escape from the incubus of Latin.

The reason for the very large number of students at the Gregorian was the prestige it enjoyed among bishops and religious congregations of men. Especially for bishops, that prestige rested on their confidence in the institution's orthodoxy. It was a safe place to send their candidates for the priesthood. Among the faculty were eminent teachers and writers. Some were seeking to push open the frontiers of theology, but for most, a strong factor in their selection was their assured orthodoxy. I am sure that my record was scrutinized and that I was pronounced safe. My unorthodoxy cropped up only later.

Faculty Fights over Catholic Social Teaching

During my twenty years at the Greg, the faculty of social sciences had little contact with students of other faculties. Catholic social teaching was the specialty of our faculty. This might have provided one link to students of other faculties, for among us there were four specialists in Catholic social teaching. The Holy See over the years had constantly exhorted theological faculties to teach the Church's social doctrine. (So, as a matter of fact, had authorities in our own Jesuit order). That voice of exhortation on the right bank of the Tiber went largely unheeded by our university on the left. For the first seventeen or eighteen years of my time, the Greg taught no course on Catholic social teaching to the students of theology, graduate or undergraduate. Students of other faculties were not encouraged to take advantage of our institute's offerings. Apparently, many of the theology faculty did not regard Catholic social teaching as theology. In fact, as it was taught by Gundlach, there was little if any theology to it. Still, at that time, the Vatican, like the Jesuit authorities, wanted theological candidates to be exposed to Catholic social teaching, even if it was taught in the more philosophical vein of neo-scholastic natural law.

I mentioned we were four specialists in Catholic social teaching on our faculty. One left just as I arrived. Msgr. Pietro Pavan deserves special comment. Pavan was already well known in Italy as a principal consultor to the Vatican, especially on trade union questions and on Catholic participation in the Communist-dominated general union. Pavan was opposed to a separate Catholic union, favoring instead participation in the general union. For their better formation on union questions as well as for their Catholic solidarity, Pavan urged that Catholics join in their own adjunct association alongside the general trade union. In 1962 Pavan prepared the final draft of John XXIII's *Mater et Magistra* (Christianity and Social Progress). He later produced that pope's *Pacem in Terris* (Peace on Earth). In the council, Pavan became widely known with John Courtney Murray for steering the decree on religious liberty through to its acceptance.

With Pavan's departure, the specialists in social teaching in the Institute of Social Sciences had been reduced to two. I was the third. A Dutch Jesuit economist, with strong emphasis on social ethics, was shortly thereafter appointed as number four. A couple years later a fifth appointment was made. Differences of approach among us were quite pronounced.

Gustav Gundlach, S.J., of Germany and Georges Jarlot, S.J., of France had continent-wide reputations; the other two, Theodore Mulder, S.J., of the Netherlands, and Jose Maria Díez-Alegría, S.J., of Spain, were highly regarded in their quarters of Europe.

The most famous name, and eventually the most controversial, was Gustav Gundlach. He was famous for at least three things. First, he had been invited onto the team drafting what was to become the encyclical *Quadragesimo Anno,* which discusses the economy. Gundlach's specific contribution was the concept of Vocational Order which, as he personally told me, offered a precisely Catholic third way between liberal capitalism and socialism. Second, throughout Europe Gundlach was widely reputed to be the main hand behind most of Pope Pius XII's written statements on sociopolitical questions. The most notable of these were nineteen Christmas messages, including the famous 1944 message which called democracy the form of government most in keeping with natural law. Third, he had been ousted from Germany because his pronouncements against Hitler's national socialism had made him persona non grata to Hitler.

Georges Jarlot had also written a good deal. Among his contributions were the introductions to the annual volumes of the *Semaine Sociale,* signed by a succession of cardinal secretaries of state. As soon as the Vatican archives were opened on Leo XIII, Jarlot undertook what became a magisterial work on how *Rerum Novarum* was produced.

Theodore Mulder divided most of his time between administrative work on the faculty and teaching economics. But he later steered a team of us through the preparation of the first draft of what became *Mater et Magistra.*

Díez-Alegría, a younger Jesuit, was added shortly after my arrival. Díez-Alegría was later dismissed from the Jesuit order for publishing and refusing to retract a volume on his personal faith which became famous in Spain and other Spanish-speaking countries. I have recently reviewed the English translation. If there is anything in it contrary to the faith, it escapes me. But then my understanding of the faith on some points has been questioned.

We spanned all possible positions on Catholic social teaching. We were a maelstrom of seething searching. Gundlach was a rock-ribbed proponent of an ultraconservative theory of natural law that claimed inerrancy because natural law was a reflection of divine law. At the other extreme, Díez-Alegría rejected natural law completely in favor of a biblical approach. His classroom notes, entitled "Christian Attitudes," suggest an approach John C. Dwyer (1987, 1) explored. Gundlach, for his part, was emphatically against Scripture in Catholic social teaching. He maintained Scripture was too "woolly" and that, in contrast to Scripture, ethical reasoning was a font of truth which all peoples could hold in common. This view was markedly illustrated by John XXIII's *Pacem in Terris.*

Pavan could not stand what he perceived as Gundlach's archconservativism in social teaching. Nor did he, as others, like an even more unpalatable trait of the German Jesuit, his way of mantling his own shoulders with papal authority assumed from the unquestioned acceptance of the drafts he wrote on invitation for papal statements. The following story, which made the rounds, is probably apocryphal, but as the Italians say: *se non é vero é ben trovato:* if it's not true, it's neatly apposite. As the story goes, Gundlach was challenged in the classroom. Whenever Gundlach was challenged he would defend his position by referring to some papal document he himself had written. On this occasion he concluded with his customary defense, "as the Holy Father has said." He then remembered that the papal statement to which he had alluded was still awaiting publication, so he revised his rejoinder to "as the Holy Father will say."

Where Was I in This Fight?

I find it hard now to place myself precisely in this controversy. In my days at the Institute of Social Order I had been ambivalent. On the one hand, I thoroughly approved the ideas of Thomas Aquinas on social morality. These riches had been wholly abandoned by neo-scholasticism and neo-Thomism. They begged, I was convinced, for a new hearing. In addition, I was largely an adherent to natural law as the centuries following Aquinas had formulated it. On the other hand, against some of the universal norms prevalent in Catholic social teaching, and to which I adhered, I assured students who found the norms inappropriate to their culture that Catholic social teaching had to be framed to their circumstances.

Now on the left bank of the Tiber (later a large part of my working day would be on the right bank) the ambivalence of my ISO days was still with me. But I tilted toward Gundlach's position and away from that represented by Díez-Alegría's scriptural approach or, for that matter, by Pavan's more contextual, more historical methodology.

I thus supported Gundlach on organicism and on natural law as being a reflection of the divine law. I went so far as to treat with respectful silence the claim this originator of the Vocational Order had written into *Quadragesimo Anno* that this middle way between capitalism and socialism was "if not of natural law at least *as if it were* of natural law." I so acted although in my doctoral dissertation on the Vocational Order I had not been able to discover viability for the project, at least in the United States. Quite apart from whether the idea is of natural law, it attracted me by its philosophical underpinnings of universal cooperation toward the common good. I was then enamored of the notion of order. I would grow out of it, but at that time my excessively orderly soul found the concept of a Vocational Order attractive. As Gundlach explained it, God had planned an ordered world. God could not be thought of apart from order. Therefore the divine mind must have an order proper to human living.

With Gundlach, and against Díez-Alegría, I was at that time a strong believer in reason. With Descartes, I agreed on the capacity of *les idèes claires* to move people to right action. If

I could only further clarify and refine the ideas of Catholic social teaching, my students would have acquired the power to change society. I also agreed with Gundlach's position that because reason is something we have in common with all humankind the human race should be able to agree on fundamental principles of social living. Our Scriptures by contrast are unknown to most of the human race. Consequently, they cannot be the basis of discourse. At that time I also believed firmly with Gundlach that Catholic social teaching was organic.

How Not to Write an Encyclical

Two events at the beginning of the sixties precipitated a change in me. The first event was preparation of an encyclical to celebrate the sixtieth anniversary of *Rerum Novarum*. The second was preparation for Vatican II. I began both preparations from the position described above.

For help in preparing the encyclical, Cardinal Tardini, then Vatican secretary of state, turned to Fr. Louis Janssens, the general of the Jesuits. He, in turn, handed the commission over to Theodore Mulder, dean of our faculty. Thus, Mulder followed the Jesuit Oswald von Nell-Breuning, S.J., who had been chosen to draft the encyclical for the fortieth anniversary of *Rerum Novarum*. (There was no encyclical for the fiftieth year, but rather Pope Pius XII delivered a radio address.)

As Nell-Breuning had at one stage or another been able to associate other Jesuits with his preparations, so Mulder associated to himself three others. Besides Gundlach there were Pierre Bigo, S.J., director of the Jesuit social institute of Paris, known then as Action Populaire, now called CERAS (Center of Research and Social Action), and myself, from the United States.

Inevitably, our work turned into a wrangling match. Bigo, who was of the school of Díez-Alegría, pushed for more Scripture and more historical openness. I, for reasons mentioned above, tended to side with Gundlach. Gundlach forcefully pushed for a document that would be faithful to *Quadragesimo Anno*. Consequently he pushed to condemn the excesses of capitalism and socialism; likewise he advocated faithfulness to the middle or third way of the Vocational Order he had managed, twenty years earlier, to get into the encyclical celebrating the fortieth anniversary of *Rerum Novarum*. The new encyclical must adhere to *Quadragesimo Anno*'s dictum that this Vocational Order was "if not natural law, as if (*quasi*) it were natural law." The German Jesuit also insisted that we uphold all other traditional teaching about natural law, such as property and state. And he wanted stressed that this new encyclical was in harmony with the corpus of Catholic social teaching.

There was much more. We especially tried to work out a final definitive statement about social justice. Gundlach's was the hand that finalized our debate. As the rest of our drafts, the section in which Gundlach resolved our debate was in a Latin that was impenetrable to me. I wondered what the Vatican would make of it. Since it was now urgent to get our draft to the secretary of state, I did not urge revision because I expected that the Vatican itself would ask for clarification.

This draft represented the attempt to address development in Third World countries. Although it was not profound, it was an attempt. Secondly, despite his vigorous fighting for his positions, Gundlach did not win on every point. When he was adamant and had some supporters he won out. Still, the other two forceful characters made their imprints.

In October of 1960 the "Jesuit" draft was submitted to Cardinal Tardini. We had done our final drafting at a villa outside Rome. I remember wondering as I returned by train whether our Latin (certainly Gundlach's) would prove, if not impenetrable, too difficult to read. Would they invite Mulder to come and explain? I took it for granted that, if the Vatican found the draft unclear or even wholly unsatisfactory, we would be invited to redraft. But the Vatican turned to another hand for redrafting. That hand, ironically, was that of our erstwhile colleague, Pietro Pavan.

Pietro Pavan turned out a decidedly different draft. Although it continued some of our ideas, there were new directions. Pavan and the pope found no difficulty in shelving the notion of Vocational Order or a notion of orders in general. Into our draft on rural, farm, and Third World development we had managed to introduce the ideas of order, ordering, and orders. While much of our writing survived, the concept of orders did not.

There were other changes as well. Our draft had carefully distinguished between social, distributive, and legal justice. The new draft used the terms more freely. *Justice* stood for all forms of justice. Sometimes justice was paired, as in "justice and love" or "justice and equity."

When the encyclical appeared, what most caught the eye was Pavan's introduction of the idea of socialization as a principle of social organization. This was a wholly new and fruitful idea that has endured. In general, the new draft was much more sociological than previous encyclicals.

Mater et Magistra proved a bombshell. Europe's most prestigious daily, *Le Monde* of Paris, bannered its appearance on the front page with the headline "End of German Jesuit Hegemony." This title heralded what by now was generally known: John XXIII had turned from Jesuits to others. It also reflected a sharp change from Pius XII's pontificate, when German Jesuits had surrounded the papal throne as advisers.

What was my own reaction to the encyclical? At first I was disappointed. But soon my dialogue with the document deepened. It was, after all, more like what Bigo and Mulder had wanted. Only a few weeks after its appearance, it was ferociously attacked by the right wing in the United States as socialist. At the request of the Jesuit weekly *America* I gladly wrote a defense, pointing out that equating socialization with socialism as conservatives did could in no way be maintained.

I must here applaud Oswald von Nell-Breuning, S.J., for declaring that papal encyclicals should not be written by relying on one or a few trusted experts (*periti*). Nell-Breuning decided, after many years of silence, to reveal in the columns of the German *Stimmen der Zeit* the story of how *Quadragesimo Anno* was written. He described the secrecy in which he was forced to work. He did manage to consult but with the handicap of not being able to divulge why he was asking. When I read that piece by Nell-Breuning, I said to myself, But of course. I repeated that sentiment more emphatically as I watched the U.S. Catholic bishops consult as they developed their 1986 economic pastoral, *Economic Justice for All.* There were over four years of wide consultation with experts and others of very diverse ideas. A dozen top economists of the country, some conservative, some liberal, were invited to testify. Revisions were followed by more consultation. What more the bishops could have done to guarantee that all useful opinions had been entertained would be hard to imagine.

The Bombshell of Vatican II

I return to the story of my personal *aggiornamento* from the rigidity of the Catholic social teaching I had embraced until 1960 or 1961. Vatican II in its unfolding, its final statements, and their interpretation was enormously influential. Three events moved me ahead. The first was a historic meeting of the subcommittee of the preparatory commission on theology. Twenty-eight theologians met to discuss how to include Catholic social teaching in a document that became *Gaudium et Spes*. Second, I was asked to write an article on Catholic social teaching for use by the council. (At least that was what Roberto Tucci, S.J., director of the semiofficial *La Civiltá Cattolica*, said when he invited me.) Third, *Gaudium et Spes* influenced me remarkably.

This historic meeting of the subcommittee featured a confrontation between Gundlach and Pavan. Because of his prestige, Gundlach had been invited to offer his views to the assembly of twenty-eight about what the council should say on Catholic social teaching. Jarlot, one of those present, related to me the following incident. During the discussion, after listening an hour to what seemed to him the pontificating of the Gregorian's authority on Catholic social teaching, Pavan pounded the table and said angrily, "That's enough of treating us like children!" Somewhat flustered, Gundlach nevertheless managed to conclude. After discussion, a vote was taken on whether to adopt the statement of Catholic social teaching that had just been offered the delegates. Gundlach's presentation got only his own vote. That was definitive handwriting on the wall for me.

Incidentally, that vote and the substantial reworking of the Gregorian's first draft for the encyclical *Mater et Magistra* were indeed crushing for Gundlach.[1]

But my struggle was not quite ended. The *Civiltá* article appeared in two parts. I still remember my reaction on its appearance: "I can't believe I wrote it." I had trotted out all the traditional ideas. First of all the article was utterly papalist: "This pope says this"; "that pope confirms"; "another nuanced while adding his authority to that of his predecessors." Reading signs of the times had not yet crossed my horizon.

That papalism was reinforced by my assertion that the Church knows what the Word Incarnate knew from the nature that he perfectly incarnated and perfectly understood. I now ask myself, did Jesus, could Jesus, have known all the history that would unfold, even in his own life? Yet at that time I assumed that Jesus had had such perfect knowledge and that this knowledge was transferred to the Church.

I then described at length the notion of a true body, a true corpus of Catholic social teaching. Indeed, I took exceptional pains to verify that, despite the newness attributed to the recently published *Mater et Magistra,* the document was largely anticipated by its predecessors and properly continued the line established by earlier papal creators of organicism.

Such organicism, such fidelity to what had been taught, was not surprising for me because fundamentally the corpus was natural law. Since natural law is only a reflection of the divine law, it carried the inerrancy of God's ordering. So, divine order and its assurance were carried forward by the Church, that is, by the popes through and from the Word Incarnate of which the Church is the extension.

There were good things in that article. But I found myself abandoning its fundamental direction. I had wavered back and forth about methodology. It seemed to have been somehow necessary to put on paper once and for all the one side of me that had dominated so that, having looked at it squarely, I could say, that is no longer me. I never learned whether, as proposed, the article was distributed to the fathers of the council. I would have been embarrassed if the project had been carried out.

The next chapter will illustrate how far I have departed from that teaching. Yet I have by no means jettisoned the entire concept of a *corpus doctrinae* nor of foundations of the human discoverable in human nature.

The third event in my personal *aggiornamento* was Vatican II's *Gaudium et Spes* (The Church in the modern world). The document urged that theologizing cease looking at the heavens and read the signs of the times all around us. While this may appear as oversimplification, nevertheless it contains a fundamental truth. The document also placed the reign of God in the world; consequently the Church and Catholics must be concerned about justice in this world. These methodological shifts brought me fully round to conversion. Just after *Gaudium et Spes* was published I received with enthusiasm the invitation to lecture on it in the summer of 1966 for the Canadian Catholic Conference and the University of Ottawa. Those lectures, edited over some months, were published by the conference.

One Catholic Social Teaching Journey: Later Decades, Right Bank of the Tiber

Pontifical Commission Justice and Peace

T he year 1967 brought a partial shift in the scene where I reflected on Catholic social teaching. In early 1967, Paul VI invited Msgr. Joseph Gremillion of the United States to become the first secretary of a new entity in the Vatican called for by Vatican II, the Pontifical Commission Justice and Peace. For that, Gremillion left his post at the National Catholic Relief Service, which he had been guiding away from its focus on aid to helping poor nations enter the road to development. Just before NCRS, Gremillion had earned his doctorate in social sciences at the Gregorian University, and before that he had had a distinguished career as a writer and pastoral guide in the Church in the United States. The commission was housed across the Tiber in an extension of the Vatican in the Trastevere quarter, about a mile downriver.

The work of the commission thrust me into a more activist role, moving around the world even more than in my first years at the Gregorian. I attended meetings with some of the sixty newly created national commissions and participated in delegations of the Vatican itself to the United Nations and other conferences. I was the Vatican's delegate at least a couple of times to the working party in Geneva which prepared a draft for the UN Charter on Rights and Duties of States. Since I had not risen to my status by the usual path of advancement within the office of the secretary of state, I did not know that I should not play an activist role unless explicitly instructed (something that did not often happen). My ignorance of protocol resulted in a delightful encounter with the ranking delegate from Great Britain. When I proposed that the charter enshrine the notion of an international common good, Her Honor avowed that that was the woolliest idea she had ever heard of. The African head of the working party was so intrigued that he invited me to explain my idea further at the next session. I did so. My woolly-headed idea, taken straight out of Catholic social teaching, is now enshrined in the UN Charter of Rights and Duties of States.

One of our tasks on the Pontifical Commission Justice and Peace was to assist (when invited) our commission members and consultors as well as our national commissions to analyze social situations and formulate social policies. This endeavor forced all of us to think anew and to analyze and reflect ideologically, since our correspondents had their own background and ideas.

I Hear New Voices

In no uncertain terms I got told off on occasion for what an interlocutor perceived as an unprogressive and unproductive idea (I have been told off just as much by conservatives). Since development was one of my fields and figured high in our program for justice and peace in the world, I inevitably got caught up in the ongoing debate over what development is. Some voices from Latin America even suggested we should be talking about liberation and not development.

My ideas about what development is and about alternatives to the development espoused by the industrial countries, the World Bank, and the International Monetary Fund have grown enormously in the fifteen years since I left the commission. I wish that the commission and my colleagues there could have benefitted from my more recent growth.

What would I have said differently about development? I would have sounded less an apostle of the UN's New International Order, which so emphasized the model of growth that seemed to the rich, industrial nations, to the World Bank, and to the International Monetary Fund as the only road to development. Although I had always clung to a notion of humaneness in development—and still do—I had not then perceived that this notion requires that people create and engage in their own development. It cannot be handed down by experts.

Over the years I became much more attuned to new voices, from the Third World as well as the industrial North, who said that the export-led model urged on the South by the International Bank for Reconstruction and Development and by the International Money Fund (some in the bank now admit to rethinking their ideas) could prove disastrous. Especially in the last years this policy has been combined with the remedies which the IBRD and IMF have promulgated for enabling the Third World to pay off its debts to the North.

In addition, I have become attuned to voices calling for development, not in terms of industrial power, but of cultural sustainment. One original model was proposed in E.F. Schumacher's *Small Is Beautiful* (1989). Paolo Freire, the Brazilian educator, provided me with another model of bottom-up education for a "Small Is Beautiful" social and cultural structure.

Contacts with the superiors general of congregations and with their staffs afforded the opportunity to test out my budding ideas on development, the Church, and doing justice as the proper task of the Christian. I had many occasions to address general chapters of congregations on the Church in the world as well as on the scriptural bases for doing justice.

How the Pontifical Commission Justice and Peace Helped Shape Me

In late 1970, the superior general of the Jesuits, Pedro Arrupe, hosted at the Jesuit Curia a small dinner to discuss the possibility of Jesuits from the United States creating in the nation's capital a new center of research and public education on justice. Present was Bishop Joseph Bernardin, then secretary of the U.S. Catholic Conference. Arrupe put to the future cardinal of Chicago the question, What accounts for the remarkable upsurge of concern for justice evident in the Church in the United States? Bernardin responded that the women religious had led the Church on this issue. This confirmed my fairly extensive experience in Rome among the hundreds of congregations of women and men headquartered there.

Shortly thereafter the Jesuit William Ryan, of the English-speaking Canadian Province, was apponted to direct this new apostolate, called the Center of Concern. His appointment shattered plans I had made with approval of the Jesuit Curia for Bill to head a work I had begun at the Gregorian. With the approval of my boss, Joseph Gremillion, and financial backing, I had established a center to raise concern for the world's problems of justice, liberation, and development among our students, who represented about a hundred nations. Gremillion and I saw the center as promoting Vatican II, especially its pastoral constitution *Gaudium et Spes.* We named the center Christianity and Development (*Christianesimo e Sviluppo* in Italian).

"Justice in the World," a Part of Me

My work at the Pontifical Commission Justice and Peace shaped me in other ways. Particularly influential was our work on that immensely influential document, "Justice in the World." In preparation for the 1971 Synod of Bishops, Archbishop Rubin, then secretary of the Commission on the Synod, invited Monsignor Gremillion to prepare a preliminary document to be discussed by the thirty bishops and cardinals of the Commission on the Synod. Whatever they agreed upon would then be sent to episcopal conferences around the world for their reflection in preparation for the synod. Our staff, of whom several had Third World experience, got to work on the assignment. To me fell the task of making the presentation to the bishops and cardinals. But I must acknowledge that several of the most innovative ideas that found their way into the final document came not from me, but from colleagues. My most important role was to shepherd them through the many phases of the year-long process that brought them to final endorsement and publication.

Two incidents during the discussions of the Commission on the Synod significantly changed the document. The first happened when I read a paragraph (each had his own copy of our text) for their approval: "The Church should not speak of justice unless it is itself perceived as doing justice." One distinguished cardinal intoned: "The Church has no injustices." Since no one else spoke out, I summoned all my courage to say, "Your Eminence, if we cannot say that we should not have a document." That broke the ice. Several intervened to support me. That section was passed with one dissenting vote. Later in the synod it was unanimously accepted and carried over into the final document. One may presume that the cardinal who declared that the Church had no sins of injustice had in mind "the spotless bride of Christ." The rest of us focused on the institutional Church.

The other incident was an intervention of Cardinal Duval of Algiers, who had secured Algerian citizenship early in the Algerian war for independence from France. Duval said that the commission's document must make a much stronger statement concerning the dependency inflicted on the poor nations by policies of the North before he would sign it. That had actually been the position of a couple of my colleagues in the commission who had lost out to some less discerning minds, including my own. A year later, in the closing hours of the synod, I met Cardinal Duval and thanked him for this important clarification. The final document sustained his view. That initial draft was sent to the bishops of the world with a questionnaire which we also prepared.

To stimulate further the Church's reflection on the draft on the doing of justice, Monsignor Gremillion authorized me to produce six brochures in English, French, and Spanish which took up various aspects of justice. In one we disclosed to the whole world the results of the Latin American Bishops' Conference held in Medellin, Colombia, in 1969. One chapter of the Medellin document was closely in harmony with Cardinal Duval's contribution. In its own language, the Medellin conference called for nothing short of liberation.

I later inserted the word *liberation* into documents published by our commission and even by the office of the secretary of state. In the latter case, inevitably the word *liberation* would be pencilled out. But in his last, great statement, *Evangelii Nuntiandi* (Evangelization in the Modern World), Paul VI used the word repeatedly, as if he had invented it.

After long months, all the comments on the draft were in the hands of the Commission on the Synod. By then I had been established as the link between that commission and ours (PCJP). Archbishop Rubin turned to me to write up the results in what would be the official report to the synod. Archbishop Haceldema of the diocese of Rosario, Philippines, was invited to deliver the *relatio,* or official opening statement, to the synod. At the suggestion of Rubin, Haceldema asked me for help preparing it.

Because of Archbishop Rubin's reliance on us, Monsignor Gremillion thought it advisable to add two theologians to our working party: Juan Alfaro, S.J., of the Gregorian, and Vincent Cosmao, O.P., of *Foi et Dèveloppment, Centre Lebret* in Paris. Cosmao was a consultor to the commission and worked often with us. The two contributed enormously to the work of the synod.

As the synod returned successive drafts to us, we welcomed the demand from the emerging, ever-increasing majority for a strong statement on justice. In their final draft the synod called for a strong turn to reading the signs of the times (a socioeconomic and political analysis which started from a Third World perspective), a theology based on the Scriptures, and an appropriate education for justice.

The Pontifical Commission Justice and Peace, at the invitation of the synod, continued to play an active role to the end of the session. The final document reflects remarkably that decisive participation. Cosmao, as I recall, gave the world the electrifying cry: "The doing of justice is a *constitutive* dimension of the preaching of the gospel." Alfaro's rendering of the idea was substantially the same, if less striking. Alfaro made many contributions to shaping the document's scriptural statement on justice.

Alfaro and I, associates on the synodal commission on revision, worked with that commission through early morning on the next-to-last day of the synod, going over the hundreds of *modi,* or suggestions for possible change. After the committee had worked its way through them, we delivered the final copy to the Vatican Polyglot Press. Miraculously, the press turned out impeccable final versions in Latin, English, Italian, and French in time for the final day's morning session.

No section of that final document—not even that containing the word *constitutive*—got less than a 94 percent approval. Despite that high percentage, in the closing hours one Italian cardinal—considered eminently *papabile*—accosted me with his forceful disapproval: "You are destroying the Church." I don't remember whether *you* meant me or the whole synodal company.

How did the synod of 1971 produce its powerful progressive message? Other synods have failed miserably; for example, the 1987 synod on the laity or the 1974 synod on evangelization (saved, however, when Pope Paul VI published his own document on evangelization, drawn not at all from the curial minority's text but largely from the cutting-edge text of the majority of the synod, a text the Roman president managed to prevent coming to a vote).

The 1971 success was, I believe, owing to the inability of the Roman curia to corral the secretary of the Commission of the Synod, Archbishop Rubin. Rubin reached out confidently beyond the inner circle to the new and innovative secretary of the Pontifical Commission Justice and Peace, Msgr. Joseph Gremillion. Paul VI liked what he saw forming.

Encounter with Paolo Freire's Thinking

Although my whole experience with the synod proved a wonderful learning experience and shaped my thinking, I was in particular grateful for becoming acquainted with the ideas of the Brazilian Paolo Freire on education. This began when two colleagues on the staff of the commission included Freire's ideas in the draft and was reinforced when I prepared the final draft of the short section titled "Education for Justice." I drew upon understanding of Freire that was fairly current.

We moved Freire's thinking on education more deeply into Church circles through one final activity based on the 1971 synod's *Justitia in Mundo*. As Monsignor Gremillion had encouraged me to prepare commentaries on the draft, he now approved of my devoting time to assemble and publish commentaries on the published document. Again, in French, Spanish, and English, we produced six reflection pieces. In addition to one of my own, Pedro Arrupe, Juan Alfaro, Barbara Ward, and Sister Mary Linscott, then superior general of the Notre Dame de Namur congregation, contributed. Linscott's was on the section "Education for Justice."

With some assistance from a member of her congregation who was an expert on Freire, Linscott advanced the short reflection the synod had devoted to this topic. One official of the Sacred Congregation on Education, assigned to review the brochure, brought to our office a score of objections. For him such ideas on education were clearly subversive. It took weeks of exchanges, after which the congregation sat on the document, before we finally forced the congregation to approve Linscott's commentary.

SODEPAX and Ecumenical Learning

Another influential work directly connected with the commission was SODEPAX (Society for Development and Peace). This ecumenical committee was created jointly by the Commission Justice and Peace and the World Council of Churches under the leadership of Joseph Gremillion and Eugene Carson Blake, then secretary-general of the council. The committee's headquarters were at the World Council of Churches in Geneva.

With immense energy and commitment the two leaders put together this ecumenical effort, which caught the attention of Protestant and Catholic worlds alike. Eyes were turned to it in hope, and it did not disappoint. An imaginative and experienced committee of Protestant and Catholic clerics and laypeople, ably guided through the first years by George Dunne, a Jesuit from the United States, propelled SODEPAX into thoughtful initiatives. As expected, not all initiatives met with full approval. Some were questioned by either the Catholic or Protestant sponsors, one or two initiatives by both. I gradually came to see that the Vatican held the most misgivings. It finally disapproved of continuing the mandate and the WCC concurred.

This is not the place to recite the impressive achievements of the joint committee or to describe its slow decline and death as it fell under the control of the two bodies that created it. I leave to historians to evaluate its operations, as well as to distribute blame for its death. My purpose here is to record how SODEPAX was instrumental in my formation in Catholic social teaching. From the beginning, I resisted rightly those rare voices within our committee who insisted that SODEPAX was created to promote Christian unity. For my part, I countered that it was clear from our mandate that we were set up to promote the humanization of life, the doing of justice, and the search for peace, although we were promoting Christian unity by doing this *together,* and we were growing in Christian unity by exercising our united love for our neighbors in need.

Late in 1967 PCJP and WCC began preparing our first joint, ecumenical, intercultural, and indeed international conference. The topic was the "Church and Development," and the conference was held in Beirut. The director of the Church and Society division of the WCC and I were to provide a joint paper on the topic. As it turned out, the paper was mine only. Invited to respond to my paper at the conference was the eminent Barthian, Albert Van der Huevel, now Patriarch of Utrecht. Van der Heuvel raised thirteen objections to my paper. They all turned on his charge of neo-Pelagianism. In his opinion, my paper manifested excessive confidence in the power of men and women to bring about development, justice, and peace. It assigned too slim a role to the Divinity.

I have now reread that paper and I am confident that, apart from an undeniable, perhaps somewhat excessive, optimism which I had absorbed from Vatican II, the theology of the paper was squarely in line with *Gaudium et Spes,* the council's pastoral constitution on the Church in the modern world. A work group used my paper as the starting point for a proposed SODEPAX statement on the role of the Christian church in development. I believe I can say that mainly the work group and the general assembly endorsed a theology that had a strong affinity with Vatican II.[1]

If I had been instrumental in incorporating Vatican II theology in the SODEPAX statement, I was not so successful in incorporating Vatican II theology in our approach to the area of development. I had joined, even taken the lead sometimes, in promoting the concept of development that emerged from Beirut, but that concept was roundly condemned in Latin America as *desarrollismo*. Liberation theologians argued that this model of development had been foisted on the poor nations by the rich industrial nations. They charged that the model was grounded in exploitation and dependency and would deepen the poverty and dependency of the Third World.

In Rome, a couple of members of the Pontifical Commission Justice and Peace heartily concurred with this criticism. Indeed, had they had more of a hand in shaping the conference they would have seen to it that a Third World perspective on development was incorporated in our analysis.

Meanwhile, two people added to the SODEPAX secretariat turned out to be strong critics of the stand the Beirut conference took on development. They urged convening a new conference (held in Montreal in the spring of 1969) to meet the mounting criticism. Although I had promoted the concept of development they criticized, I had to draft the preliminary paper that set out a new approach to development. Since I had, happily, learned a lot, my work for the 1969 Montreal assembly was much more satisfactory. SODEPAX saw to it that a couple of Latin American experts in development were present at the Canadian conference.

Enter Gustavo Gutierrez

Having improved its statement on development, in the fall of 1969, the same year as the Montreal conference, SODEPAX held another conference to advance its concept of the theology of development. Building upon the Beirut conference, this one, held in Cartigny, Switzerland, explored the Church's and the Christian's role from the perspective of the victims of poverty and oppression. These victims sought a *liberating* Christ. They asked too for a Church that accompanied them in their poverty and oppression.

A roster of well-known Protestant and Catholic theologians were at Cartigny: from Latin America, Protestant Ruben Alves and Catholic Gustavo Gutierrez;[2] from France, Dominican Vincent Cosmao, mentioned above; and Charles Elliot, SODE-

PAX's British Anglican priest who was also a bright professional economist at Oxford and a thoroughly grounded theologian. Elliott (1970) drafted the final report in addition to his insightful evaluation of the theologizing at Cartigny. Also present were Canon Ronald Preston (who with me and Cosmao began the planning for the conference) and Paul Abrecht, director of the WCC's Church and Society. The conference was chaired by John Bennett, then president of Union Theological Seminary in New York. In the closing session Bennett remarked that, for the life of him, he could not, on the basis of the discussions, set out a Protestant position against a Catholic one: Catholics had joined Protestants in arguing both sides of the debates.

Vatican Delegate for One Day

One other incident stands out in particular in the final months of my Roman stay as an influence on my development in Catholic social teaching. This incident actually ended my stay. I was invited by the office of the secretary of state to attend the UN Conference on World Population, slated for Bucharest in the fall of 1974, as a member of the Vatican delegation. I never got there.

To begin with, that delegation had—something I had never heard of—two heads. Archbishop (now Cardinal) Gagnon was what can only be described as a titular head. He had to head the delegation because the conference was on population, and in the eyes of the Vatican that suggested that Gagnon, the president of its secretariat on the family, should head the Holy See's delegation. But the Holy See also believed that the delegation needed a sturdier and more politically seasoned guide for such a delicate matter as population. Hence, it appointed a co-chief, Henri De Riedmatten, a Swiss Dominican and long-time permanent observer of the Holy See at the United Nations in Geneva. De Riedmatten was the real head.

I lasted a couple of days. De Riedmatten had circulated a paper indicating the positions on the United Nations' provisional statement for discussion, which all delegates had to support. I had reservations, especially on the absolute no to any governmental policy on population control. So I asked Gagnon if I might circulate an alternative to the members. He gave his *bene placitum*. De Riedmatten was, to say the least, upset when he learned of my audacity.

At the first and only preparatory meeting which I attended, Msgr. Giovanni Benelli, pro-secretary of state, came to read us a letter of instruction from the hand of the secretary of state, Cardinal Villot. I could not believe my ears. We were instructed not only against disparaging the encyclical *Humanae Vitae*'s absolute prohibition of all artificial birth control means but also to defend it. That was fine by me. As a member of the delegation I should not be seen in opposition to *Humanae Vitae*. Furthermore, so far as I had opportunity, I should defend it. But Cardinal Villot's letter further exhorted us to promote the encyclical at the Bucharest conference. *Le pousser* were the cardinal's words.

Benelli read the cardinal's message and departed without any discussion. The members of the delegation did not seem disposed to discuss the letter. I finally broke the silence to ask if I had heard aright. Because, I went on to say, while I highly esteemed the encyclical and would surely never give anyone present at Bucharest indication of reservation, I did have reservations on the two paragraphs which promulgated the absolute prohibition of artificial birth control. My reservations? I found it impossible to accept the anthropology elaborated in those two paragraphs.

Neither head of the delegation said a word. But the very next day my superior in the Pontifical Commission Justice and Peace called me to his office to read me a letter he had just received from the cardinal secretary of state. It demanded that before witnesses Father Land attest his total loyalty to the encyclical. I assured my superior that he could assure the secretary of state that I had complete loyalty to the encyclical, adding "according to the norms of Vatican II."

I learned the next day that was not enough loyalty. The new, phoned message was that Father Land again, before witnesses, must attest that he had no question about *Humanae Vitae* either in *foro externo* or *foro interno*. While the former refers to my communication with others, the latter is my conscience. I could not believe my ears: I could have no reservation even if I kept it to myself. On the one hand, I could not quarrel with the Vatican's laying down whatever conditions it thought appropriate for membership in its delegation. If it wanted only people who held to the encyclical unquestioningly, that was its right. I was prepared to accept or try to accept the condition. But suppose there were no truly qualified demographers among Catholics who did not have some question? And suppose that norm were applied to the appointment of bishops? Then only priests who had no question at all about the encyclical could become bishops. But how many truly qualified candidates would be excluded! And suppose unquestioning adherence to all encyclicals were required? *Veterum Sapientia,* which had ordered that all theology be taught in Latin, had been ignored virtually throughout the Catholic world. These questions I was to mull over in the days to follow. But at that moment I turned to our presiding officer and said, "Tell the good cardinal that I will stay home and pray for the delegation."

Thanks be to God, I did stay home. I would have been mortified beyond all words to have been seated among the delegates of some 140 nations to hear the Holy See represented by De Riedmatten cast the sole vote against the final document. He could have voted in favor with reservation and stated the reservation. He could have abstained. But the Holy See went on record as rejecting in toto the effort of the world's nations to understand the problem of population and to cope with it.

I've Had It

From that time on, my activities in the Pontifical Commission Justice and Peace were sharply circumscribed. As I interpreted the situation, I was virtually boxed up in my office in the commission's secretariat. Gone were the usual calls on my expertise. Former outlets were closed. At one moment I said to myself: "Land, you have done a lot of talking about justice, but you've never suffered for it; now you are going to learn to suffer for justice." So I did for a considerable period.

But the day came when I found myself asking whether our commission was any longer a true witness to justice. It seemed that at the least, we were no longer witnessing to justice by doing what had come to be expected of us. From being an organization actively engaged in the struggle for justice we were in effect being reduced to a study group.

I decided matters had come to the point where I no longer fitted in; I felt I was a counterwitness. I communicated to superiors in the commission (Monsignor Gremillion was by now back in the United States) and in the Jesuit order my desire to leave. There were remonstrations by my superiors and assurances that the Vatican did not want me to leave. Now, fifteen years later, I would have to confess that I may have misread the signs that the Vatican could well do without me.

As my thoughts now turned to departure, I looked back over my eight years with the Pontifical Commission Justice and Peace. All the years, including those of some harassment, had been years of warm relations with the president and staff there. The earlier years of collaboration with Joe Gremillion, whose imagination and initiative shaped the commission into an ecumenical and a world force, were particularly intimate, encouraging, and enabling. Many an early morning, before the rest of the staff had arrived, we would sit at a cafe in the lovely piazza of Santa Maria in Trastevere with its fountain and the facade of the church before us as we drank our cappucchino and discussed ideas and planned programs. I still treasure his friendship, his strong imaginative leadership, his courageous support of his staff, including me, when our missteps displeased someone or other of the Vatican. He fought down to the wire on a couple cases.

The rest of the staff and I were not always in agreement. With time I came to recognize that on some issues they had been right and I wrong. The research and administrative staff held together as a team. I admired Gremillion's successor, Msgr. (now Archbishop) Andrea di Montezomolo. At the commission, besides Gremillion, another former student of mine from the Gregorian was Archbishop Ramon Torrella y Cascante, the vice president. Here too was a warm personal friendship and strong support.

Was I right that this was the time to go? Another person in whom I had great confidence agreed it was time to leave. This was the eminent British writer and authority on Third World development, Barbara Ward (Lady Jackson, Grand Dame of the Republic). She had entered most generously into the work of the Pontifical Commision Justice and Peace. I recall her writing a lengthy study for Gremillion which did not even bear her name. It could very well have become one more of her books. Among her many contributions was her assistance in the final shaping of *Justitia in Mundo*. At that time, Barbara Ward held the Albert Schweizer Chair of International Economics at Columbia University.

At the age of sixty, five years before my actual departure from Rome, I first thought of leaving the Eternal City to start something new. It happened that I accompanied Barbara Ward from the Rome airport for a meeting. I had by then so much confidence in her and her judgment that I laid before her my musings. Her response was, "Don't you ever think that again!" That was enough to make me drop the thought for all the years until the Bucharest conference.

During the aftermath of Bucharest and while I was deciding about leaving the commission and weighing the implications for also leaving the Gregorian and Rome, I was invited to dinner with Barbara Ward at the home of my old friend Luigi Ligutti, now retired as permanent observer of the Holy See at the Food and Agricultural Organization of the United Nations. I laid out for them the state of my soul, my reasons for believing that I should leave the commission. This time Barbara Ward (as did Monsignor Ligutti) agreed. And again her word was enough for me.

From the Banks of the Tiber
to the Banks of the Potomac

But how did I get to the Center of Concern? I had received approval of my superiors in Rome to depart. The Gregorian did not put up much of a fight, either through magnanimity or because they felt they simply could do without me. As I was pondering my options, an invitation from Bill Ryan, S.J., to join the Center of Concern came unexpectedly. Ryan had no knowledge of my decision to leave my two works in Rome. Thus the invitation had all the marks of Providence, and I welcomed the invitation and the opportunity to work with another of my former students.

At the age of 65 I came to Washington and began a career of fifteen years with the center. En route to Washington, I stopped in England to journey down to Barbara Ward's home in Sussex where she was dying of cancer. She was ever her gracious, serene self as she faced the end of her brilliant career, cut off by cancer at sixty. She was for me another saint of our times in a niche alongside Dorothy Day.

Fifteen years at the Center of Concern, which celebrates its twenty-fifth year in 1995! What a wonderful lot of companions in the service of God and the world! If I do not name them because of the limits of this project, I do lift them up in memory. More to the point, I must salute them for the contributions they made to my ongoing formation. One day a few years back—Bill Ryan, S.J., was still director—we voted to halt all our activity and gave ourselves a six-month sabbatical to reflect. We explored method. What did reading signs of the times mean, sociologically and theologically? We asked ourselves whether there were cultural and religious symbols more relevant to our projects than those we were employing.

Even while I was saying my piece on a number of platforms I was learning as listeners challenged my ideas and my method. I even came to understand that they were not passive recipients into whose heads I could pour prefabricated ideas. They taught me to learn from them, from their way of reading the signs of the times, from their way of stating the problematic.

The pastoral circle, which I will describe in chapter 9, soon became second nature to most of my companions at the Center of Concern. To me it is a procedure that stood much of theological method on its head.

I am convinced that I read more theology in those fifteen years than in my twenty Roman years, perhaps even than I read in my four years devoted to earning a licentiate in theology—if not more works, at least more relevant theology. And yet, many of the themes I now read with renewed assiduity were theological themes on which I had already written. I guess what I am saying is that they had now become more solidly mine. I felt more assured about theological positions which I had tentatively adopted, but was prepared to back off if I could not find adequate support for them from a solid majority of the theological community.

One of the great gifts to me was the appearance of Karl Rahner's *Foundations of the Christian Faith* (1978). The Rahner I had been reading in disparate articles of his *Theological Investigations* and other slimmer volumes (to deepen my understanding of that narrow band of theological themes I felt I must pursue) were now offered to me in a single volume. The same publishing house shortly thereafter presented to me a precious commentary on Rahner's *Foundations* (O'Donovan 1980) done by a notable group of Rahnerian scholars. I refer to it often in these pages.

One further note before concluding this description of my journey. Five years back I put into the computer much of the substance of this chapter and several other chapters of what I called "My Autobiography in Catholic Social Teaching." I abandoned that writing altogether to undertake a book-length study (and defense) of the U.S. Catholic bishops' economic pastoral, *Economic Justice for All*. When that and a few other writing assignments were completed, I came back to the project of the Catholic social teaching autobiography.

To my surprise, I found that first draft singularly unappealing and inadequate. I had not put on paper the methodological changes that had become central to my current lectures. For example, there was nothing in that original draft about contextual theology, *praxis* theology, political theology, and liberation theology. Furthermore, that first draft, though it had chapters that disclosed my theological orientation, was excessively philosophical. I wondered if whether I was more philosophical or more theological on a given day depended on which side of the bed I got out of in the morning, for where the two disciplines were reported in that first draft they appeared quite independently, side by side. There was nothing of the dialogical character which I hope the pages that follow will reveal.

Reflection on
Chapters 1-3

T his chapter of quick review of the events as my thinking and doing unfolded over those long years depicted in the first three chapters presents themes that are developed in the chapter to follow. This chapter reveals both thematic and methodological shifts. My present perception is that the thematic changes were largely stimulated by the methodological changes.

Four Methodological Shifts

1. **Turning to the person, the social person**. The entire chapter 7, "Moral Making in the Social Order," is devoted to this shift. The bulk of that chapter is based on Rahner. Even though Metz and others argue that Rahner's treatment of the subject did not include a social subject, in chapter 6 I reply that Rahner, if not explicitly, did lay profound grounding for this shift, and I draw attention to his profoundly insightful article on the unity of love of God and neighbor (1974).

2. **From thinking about doing to doing and thought derived from doing**. At issue here is a diminishing attention to thought about social living accompanied by a corresponding increase of concern for living, for "doing social action." Says my confrere,

James Hug, S.J. (1983), "The goal of this theological reflection is Christian life rather than Christian truth, or perhaps better, it is lived Christian truth rather than articulated Christian truth."

This seems to me to correspond to the familiar distinction between right living and correct living (Fuchs 1989).[1] Chapter 11, "Moral Rightness of Social Action," explores this bipolarity, the one throwing emphasis on doing. Here I need only note that the essence of morality is the free choice one makes in one's conscience, as has been profoundly vindicated by the Second Vatican Council (on which more later).

The only point to be dwelt on here is that conscience links rightness and correctness, for Catholic moral theology has always recognized that one could make an erroneous judgment about an action without nullifying the goodness of that action. That action, so long as the judgment is made with honest effort and care to be correct, would be a good choice.

Dermot Lane (1984, 29) builds on the distinction of right living and correct living. For him the primary emphasis of Catholic social thought is on right living in the social sphere, that is, "to transform the Church into a more effective instrument of social change, a transformation that may be blocked. The apparent ineffectiveness of the Christian message in the public forum and the social domain [results from] its highly theoretical character." This language seems to warn against excessive concern for the *correctness* of a moral decision.

All of this may be saying only that correctness identifies with the tradition of deductive morality, rightness with a *praxis* orientation. The latter starts its search for truth in the social context. *Praxis* theology (to use a term familiar to readers of Lonergan) finds meaningfulness in the doing and in the suffering. "Such an understanding of *praxis*," argues Lonergan,"if realized individually and communally, provides religious and intellectual foundations for an understanding of Church doctrines as sets of meanings and values which should inform Christian living." Meaningfulness streams from many fountainheads.

Meaningfulness is essential for morality and indeed for salvation, but it is not to be subordinated to concern for social change. However, *praxis* theology will insist with *Gaudium et Spes* that social concern stems from the salvific love of neighbor, which embraces concern for the humanization of social life (*GS* 39, 43; see also *GS* 34, 57). If I am correct, an option more fundamental than the option for the poor is grounded in the love of neighbor. This option embraces the option for the poor and is the option for the other, the neighbor, the sister, and the brother.

3. **From revelation about social living found solely in human nature to revelation about social living found in Scripture.** In the second chapter I related the incident of a group of ue a social encyclical celebrating the sixtieth anniversary of *Rerum Novarum*. There I recounted how two of the four sharply dissented on whether Scripture should be regarded as a fount of truth about social living. Gustav Gundlach held out strongly against it, saying Scripture was not intended to set norms for social living and that revelation given in human nature, in natural law, was totally adequate. After all, he argued, natural law reflects divine law, God's ordering of humans in society. Besides, it is a revelation which we share with other faiths and a foundation we can build on together.

Pére Pierre Bigo fought mightily but unsuccessfully to introduce norms and attitudes from Scripture into our draft. Bigo, then director of Jesuit *Action Populaire* in Paris, would have the Catholic world as well as the Protestant decidedly on his side today. That Jesuit text dutifully repeated the time-honored formula about Catholic social teaching being derived from "reason and the gospels," but biblical norms were exceedingly sparse. Biblical norms will abound in the chapters to follow.

Perhaps a word might be added about attitudes—biblical in origin but also humanly grounded. As mentioned earlier, whereas others of us in the Gregorian's faculty of Social Sciences emphasized the norms, one, Jose Maria Díez-Alegría, titled his lectures on Catholic social teaching "Christian Attitudes." This would be closer to Lonergan's "meaningfulness," that is, what meaning for social living do I get out of my context? A few examples of powerful attitudes in society are the option for the poor, love of neighbor, and seeking justice. Such Christian attitudes appear extensively in the pages that follow.

4. To reading signs of the times. Where do we find God's revelation about social living? Before the council we would never have thought of looking for it in our social context. We would have found it only in the Church's social teaching, possibly also in our hearts, but not in the hopes and fears of our contemporaries, not in the movements of our times.

Let me devote only a couple paragraphs to this shift in methodology to place it in the perspective of this book. I offer two classic statements on it.

First, from Vatican II's constitution on the Church in the modern world, *Gaudium et Spes:*

> The Church has always had the duty of scrutinizing the signs of the times and of interpreting them in the light of the Gospel. . . . We must therefore recognize and understand the world we live in, its expectations and its longings, and its often dramatic characteristics (*GS* 4).
>
> The People of God . . . labors to decipher authentic signs of God's presence and purpose in the happenings, needs, and desires in which this People has a part along with other men of our age (*GS* 11).

Fully supporting this conciliar line, Paul VI in his encyclical *Octogesima Adveniens* (Eightieth annivesary of *Rerum Novarum*) wrote "it is up to the Christian communities to analyze with objectivity the situation which is proper to their own country, to shed on it the light of the gospel's unalterable words and to draw principles of reflection, norms of judgment and directives for action from the social teaching of the Church" (*OA* 4).

This striking shift in methodology for Catholic social teaching is particularly notable in Paul's statement, for it explicitly links Catholic social teaching and a prior analysis of the situations in which people find themselves. Much of this link will be developed in the chapters that follow.

I want to devote the rest of this chapter to one way to read signs that seeks not so much directives for the normative but rather where in the sociopolitical world of our day God is calling. This search is based on the invitation of the council to the people of God to "labor to decipher authentic signs of God's presence and purpose."

Reading the signs to seek the authentically human as the foundation for social thinking and doing pervades the remaining chapters, even while not specifically mentioned. But reading the signs to ask where God is calling us does not. Therefore, I want to elaborate on this idea here.

"Authentic signs of God's presence and purpose." Those words appearing just above open an alluring vista for revealing God's vision for society, his reign in the here and now, as Shalom, the city of God.

I have just read the fortieth chapter of Isaiah, in which God calls the people of Israel, who are in bondage in Babylon. The prophet uses the metaphor of a people exiled in a desert: "Make straight in the desert a highway for our God . . . (so that the) glory of God can be revealed." The desert is of their own making. Because of Israel's sinfulness, their God let them be taken in captivity to Babylon for several decades. But the God of the covenant is prepared to return them to their land and their status as partners under the covenant. For that they have only to return to God and prepare the road for him to meet them and lead them back to their own land, to the temple of Jerusalem.

The fortieth chapter of Isaiah increasingly favors the metaphor of the Babylonian captivity, including God's will to renew the covenant, but continues to use the metaphor of the Exodus and God's deliverance through Moses, which formerly predominated. A recent book, *Kairos: Three Prophetic Challenges to the Churches* (Brown 1990), presents three *kairos* documents of our times. The first challenge, a prophetic statement partly written by the eminent Dominican theologian Albert Nolan, called the churches of South Africa to do penance for their sin of apartheid. The second, similar in substance, came from Central America. The third, *The Road to Damascus: Kairos and Conversion,* was signed by hundreds from South Korea, the Philippines, and Central America. The title, drawing its metaphor from the story of Paul's conversion, is a call to the people and their society to conversion.

Reading Socioeconomic Signs in the United States

This section may seem peripheral to our focus, methodological change. But it appears to me rather as one application of one methodological change, reading signs of the times, in the United States today.

Theologian Robert McAfee Brown asks: "Do we in the United States live in a *kairos* situation [that is, a moment of call to conversion]?" Or, he goes on, "Are we something of an exception, doing pretty well at a time when others are stumbling? Would it not be guilt-mongering or at least gloom-mongering to paint our situation as darkly as theirs?" (Brown 1990).

The concept of a *kairos* situation in the United States is immensely relevant to social living and Catholic social teaching, for it is founded on God's direct revelatory action at the core of our individual existence, his call revealed in an honest reading of the signs of the times.

How might the signs read now? Contemporary signs in the United States might read like this: Our children are not getting enough of the right education. Those not going on to college will have less income than their parents because their education has not prepared them for today's jobs. But even those who do go to college have no guarantee that they will do as well as their parents. The number of college graduates who, because of low job earnings, are forced to live with their parents is growing. Couples in their thirties, even those with two incomes, ask whether they will ever be able to afford a home of their own. Low national investment in our children during the Reagan and Bush years accounts in good part for the inability of our school system to educate our children adequately. It also explains in large part why the United States is falling behind in scientific competition with Germany, Japan, and other nations.

In *Shaping the Welfare Consensus* (1988) I portrayed poverty in the United States and its causes, as well as unemployment and its causes.[2] As I predicted, conditions have worsened. At this moment (October 1991), the recession, which President Bush repeatedly proclaimed was ending, now looks as if it may become a double-dipper. If not quite that, then at least the recovery will be so slow and slim that for very many it will appear an illusion.

Has the American dream become bankrupt? You would not know it from the copy of Madison Avenue. The countless millions whose hopes of a better income have dimmed are daily bombarded by commercials that assure them they have a right to the good life. An emphatically consumer society defines the good life by what one eats, drinks, and wears and how one travels and entertains. While the pitch for the good life shouts, the indexes of consumer confidence in the U.S. economy show a sharp decline. Where is God calling now?

Paying interest on the national debt severely restricts government efforts to brighten our gloomy economic outlook. In ten years, our national debt has grown from one trillion dollars to two and a half trillion. Hundreds of billions are owed, not to U.S. nationals, but to other nations. According to one estimate, the increase in the nation's debt per person from 1980 to 1990 costs each taxpayer $1,300 every year. Lower interest rates might stimulate business, but if the Federal Reserve Board sets interest rates low enough, foreign investors will dump their holdings of U.S. bonds. Lowering interest rates to reduce capital gains will not induce businesses to invest if consumer demand is weak. Our two recent supply-side presidents ignored this fact.[3] Lower interest rates for consumers might be proposed to achieve the stepped-up buying that manufacturers need. Increased consumer sales are normally a stimulus in recessions, but in this recession people are so concerned about pink slips that they avoid borrowing.

The fond hope that reducing the defense budget would pay a social dividend has thus far been illusory, especially after Republican presidents pushed for their outrageously costly weapons systems for the future.

Newsweek's Robert Samuelson, who is largely pro-business, rhetorically asks, who benefits from government? He answers, the rich. We are, he adds, in plain language, a plutocracy, a rich man's governing club. So, where is God calling in this plutocracy?

War and a Reading of Signs in the United States

In January 1991 President Bush decided to open armed hostilities in the Persian Gulf. Is it totally impermissible to see *kairos* in our war engagement? To hear our God questioning us? To see another idol that needs to be cast out?

This questioning need not imply disrespect or misunderstanding of motives or disaffection for our troops. We hoped and prayed that all of them would return safely, just as we hoped the Iraqi troops would. But, as an editorial in *America* (February 2, 1991) stated: "Sanctions and diplomacy were not the road taken. . . . War is now the *evil* reality" (emphasis added).

Evil reality. Was the language of our president that of a nation on the road back to the covenant? True, the invasion of Kuwait was an evil deed, even granting Iraq's claims to the long-disputed territory between the two countries. But did Iraq's invasion justify resorting to arms to liberate Kuwait?

Why were we obligated to intervene? Were our obligations greater than, say, those for liberating Lithuania from its long years of subjection to Soviet power?

There were ancillary motives. Hussein threatened to acquire nuclear weapons. Granted that the United Nations investigations substantiated this threat, does that justify a war and killing 100,000 to 150,000 people? It was surely not justified on grounds of a military threat to the United States or even to Israel (which has a considerable stockpile of nuclear weapons). Furthermore, if nuclear weapons in Iraq would be a menace to its neighbors, is it inconceivable that the United States and the United Nations could have neutralized that threat? If Iraq was disarmed because it posed a nuclear threat, then what about Israel and all the other nations that possess nuclear weapons? Was Bush afraid that possession assured use? Only one possessor did use it—the United States.

That war brings us to the theory of a just war. I have already alluded to it when discussing social living and loving one's enemy. The theory of just war and especially its condition of proportionality enabled me to say no to the war in the Persian Gulf and to picket the White House on several days during the weeks before the United States sent in the troops. I am also convinced that in time economic sanctions could have induced Hussein to withdraw from Kuwait.

But I find myself coming round to the position of Pax Christi that just war is a hopelessly useless guide because before actual conflict begins we cannot estimate the proportion between the destructiveness of war with today's weapons and the good to come from winning the war. That conclusion has recently been affirmed by no less an authority than Cardinal Ratzinger, president of the Sacred Congregation for Promotion of the Faith.

In this war, the harm to weigh includes "collateral damage" (euphemism for civilian deaths), the destruction of Iraqi infrastructure, the impoverishment of the Iraqi people, the undying hatred of Arabs for the United States, and the unlikelihood that any new political arrangement in the Gulf would proportionately improve the situation.

A *Kairos* Moment

So, what is God calling us to do? To shatter another idol? President Bush promoted a New World Order. Was oil another idol? Was the power of the United States to settle disputes? Was the role of the United States as world policeman? Was world recognition of the United States as the most powerful, the most benign of nations, the chosen people of God?

One component of that New Order, in Mr. Bush's perception, was already in place, that is, democratic reforms and demilitarization, not only in the USSR and Eastern Europe, but on other continents. Mr. Bush hailed democracy and demilitarization as the triumph of his own containment policy, especially his neoliberal economics. He claimed socialism had been defeated and capitalism had won out. Mr. Bush and conservatives in the United States believed that they had the pope on their side on this issue.

So, where is God calling us as a nation, as churches, as the Roman Catholic church? Do we have idols to shatter? War? Power? Receiving world tribute as Number One? Our role as guarantor of God's recent gift, the triumph of capitalism, that is, of neoliberal economics, over socialism?

Facing *kairos* reflects one of the social dimensions of Christian living; *kairos* is the proper matrix of Catholic social thinking. It is the doing of what Catholic social teaching is thinking, and the thinking is much better because the doing carries on that thinking.

The last section discussed the revelation discoverable by reading signs of the times. Although formerly Catholic social teaching perceived revelation only in the norms discoverable in our God-given nature, contemporary Catholic social teaching attends to God's revelation in the events and crises of our times. Having said that, it is worth recalling that the focus of this chapter is Christian living—a Christian living that is decidedly social, that is the accomplishment of the reign of God in our time, which will be fully established in the reign beyond time.

Summing Up

One theme of this chapter is the several ways the social vocation may be revealed. One is long honored as unique by neo-scholasticism, the nature God gave humankind. In addition, several revelations can be drawn from Scriptures, notably the revelation made in Jesus Christ. Finding revelation by reading signs of the times was the way most prominent in the post–Vatican II Church.

Perhaps reading signs of the times reveals less about norms and more about the social vocation. What is God calling us to in our social and economic situation? Where is God's call when we deliberate about going to war? Is this country's New Order, as its proponents seem to believe, a vocation from God? Or are war making and the New Order idols God calls us to tear down? The brief probing of this chapter—there are other probings elsewhere in this book—lays down a foundation for the response of Catholic social teaching to issues of our time.

Catholic Social Teaching 1

F irst, three words apply to all the chapters that follow. I had conceived the preceding chapters as telling my story, that part of my life that is relevant to living, loathing, and loving Catholic social teaching. This discourse, I must say again, is much more methodological than thematic. But the chapters ahead do continue the autobiography whether they are thematic chapters, as the next three, or methodological, as the rest of the volume. The methodology sometimes confirms themes, sometimes qualifies or enlarges them.

Second, do I not contradict a premise of my preface, that is, that I have largely abandoned the purely speculative in favor of the historical? If these are universal themes, how do they square with the particularity of the historical? My answer is that the next three chapters are like what Rahner typified as irreducibles of human nature (not that he proposed my set of norms). But these irreducibles, I hold, are heavily drawn from ages of experience, and they are much more like what Aquinas called *ius gentium* (law of nations)—truths people generally hold—than purely deductively drawn universals.

Third, this book is decidedly anthropocentric, even though one of the things I loathe about Catholic social teaching is its failure to place humans properly in the universe. In this book I discuss creating on this earth the *oikos* (home), the *shalom* (peace), the habitat of justice, friendship, peace, and communal living. I discuss human rights and the common good.

But what about the common good of the planet? Indeed, can the common good of the human community stand without that wider planetary common good? Do animals and other components of the universe have no rights, or some analog to rights? Can the *oikos* of the human survive if the *oikos* of the environment is neglected, even destroyed, as humans are presently doing? Some say that we shall shortly destroy the basis of our human *oikos*. *Oikos* can mean management of the household and home economics. Human economics had better start with the economics of the earth, our home. I present chapters rich in religious truth for building the *oikos,* but none that offer religious truths drawn from our Scriptures and theology about loving, caring about, and sharing God's universe or viewing the cosmos as a sacred whole.

I can only submit that this is an incomplete project indeed. One could well argue, for reasons given above, that this is the least important project. Yet, all I say about building the human *oikos* within the cosmic *oikos* is still very relevant. Fortunately, very much is being written about that wider project, and this less significant one could well be integrated into it.

The topic of this chapter, Catholic social teaching, is a body of concepts, more or less organically connected, about human beings living in society.[1] That tradition once found its building blocks only by reflecting on human nature. It viewed humanity as a universe yielding universal and, hence, unexceptionable, norms.

This book carries on a dialogue with that tradition in two ways. First, method: how does reflecting on human nature arrive at norms? Does it consider human nature in a purely deductive way or historically? Second, sources: does it rely exclusively on that disclosure of human nature? Or, does it draw also upon Christian revelation? If so, does it draw upon a God who reveals himself in society? Does it reveal human comportment in society? Most of this book responds to these two sets of questions.

One caveat: If God is active in the social and political order, that truth should not be interpreted to mean that human beings are nothing more than objects of divine manipulation, like puppets. No, God does not want us to be passive receivers of divine law and ordinances, of preordained norms, following the dictates of nature and divine interventions. We are to create our morality, our moral being. That is our responsibility.

If God is active in our world, it does not mean that we dismiss essential ethics, all objectivity of nature, or essential channels that flow from our bodiliness and our sociality. But as we pursue essential ethics, the moral quality of social acts, we are conscious of the limits on our freedom. Natural law, I explain later, deals with what grounds a free peron's activity and empowers it, as well as what limits it and channels it.

Since these pages treat norms traditionally derived from contemplating human nature, norms which are labelled Catholic social teaching, it seems appropriate here to set them forth, if only briefly. We turn in a moment to the following: dignity and freedom of the human person, the social nature of the human person, solidarity, the common good, rights as imbedded in the common good, justice (especially the obligations of social justice), social love, participation, equality, the hierarchy of values, and subsidiarity, which relates the state to the individual and to intermediate organizations. The substance of these topics has received traditional statement as natural law. Karl Rahner remarked that the natural law is not something extra, superimposed on norms inherent in reality, but the expression of these norms as something to be respected according to the will of God. Right relationships with persons and reality are materially identical with the moral norm.

Without destroying their value, these norms have gradually enveloped that other matrix, revelation, during the last half century, culminating in Vatican II. Gilleman, who is often mentioned in these pages, was important in balancing norms and revelation. One of the most notable figures, however, was Henri de Lubac. This eminent precursor of Vatican II bases his study of person and society (1938) on theology.

An extraordinary witness to this process is John Paul II's latest encyclical: "Thus the Church's social teaching is itself a valid instrument of evangelization. As such, it proclaims God and his mystery of salvation in Christ to every human being, and for that reason reveals man to himself. . . . In this light and only in this light does it concern itself with everything else: the human rights of the individual, and in particular of the 'working class,' the family and education, the duties of the State. . . . " (*CA* 54). The pope emphasizes: "Christian anthropology therefore is really a chapter of theology, and for this reason, the Church's social doctrine, by its concern for man and by its interest in him and in the way he conducts himself in the world, belongs to the field of theology and particularly of moral theology" (*CA* 55).

This Christian anthropology of action in the world seems to be equivalent to doing justice as a Christian vocation. Doing justice in Christian anthropology is doing justice in love. I formulated this statement recently for a dictionary of theology (Land 1987). I began: "Let justice roll like a river." Before Vatican II, no Roman Catholic treatise on justice would have begun with a quotation from Scripture. It would have taken its start from the definition of justice—*suum cuique tradere*—to render to each one his or her due. I next said: "With Vatican II, but especially with the 1971 synod's *Justitia in Mundo*, justice becomes a call to the Christian from the God of the two Testaments."

Noting that the idea of justice as a vocation was not foreign to an earlier Catholic tradition, I observed that the 1971 synod moved decisively from concern for rational definition to its commitment to doing justice. Moreover, this commitment is linked to stronger emphasis on love as the form of justice, thus providing new interior force and motivation. Justice, I said, was now being proposed as the first requirement of love, and Christian love radicalizes the doing of justice.

The 1971 synod took up justice as proposed in the two Testaments. In the Hebrew Scriptures, according to the synod, God reveals himself as the liberator of the oppressed and defender of the poor, demanding from human beings faith in him and justice toward one's neighbor. It is only in the observance of duties of justice that God is truly recognized as liberator of the oppressed (*JM* 6; Gremillion 1976, 513–39).

Turning to the Christian Scriptures, the synod asserts that "in his preaching Jesus proclaimed . . . the intervention of God's justice on behalf of the needy and oppressed" (*JM* 31). Further, Jesus identified with his least brethren: "Insofar as you did this to one of my least brethren you did it to me"

(Mt 25:40). Hence, says the synod, "for a Christian, love of neighbor and justice cannot be separated. For love implies the absolute demand for justice, recognition of dignity and the rights of one's neighbor" (JW 34).

In the same article, I made two more points pertinent to our present discussion. First, "it is obvious how far the language of scripture and synod is from that minimalizing of justice which derives from treating the Beatitudes as an ideal or optional work for those seeking perfection, while assigning to the main body of believers a minimal ethic of justice in free exchange between individuals." Second, "Biblical justice embodies the principle: 'To each according to need.' It calls for a very large degree of opportunity and of life style" (Land 1987, 550).

Justice, then, is a vocation. And that is what Catholic social teaching is all about. From the perspective of the God who does the calling, the reign of justice can be named the reign of God. From the perspective of the people living it out, it could be variously named. It is the *shalom* of the Hebrew Scriptures wherein the needs of people are met, including widows, orphans, and strangers. It is Karl Rahner's unity of love of God and love of neighbor. It is Augustine's ancient *"pax: tranquillitas ordinis,"* the right relations of Christians and others in human society, a right ordering that must now be extended beyond the human to embrace the cosmic whole of creation.

Another description that appeals to me is this: the vocation of justice is the call to build the *oikos,* the human habitation where all have access to resources to meet their basic needs, which offers meaningful work to all in a community of peace in an ecologically sustainable environment. The values and supporting institutions one desires are known as alternative in the literature of social change.

Building the *Oikos*

Catholic social teaching can be formulated as an orderly procession of ideas, all elaborating the central notion of the social nature of the human (the manual approach). Another formulation is as an answer to the particular question one puts to the tradition. For instance, in a recent book (Land 1988) I put the question: What does Catholic social teaching have to say about welfare, including unemployment, poverty, gross inequalities of income, property, assets, education, and medical insurance?[2] Another approach is to begin with how Catholic social teaching responds to a particular conflict of social living, such as the spotted owl versus the timber industry, or to conflict resolution generally.[3]

Although these other approaches to the formulation of Catholic social teaching are attractive, my purpose is not to provide an exhaustive treatise on Catholic social teaching, but rather to illustrate the fecundity of its noetic or philosophical component. I choose to formulate Catholic social teaching according to its contribution to building the *oikos*. I may bring a narrow, human anthropology to bear, but I do want my view of *oikos* to embrace ecology.

Some aspects of the reign of God and other theological metaphors are most pertinent to Catholic social teaching. However, I reserve these metaphors for later chapters. Here I focus on an anthropology that derives from the social nature of the human.

This approach is starkly noetic, that is, conceptual. In a day gone by, the noetic was all there was to Catholic social teaching. Indeed, if we had to stick narrowly to the name of our discipline, it says it is teaching and nothing but teaching. As I said above, its actual practice is much more than a noetic exercise. In this chapter, however, we may confine ourselves to the noetic.

In the papal documents of Catholic social teaching, *oikos* has largely concentrated on the industrial order in the North Atlantic nations and in nations drawn into their trading orbit. It is predominately male and urban. This vision of official Catholic social teaching has to be broadened. Because Catholic social teaching concentrated on Western industry and its structural deficiencies, it focused on structure and neglected culture. My vocation to justice addresses the cultural as well as the structural changes required to build the *oikos*.

Building Blocks of Catholic Social Teaching

Dignity of the Human Person

The ground of the dignity of the human person is that he or she has been created in the image of God. "So God created man in his own image, in the image of God he created him: male and female he created them" (Gen 1:27). Therefore, the human shares being with God. Men and women do not have being from themselves; they "borrow" it from God. Still, they are beings made in the image of God. They are therefore not objects but subjects, self-reflective and free, with all the responsibility of freedom. The question that Catholic social teaching raises on every social program or political process is how does it affect the human and the rest of creation? Traditional Catholic social teaching treated the ground of human dignity in philosophical terms: this dignity is imbedded in human nature by its Creator. But the Second Vatican Council opted for a much more theological statement, rooting human dignity in the Incarnation. In *Gaudium et Spes* the council asserts: "Since human nature as He assumed it was not annulled, by that very fact it has been raised up to a divine dignity in our respect too" (*GS* 22). The whole of paragraph 22, "Christ as the New Man," is a rich exposition of the implications for the human race when Jesus wholly assumed our human nature and thereby identified himself with each person. Human nature was elevated when Jesus as God identified with us in and through our human nature, which is his human nature.

Social Being

In natural law, social being has been explained in terms of human sociability or sociality. God designed the human person to live for others and not just for self. As John Donne wrote, "no man is an island." Vatican II, in one example of Christian anthropology, laid the ground for that sociability in the social life of the Trinity.

Another example of Christian anthropology is the way Christ celebrated the table as a symbol of the sociability of our human nature and of Christian fellowship. Our word *companion* comes from the Latin *cum pane,* which means "with bread." How often Jesus resorts to a table of fellowship to expound his message and to live that message! Luke's Gospel is full of instances. For example, the Gospel account of Jesus telling the story of the prodigal son begins with "Now the tax-collectors and sinners were drawing near to hear him. And the Pharisees and Scribes murmured: This man receives sinners and eats with them" (Lk 15:1–2). The same Gospel account ends with another banquet, which signals the eschatological wedding banquet: "Bring the robe, the ring, and shoes. . . . Bring the fatted calf and let us eat and be merry" (Lk 15:22–23).

Passing over many other uses of table (such as the breakfast prepared by the risen Christ for his disciples), I come to the Last Supper. Jesus chooses, not a temple scene, but a familiar Jewish family rite of celebrating Passover at table. "While they were at table . . ." In table fellowship Jesus gives his community a form of worship. He also presents the eschatological time as a continuous banquet: "Henceforth I will not drink of this cup until I drink it with you in the eternal Kingdom" (Lk 22:16).

As human persons we are destined to be and to be socially. The substance of our being is goodness, the good of the human. That common or social being has often been called by John Paul II solidarity, which is surely a more emotive word and one richer in symbolism. John Paul's solidarity echoes an earlier tradition, developed by the German Jesuit Heinrich Pesch, who named it *solidarismus,* or the good of social being.[4]

The Common Good

The common good is often described as the total of all those conditions of social living—economic, political, and cultural—which make it possible for women and men readily and fully to achieve the perfection of their humanity. But much more fundamental about the common good than creation of these conditions is the consideration that social being (that is, social good) is another name for the common good. It is first and foremost being together. It is "life-giving community which creates space for individuals."[5]

This, I submit, is not different from one of the purposes of government described by our Founding Fathers, "to promote the general welfare." Aquinas took a teleological approach to the common good. It was that "order" in which human beings attain their ends. This view accords with our approach because the end is the fullness of human good. This is a common good because it is the good of all humanity.

I find my insistence on common good is much more than insistence on a set of conditions promoting social life. That common good is shared life or being is corroborated by John XXIII in his encyclical *Pacem in Terris*. Thus "they [individuals and intermediate groups] must bring their own interests into harmony with the needs of the community" (*PT* 53). Interests are manifestations of being, of life. They are ways in which I choose to live. I am interested in music. I like to read novels. I like hiking in the mountains.

John XXIII's successor, Paul VI, uses only slightly different language to convey this commonality of being, this way of perceiving the common good as not just *conditions* for being, but communal being itself. In his encyclical *Populorum Progressio* (Development of Peoples) the development the pope advocates is "personal and communal" (*PP* 18). What is this development? It is "a transition from less human conditions (of living) toward more human conditions" (*PP* 21). Social ethician Drew Christiansen, S.J. (1989, 63), in a perceptive article on the common good that compares the treatment of common good in *Mater et Magistra* and in *Pacem in Terris*, argues that "Indeed, it becomes clearer (in *Pacem in Terris*) than it had in *Mater et Magistra* that the good of the whole is conceived largely as the individual's share in the well-being of the society."

Christiansen continues: "The common good is injured if classes are excluded from participating in it. Hence, promotion of entitlements, provided it be within the common good, is not favoring one group or allowing them to 'elbow-their-way-in.' If the privileged classes resist, promotion of entitlements may require that government step in to enforce the right of the underprivileged to a fairer share. The common good may indeed require some to relinquish their privileges for the sake of the common good in which they share and which secures their own rights.

I am aware that some liberals rightly charged with promoting rights and entitlements totally ignore public responsibilities. On the other hand, neoconservatives often act to strike out of United Nations charters on rights any reference to social and economic rights. The only rights the conservatives accept are political.

Obviously, relinquishment flies in the face of the American dream of ever-upward mobility. It is contrary to the economic optimism that all boats rise on a rising tide. It is contrary to the approach to taking care of the poor by increasing the gross national product so that income will trickle down to them. This position is still held after a decade in which the rich have grown richer and the poor poorer. What about the chances for the rest of the world? Can they make much headway while 6 percent of the world's population consumes 40 percent of the world's resources and is the greatest polluter of the world's atmosphere? Are we not called upon to reduce our consumption and waste for the sake of humanity, for the sake of the international good, and for the sake of the cosmic good? Is this not what is meant by the slogan, *be rather than have?*

To help the poor, it may be politically necessary to pass laws that affirm that the middle class has certain entitlements, as is common in European social legislation; for example, laws that provide family or children's allowances.

It should now be apparent that pitting individual good against the common good can be done only if the common good is not viewed as also the good of every individual. Downward mobility for those in grossly high incomes can be considered a sacrifice of individual good in favor of the common good from only a narrow viewpoint. First of all, it enhances the rich as individual human persons because their sacrifice enriches them as mature members of society. Second, it enhances their common good, their common being. The same is true of levying taxes and of asking the very poorest not to fall into a welfare mentality of wanting that everything be done for them and not acting for themselves.

The same will be so, *mutatis mutandis,* of localities and nations in relation to the global common good. Local groups and nations have responsibilities to the global, for example, and they also benefit from it when another dimension of the local or national being and good is realized in common. In Christian terms, because the common good is realized in our redemptive order, the relinquishment required of us is redemptive. As the poor are gradually empowered, they force on the rich a downward mobility if the latter cannot be induced to share their wealth freely. Thus the rich are redeemed. The same is true when multinational corporations are divested of abusive rights, privileges, and power.

This Christian perspective on the common good was introduced by Vatican II in *Gaudium et Spes.* For the council fathers the perfection of the human calls for communion with God and mutual bonding with all on this globe. Reflect for a moment on my insistence that the common good, beyond signifying the availability of conditions necessary for social life, focuses more fully on that social life itself. It is common being. The ultimate of our being is found in God. God becomes our common good. Seeking to achieve our common good, social justice reaches beyond to establish the reign of God here and now.

The U.S. Catholic bishops in their 1986 pastoral *Economic Justice for All* agree: "Human life is life in community and Christians look forward with hope to a true communion among all persons with each other and with God. The Spirit of God labors in history to build up the bonds of solidarity among all persons until that day on which their union is brought to perfection in the Kingdom of God" (*EJA* 64).

The potentiality of the principle of common good contributing to social order could be illustrated in several ways. Let me adduce just one. The perennial debate between Right and Left in U.S. society asks how best to secure material well-being for our population, while securing as much individual choice as possible in decisions about one's goals. For our purpose the Right can be simply designated as neocapitalism (conservative capitalism) and Left as welfare capitalism (progressivism). Welfare capitalism, like neocapitalism, supports the capitalist industrial processes, including the market, although, as we see, its modified market is rejected by neocapitalism.

Neocapitalism minimizes the role of government in forwarding the economy, in bringing about the abundance from which all will be served. That is best left to the free market. True, it will pile up riches for the business community. But from that community it will trickle down to benefit all. Welfare capitalism calls for much more state intervention to control market forces and to ensure more equality of fortune in the nation. However, keep in mind that the thrust of both neoliberal capitalism and welfare capitalism is to maximize the good of individuals as individuals. It does not suggest any common good as an objective.

For both, this individualism is rooted in their adherence to the Enlightenment and the utilitarianism of the seventeenth and eighteenth centuries. The Enlightenment had a positive side, but this we set aside to focus on how it bred individualism. The Enlightenment was a reaction to the prevailing mercantilism, which accorded the dominant role to the state as promoter. It was also a reaction to the stifling of freedom of thought by political monarchies, traditional cultures, and the Church, the latter perceived as in league with the others. It was thus a liberating force. For that reason its proponents were known as liberals. The Enlightenment philosophers proposed that human reason dominate nature, traditional culture, and dehumanizing forms of religion.

For its part, the accompanying utilitarianism taught that the useful (pleasurable) is the goal of life. Each individual—as an individual—seeks to maximize utility (pleasure) over disutility (pain). The aim of states was to maximize the good for the greatest number of individuals, again as individuals. However large the aggregate of utilities might become, they never would amount to common utility or common good.

When these liberals (today in the United States they would be called conservative capitalists) began to think of an alternative economics to mercantilism, they drew heavily upon Newtonian physics, using its prestige to advantage. Newton's system successfully described free movement of energies in a beneficent physical world. Liberals translated that into free flow of market forces in the economy. Thus was born laissez-faire economics: Let the state keep its hands off and allow the free market to work its magic.

Whatever good results the free market had (indeed there surely were such), the industrial world soon became a horror for the masses of industrial workers and their dependents. As such, it was roundly condemned by new social voices. Among these were the papal voices of Leo XIII and his successors. For them, *liberal* became a bad word. So, in Europe the conservativism of the Church remains today. Europeans reacted to their own liberal, laissez-faire economics in a movement variously denominated socialism, state welfare, progressivism, and, in West Germany, as social-market economics. Catholic social teaching is a variant of this more socially minded reaction to Continental liberalism.

On this side of the Atlantic, Continental liberalism became known as capitalism or conservativism. Europe's socially minded philosophy became known as progressivism, welfarism, or welfare capitalism. As in Europe, Catholics here labelled their social ethic Catholic social teaching.

But coupling Catholic social teaching with welfare capitalism may be misleading. It sounds as if they were the same. As said above, Catholic social teaching does not make the individual good the supreme good of the nation, whereas welfare capitalism and neocapitalism do. True, welfare capitalism (liberalism in the United States), viewing the history of neglect of the downtrodden, was filled with compassion. Its individualism became tempered by concern for the victims of industrial capitalism. Their concern extended, too, to the ill effects of monopolistic growth. They were concerned about the uneven positions of capital and labor. In their compassion and concern they increasingly turned to government for remedies. Government had to stand on the side of labor in its uphill battle against industrial employers. The concept of countervailing power was born, although its meaning shifted according to the powers in play. It could be a countervailing use of power between capital and labor to prevent one from dominating the other. It could also be a countervailing use of the power of the state against the powers of capital and labor to prevent them from dominating society. In any case, the countervailing powers were not perceived to represent any good other than that of the collection of individuals on the one side or other. There is for progressives as for neocapitalists no intrinsic ordering of the protagonists of society and their social functions. There is no organic integration of social components. There is only mechanical balancing, as power shifts from one individual or interest group to another. By contrast, Catholic social teaching has considered the social order in terms of an organic whole. (That is, so long as the word *organic* is not taken in a literal sense, as a few Catholic social thinkers, especially German, have done. Each part has its rights and responsibilities for the growth and improvement of the social order as a whole. From that social good each individual has a right to draw, not only in the political and civil order, but also in the social and economic. It would be unfair to the progressive tradition to fail to overlook a line that moves away from individualism. This line marches under various banners, not all having the same content: workplace democracy, democratic socialism, and post liberal or radical liberalism. All of these are apprehensive of excessive welfarism. All stand for a society that is decidedly more communal, but mostly they support a strong, positive role for the state in achieving welfare.)

Two final questions on the common good: First, does acting for the common good mean that one must aspire directly to achieving it and, conversely, that one may not seek to further a special interest? Can I not advocate improved health care for the elderly? Of course I can. Such advocacy will serve the common good provided that it does not clash with the rights of other age groups to health care, and provided that this specific good is sought within the general good. Concern for the environment will serve the common good, provided it is weighed against legitimate counterclaims. Union workers legitimately seek better wages and demand legislation to protect their jobs when they strike on a legitimate issue.

The second question turns on another problem of practicality. What in the concrete will this good be, this communal living? Surely, it is not enough to say that it will be sharing in solidarity, with cooperation, with relinquishment of individual good if and when required for the common good, for the questions remain: share precisely what? cooperate in what way? renounce what and how much and why?

This problem I reserve for the final chapter. For its resolution I return to Thomas Aquinas's moral making. My return there proceeds in two stages: First, I retrieve Aquinas's practical reason (*ratio practica*) as the process of getting from general norms to more concrete norms bearing on the specific decision to be made at one particular moment of history by one particular individual or group. Second, I move from the moment of decision to a judgment that a certain action must be done. This final stage Aquinas works out for the political order through several rules of practical wisdom.

Individual Rights

Individual rights, so often defined in terms of prerogatives against the state, are at a deeper level the God-given enfranchisement to be and to pursue the development of one's being. *Ius ad bonum suum,* the right to one's good, to one's total being, is the Latin expression. In this sense, rights are properly said to be founded on human dignity. These rights are titles to possess one's total good. If, then, I note that individual rights cannot exist apart from the common good it is not because the common good creates individual rights. It is only because individual rights exist in solidarity. The good of the commonality is the sine qua non for the actualization of individual rights.

Human rights do not exist anterior to the existence of the human community nor independently of it. Further, human rights are imbedded in the common good, in the communal life. But some papal language seems to put rights before the common good. Thus: "it is agreed that in our time the common good is chiefly guaranteed when personal rights are maintained" (*PT* 68). Similarly, "the public and universal authority must have as its fundamental objective the recognition, respect, safeguarding and promotion of human rights" (*PT* 139). The common good for John XXIII, it appears, is defined in terms of support for human rights.

Yet, as Drew Christiansen pointed out above, the good of the whole is conceived largely as the individual's share in its social well-being. The solution to the conundrum seems to reside in the fact that human rights do arise from personhood, but from a personhood that is essentially social. Rights are possessed, shared, promoted, guaranteed in and through the existence of commonality, communal being, and solidarity.

There is a God-given *ius ad bonum suum* (but a *bonum suum* that is communal). Accordingly, there must also be the concomitant right to the means for achieving this good (*ius ad media*). This right may translate into rights to basic needs, that is, food, shelter, work, health, education, and means of spiritual nourishment, such as leisure and contemplation.

Right to Development

The right to development is only another specification of the right to one's total good. It says that the individual has a right to grow. In the language of Paul VI's 1967 encyclical *Populorum Progressio*, individuals have a right not to have more but to be more. When treating the common good I have explored, if briefly, the centrality Paul VI accorded to the right to development, to become more human in relation to all other rights.

Economic Rights

Each person, as a social being, has certain basic rights. Among these are socioeconomic rights. Conservative Catholics in the United States strongly resisted introducing economic rights into the U.S. bishops' pastoral, "Economic Justice for All: Catholic Social Teaching and the U.S. Economy." According to these conservatives, there are no rights except of a political and civic nature: the right to freedom of speech and of assembly, the right to be free of unreasonable government searches, the right to elect officials of our own choosing, and so on. These are, of course, classic freedoms enshrined in the U.S. Constitution's Bill of Rights. For Catholic conservatives, the suggestion of economic rights is too close to the idea of "economic democracy." It suggests that the state is given the right and responsibility, under whatever circumstance, to provide everyone a living. That—according to the conservatives—is socialism.

Nevertheless, long before the U.S. bishops' pastoral on the economy, Catholic social teaching had recognized the importance of economic rights. A classic enshrinement in Church social teaching of socioeconomic rights alongside civic and political rights is found in John XXIII's *Pacem in Terris*. The same central themes reappear vigorously in John Paul II's 1981 *Laborem Exercens*; chapter 4 is entitled "Rights of Workers within the Broad Context of Human Rights." These economic rights are more than rights to participate in a certain economic system, such as the right to engage in contractual arrangements or the right to employment. Economic rights in this sense are rights that relate specifically to the economic well-being of the individual.

Such rights include those to life, bodily integrity, and the means necessary to sustain them. In addition, there is a right to the means necessary for development of a proper life. Economic rights therefore include the right to food, clothing, shelter, medical care, and to "necessary social services." A recognition of these rights also appears later in Vatican II's *Gaudium et Spes* (see *GS* 67–71).

The "necessary social services" are those things which a state is expected to provide for its citizens to ensure a proper and adequate life. Such social services include security in event of sickness or disability, or widowhood, old age, or unemployment. Other economic rights are the right to work, to suitable working conditions, and to a just wage. Finally, there are those economic rights more readily recognized by conservatives: rights to take initiative, to hold private property, and to make contracts. All these human rights that flow from work are included in the fundamental rights of the person (*LE* 16).

The enshrinement of social and economic rights alongside civic and political rights also appears in documents of the United Nations which have been recognized and praised in Church social teaching. There are two instruments of the United Nations' approach to rights. The first is the 1948 Universal Declaration of Human Rights, adopted by the UN General Assembly. This declaration is not a binding treaty but a standard by which the nations of the world can measure their sensitiveness about rights. The United States is a signatory to this declaration.

The other United Nations instrument is actually two distinct covenants: one covers civil and political rights, the other enunciates economic, social, and cultural rights. (The United States has long been recalcitrant about signing either. Finally, in 1992 the Senate ratified one, the civil and political covenant.) Among the economic, social, and cultural rights enumerated by the other covenant are the following:

the right of everyone to an adequate standard of living for oneself and one's family, including food, clothing, and housing (Art. 11)

the right of everyone to form trade unions and to join in the trade union of one's own choosing (Art. 8)

the right of everyone to social security, including social insurance (Art. 9)

the fundamental right of everyone to be free of hunger (Art. 11)

the right of everyone to enjoy the highest attainable standard of physical and mental health (Art. 12)

the right of everyone to education (Art. 13).

The social systems that emerge from the collection of individuals, then, must recognize and guarantee these human rights. Church social teaching seeks to address the development of human systems from this perspective, with the additional consideration, to be detailed later, of the option for the poor. Thus there is a fundamental difference between the approach taken by Church social teaching in evaluating social systems from the moral perspective and the approach taken from a purely political perspective.

The above discussion of rights has avoided using the word *entitlement*. This term can be the equivalent of right conferred by nature or nature's Creator. But for many an entitlement is some title specifically conferred by the state. The position taken here is that basic rights—those described above—are inherent in human nature, although their implementation may require state initiative. For instance, certain inequalities deriving from the market may need to be corrected by redistributive actions of the state, prompted by distributive justice. But entitlements thus achieved may appear to many to originate wholly within the state. Then the more conservative may fear that the state will be required to meet any entitlement a liberal can think up. Catholic social teaching, however, precludes that position. Moreover, this body of teaching insists that the rights or entitlements of the middle class—indeed all classes—must be prompted by the state. The following addresses the critics of economic rights, notably Michael Novak.

Critics of Economic Rights

Michael Novak (1985) argues that citizens of the United States are at different levels of discourse when they speak of civil and political rights on the one hand and of social and economic rights on the other. To the former they accord an exalted status. These are in the realm of courts and constitution. Not so for "so-called economic and social rights." The bishops, clearly, accord the latter the same status as the former on the basis of their derivation from the sacredness of human nature. Novak charges that the bishops run the danger of excessive state intervention. "It may well position the Catholic church in a preferential option for the state that will more than rival that of the Constantinian period."

The bishops had noted in an earlier draft that a number of rights mentioned in John XXIII's *Pacem in Terris* are specifically of an economic nature: rights to life, food, clothing, shelter, rest, and medical care. Novak asserts that this affirmation is not made in that encyclical. Where the pope mentions these rights he does so only in a section on "rights to life." But when he speaks explicitly of economic rights he does so in a passage labelled *economic rights*. What appear there are the classical economic rights in the United States to free initiative and private enterprise, the right to (that is, not to be hindered from) work, and to private property. The bishops were not impressed with Novak's argument. In their final draft they reaffirmed the economic rights noted above.

Novak in the article makes two points. First, where the pope speaks of rights to life, food, clothing, medical care, and so on, he observes that these "life rights, not economic rights" are—he quotes *Pacem in Terris*—the responsibility of government only

when "through no fault of their own some are incapable of realizing them." The second point, seen above, is that what appear
in a paragraph labelled *economic rights* are only the traditional
rights recognized by the United States, such as private initiative.

But not all of John XXIII's cases of need are those owing to
personal fault. They are much more those which John Paul II
deems the ordinary responsibilities of the state. Thus, the
encyclical reads: "sickness, inability to work, widowhood, old
age, unemployment" and "other cases in which persons are
deprived of the means of subsistence through no fault of their
own." Think of frictional and cyclical unemployment, plant
closings, and community abandonment when industries flee
to cheaper labor markets. Think of poor health, lack of education, and inadequate training for new technologies.

Novak should not make so much of the title "economic
rights" that introduces the English text of paragraphs 16–20.
That title is not of the pope's doing. It is the work of the editor of the English version. The official Latin text, appearing in
the *Acta Apostolicae Sedis* (the official commentary of the Holy
See), does not have this or, for that matter, any other heading.
More to the point is to compare the two lists of rights in
Pacem in Terris paragraph 11, the "rights to life," with those
in paragraphs 18–22, the rights in "the economic sphere."
From such a comparison it appears that, apart from the addition in the second set of the rights to initiative, enterprise, and
property, the two correspond. "Both are substantively economic and both are to be guaranteed by the state."[6]

That the rights are indeed parallel, including that of govern-
ment-guaranteed security, becomes most explicit in a later
section of the encyclical to which, astonishingly, Novak makes
no reference at all. In a key section of *Pacem in Terris,* John
XXIII treats the role of the state in promoting what are precisely the economic rights noted by the bishops. "The whole
reason for the existence of the state is the realization of the
common good without preference for any single citizen or
group," though "justice and equity can at times demand . . .
more attention to the less fortunate." This common good
embraces "the sum total of those conditions of social living
whereby persons are able to achieve their own integral perfection more fully and more easily" (*PT* 63–65).

Linking the common good to rights, *Pacem in Terris* emphasizes that the common good is chiefly guaranteed when personal rights and duties are maintained: "The chief concern of civil authority must be to ensure that those rights are acknowledged, respected, coordinated, defended and promoted" (*PT* 60). Lest one imagine that this activity of government does not apply in the economic sphere, the encyclical asserts further the "obligation of civil authorities to take suitable action with regard to economic, political, cultural matters." To achieve this, the state must create essential services (*PT* 60–72).

It is therefore necessary that the government give wholehearted and careful attention to the social as well as to the economic progress of citizens, and, in keeping with the development of the productive system, to the development of such essentials as roads, transportation, communication, water supply, housing, public health, education, unrestrained practice of religion, and recreational facilities. Government must see that insurance is available to the citizens, so that, in misfortune or increased family responsibilities, no person will lack a decent standard of living.

The government should make similarly effective efforts to see that those who are able to work can find employment in keeping with their aptitudes, and that each worker receives a wage in keeping with the laws of justice and equality. It should be equally the concern of civil authorities to insure that workers be allowed their proper responsibility in the work undertaken in industrial organization, and to facilitate the establishment of intermediate groups which will make social life richer and more effective. Finally, it should be possible for all citizens to share as far as they are able in their country's cultural advantages.

The government has further responsibilities for employment and unemployment benefits, and the state will serve economic rights, such as wages, social benefits, health care, pension, old age insurance, and "within the sphere of these principal rights a whole system of particular rights" (ibid.).

That Novak does not refer to this full and important discussion of economic rights in this latter section of *Pacem in Terris* is evidence of the shallowness of his charge that the pastoral is out of line with papal teaching. Similarly weak is his complaint that the bishops endorse the United Nations Universal Declaration of Human Rights, which contains economic rights. But here again the bishops are in line with papal support of the UN declaration. John XXIII in *Pacem in Terris* had already made this point and John Paul II repeated it in his 1979 *Redemptor Hominis* (Redeemer of Humankind). John Paul II praised the United Nations for its initiative in describing economically related human rights in his October 2, 1979, address to the thirty-fourth session of the United Nations General Assembly. In that address, he placed civil and political rights on an equal footing with economic and social rights. In listing rights "universally acknowledged," the pope mixed together these two sets.

To sum up, rather than being outside the thrust of papal documents and other Church social teaching on economic rights, the economic pastoral is fully within the mainstream. How the United States will view economic rights and whether they will have the same status as civil and political rights are among the crucial questions in the coming decades.

Economic rights create a problem not experienced in political and civil rights. How can it be meaningful to discuss rights if they cannot be implemented? How can society have responsibility to provide adequate food, clothing, and shelter if it manifestly lacks the material resources to accomplish this? Where is the right?

It seems to me that the inability of society in certain circumstances to implement this right does not negate its existence. The right, as all rights, is not an absolute. It does not assert a categorical obligation to do the impossible. But neither is it just an ideal. It would be nice if all could have adequacy. But as with all other ideals, one should not make an outcry over this one. No, this economic right is an objective characteristic of the human. It belongs to the human. Social justice demands effort toward its realization.

At a minimum, economic rights demand that a society seriously reflect on whether maldistribution of its wealth does not prevent the poor from achieving economic well-being. It demands that the wealthy north side of the world ask whether its consumption patterns (the United States consumes 40 percent of the world's resources) do not impede the south side from realizing its economic rights. It suggests reflecting on whether our society favors wants of the better-off at the expense of meeting genuine basic needs of others. Using the term *basic needs* raises the problem of who is to determine what basic needs are, but a poll of the human race would, I think, identify basics quite reasonably, even though different cultures would articulate them differently.

Economic Democracy

My discussion of economic democracy in Catholic social teaching is entirely in terms of the Catholic bishops' pastoral on the United States economy, *Economic Justice for All*, because it was only during the years of drafting that document that economic democracy as a specific theme of Catholic social teaching came to my attention. Until then I had treated it as equivalent to the right to participate. Sometime during the preparation of the pastoral, Archbishop Weakland remarked that the heart of the document is "economic democracy." With that achieved, Weakland asserted, the people of the United States will have matched their political democracy.

Use of the term *economic democracy* raised a furor in more conservative Catholic circles. For many, the term is nearly synonymous with *socialism*. Once again, Michael Novak was a principal speaker for the critics. For example, in a debate with former U.S. Rep. Robert Drinan, Novak made these strong remarks about economic democracy: "Explain why they [the bishops] use Tom Hayden and Jane Fonda's slogan "economic democracy"? There's a program attached to that. Do they buy the whole program? Or do they mean what Olaf Palme, the Swedish socialist, meant by it? He's been arguing for fifteen years and he says exactly what the bishops say."[7]

Concerned that using the term *economic democracy* would, in the eyes of many, prejudice what they wanted to say about the fullest possible economic participation at every level, the bishops omitted the phrase from later drafts. But it is very clear that they in no way pulled back from the fullness of content that the term *economic democracy* had for them.

Here is the original language of the first draft. It is prefaced by pointing out the greatness of the United States' achievement in establishing the concept of political rights for all. "We believe the time has come for a similar experiment in economic democracy: the creation of an order that guarantees the minimum conditions of human dignity in the economic sphere for every person" (*EJA* first draft 1984, 89). This, the bishops add, would be the topic of a later section, "A New American Experiment."

Just why such strong and fearful reaction should have been generated by this language is not easy to understand. What could be wrong or threatening in the proposition: The United States has achieved, even if imperfectly, political democracy; now let's work on the same fullness of participation for everyone in the U.S. economy? Whatever might be meant by the term *economic democracy,* it is clear that for the bishops it meant nothing more than full participation in economic life, including participation in decision making at all levels.

Note the language introducing the same idea in the pastoral's final draft: "The nation's founders took daring steps to create structures of participation, mutual accountability and widely distributed power to ensure the political rights and freedoms of all. We believe that similar steps are needed today to expand economic participation, broaden the sharing of economic power and make economic decisions more accountable to the common good" (EJA final draft 297). The commitment to economic democracy has certainly not been watered down.

Toward this economic empowerment of all, the bishops propose "A New American Experiment." At the level of the local workplace this calls for a new partnership between workers and managers, cooperation of all in discovering new businesses and new jobs, and such standard items of Catholic tradition as sharing in management, profits, or stock. Within industries and plants collective bargaining—again very traditional Catholic teaching—should be less adversarial. Further, any power possessed exclusively or disproportionately by one group should be reduced; for example, a group whose power protects it from sharing sacrifices when factories close (*EJA* final draft 303). What will efforts at more democratic participation in the economy mean at the national level? The pastoral proposes that individuals and groups cooperate with government to develop national policies.

Perhaps now conservative fears may be aroused because of urging that "society make provision for overall planning" in the economic domain (*EJA* final draft 315). The pastoral notes that those words are borrowed from John Paul II (*LE* 18). It adds: "The Pope's words cannot be construed as an endorsement of a highly centralized form of economic planning, much less a totalitarian one" (*EJA* final draft 316). It is rather a question of "a just and rational coordination" of the endeavors of many economic actors to create new forms of partnership and participation in shaping national economic policies. Planning does exist. The challenge is to make sure that the planning is begun and carried through democratically, with the full and effective participation of all those affected.

Preferential Option for the Poor

Preferential option for the poor, like *economic democracy,* is a new expression, but the concept has a long tradition in Catholic social teaching. One of the more forceful expressions of this newly stated theme of Catholic social teaching is, again, the bishops' pastoral on the U.S. economy. For this reason and because it embodies other official statements of the same theme, I again frame my discussion in that source.

The preferential option for the poor is fundamental to the Catholic perspective. There is no doubt that the U.S. bishops have made this fundamental option the key to their economic pastoral. Recalling Vatican II, the bishops write that the griefs and anxieties, especially of the poor, are the griefs and anxieties of the followers of Christ (*EJA* 10). The poor, the pastoral adds, "have the single most urgent economic claim on the conscience of the nation" (*EJA* 86). "As individuals and as a nation, therefore, we are called to make a fundamental option for the poor" (*EJA* 87). Again, "The fulfillment of the basic needs of the poor is of the highest priority" (*EJA* 90).

Making this an option for the poor will call on the citizens of the United States to examine their way of living in light of the needs of the poor (*EJA* 75). The entire thrust of the pastoral's sections on poverty (*EJA* 170–215) is a description of how to put this option into practice in society today. Even investment decisions ought to be worked out scrupulously in this perspective. According to the bishops, policies governing the investment of wealth, talent, and human energy "should be specially directed to benefit those who are poor or economically insecure" (*EJA* 92). (Quite opposite to this perspective is columnist Charles Krauthammer's derisive retort: "Capitalism is the option for the poor.")

Several strong objections have been raised against this option. A whole school of business-oriented thinkers dismiss the bishops outright as woolly-headed do-gooders. The working hypothesis of these critics seems to be: "Leave the capitalist system alone and it will effectively take care of the poor." But that easy supposition is of course precisely what the bishops, in union with many of today's best economic thinkers, are challenging. It is also alleged that the bishops want to eliminate any and all inequality, ignorant that in doing so they would kill the goose that lays the golden egg. But in truth the bishops, as noted earlier, clearly recognize that some degree of inequality may be productive. What they object to are the sharp extremes in society (*EJA* 183–85).

Of more substance are two related questions which have been raised by critics of the pastoral's option for the poor. The first is that the fundamental option ought to be for the common good—not for one particular segment of society. The second is that the pastoral seems to be written as if there were only the marginalized poor exploited by the rich. But what about the vast middle class? What about its economic problems? Is the middle class to be considered, alongside the rich, responsible for helping the poor? We must look at these charges.

The Option for the Poor and the Common Good

Some critics charge that the bishops, in their expression of the option for the poor, ignore the essential thrust of social justice toward the common good. But the pastoral letter does indeed clearly recognize the central place of the common good. It makes its own Pius XI's statement, "It is of the very essence of social justice to demand from each individual all that is necessary for the common good" (*EJA* 71). So, it has some sense that achieving the common good is indeed the primary option of a community. It is also in and from the creation of this common good that all society may share and should share. Nevertheless, the bishops—as John Paul II, other episcopal conferences, and many religious congregations—insist strongly on the priority of the option for the poor. They agree with the synod of 1971's *Justitia in Mundo* that this was also the option of Jesus (*JM* 31ff.).

The economic pastoral links the option for the poor with the common good in an important way. In their introductory Pastoral Message,[8] the bishops state that the option for the poor is a way of "strengthening the whole community by assisting those who are most vulnerable" (*EJA* 16). In a key passage the pastoral seeks to meet directly the objection that exercising the option for the poor would hurt the common good. This deserves to be quoted in full: "The prime purpose of this special commitment to the poor is to enable them to become active participants in the life of society. It is to enable all persons to share in and contribute to the common good. The 'option for the poor,' therefore, is not an adversarial slogan that pits one group against another. Rather it states that the deprivation and powerlessness of the poor wounds the whole community. The extent of their suffering is a measure of how far we are from being a true community of persons. These wounds will be healed only by greater solidarity with the poor and among the poor themselves" (*EJA* 88).

This formulation is a strong echo of the response given to the same question by John XXIII in his *Pacem in Terris*. He calls for "the common good of all without preference for any single citizen or group." But he adds the qualification that "considerations of justice and equity can and sometimes do demand . . . that more attention be given to the less fortunate members of the community" (*PT* 56). In no way does the option for the poor undercut the promotion of the common good. Rather, the option amplifies its scope and strengthens its bonds.

The Option for the Poor and the Middle Class

It is true that many of the middle class, especially the lower middle class, have felt left out of the consideration of the bishops. There is not in the pastoral, they believe, enough concern for "the common good of all without preference." Many in this group are struggling to raise their families and meet the tuition demands of college. Even two-earner families may be working extra hard not to lose mortgaged homes and to do a bit of saving for the future. Some face large medical bills for their aging parents. Large numbers of them are only a lost job or an expensive medical emergency away from poverty. Widowhood, divorce, or separation have thrust many middle-class women into the labor market at wages near or below the poverty line.

The Institute for Social Research at the University of Michigan, which has studied poverty for many years, has discovered that the permanently poor are—at least up to recent times—a very low percentage of the U.S. population (Duncan 1984). The largest number of people below the poverty line are those who have spent—and will spend—time out of poverty. Indeed, it is estimated that one-fourth of the U.S. population has at one time or another been below the poverty line. Because of these statistics, some argue that the option for the poor would make more sense if the pastoral were being written in Brazil, where 80 percent of the people are poor.

What the U.S. bishops have in mind, however, touches two important points relevant to U.S. society. First, they do recognize the economic pressures felt by the middle class, especially the lower middle class, who "are barely getting by and fear becoming victims of economic forces over which they have no control" (*EJA* 85). The bishops are sensitive to middle class concerns. Second, they also acknowledge that the middle class in U.S. society needs to be challenged. Archbishop Weakland (1985), chairman of the pastoral drafting committee, addressed this issue: "The phrase 'preferential option for the poor' is not meant as a slogan to polarize our society, but as a challenge to all—including the middle class. In attempting to build bridges of responsibility between the poor, the middle class and the affluent classes, one must also challenge many middle class values in the United States, and not leave the impression that all is well."

The pastoral does present a challenge for the United States to examine life-style in the face of the needs of the poor. The American dream needs to be reevaluated, since "Christian faith and the norms of justice impose distinct limits on what we consume and how we view material goods" (*EJA* 75). Moreover, the pastoral, in the name of the option for the poor, calls for more sharing on the part of those who currently possess economic power and privilege. In so doing, it echoes the strong words of Paul VI: "In teaching us charity, the Gospel instructs us in the preferential respect due the poor and the special situation they have in society. The more fortunate should renounce some of their rights so as to place their goods more generously at the service of others" (*EJA* 87).

It is simply not fair to criticize the bishops' endorsement of the option for the poor by saying that it goes against the middle class in this country. But it is also necessary to be honest in admitting that this option does have serious consequences for the business activities and life-style of the middle class. This will be one of the significant challenges in implementing the pastoral.

Labor Unions As an Organizing Principle

I am writing these paragraphs in a moment of widespread, even general, indifference to labor unions and, increasingly, of downright hostility on the part of business. Chapter 1 reveals that immediately after ordination I persuaded my provincial superior that, rather than go to Toronto's medieval institute to prepare to teach philosophy to Jesuits in formation, I believed I had a vocation to start a Labor School at one of our two universities in the Oregon Province of the Society of Jesus. The provincial blessed the project.

What a Labor School was is explained in that first chapter. Some twenty flourished in the early forties. Their existence spoke convincingly about the enthusiasm of the Roman Catholic community for unions in the three decades immediately preceding Vatican II. Many bishops encouraged the

spread of these institutions. A sizable number of priests—
diocesan more prominent than order priests—made them
their apostolate. Chapter 2 narrates the circumstances which
shifted me away from my first love, helping workers discover
through schooling ways of running more successful unions.
My professional life from then on would be quite other. It
would be in research, teaching, and writing on questions of
social ethics and social *praxis.*

Indeed, as a matter of division of labor in social ethics and
social *praxis,* it fell to others—not to me—to study the ethics
of union questions. Still, as the years rolled on, I kept an
eye, a disquieted eye, on the crumbling fortunes of workers'
associations.

So, it is a matter of dismay for me first of all to see the percentage of unionized workers falling from roughly one-third of
the total work force to a depressing low of 13 percent. It is not
for me here to try to explain that phenomenon. Suffice it to say
that significant factors in that precipitous decline of unionization are the following: First, a pervasive indifference to unions
or downright hostility diffused through the public. Gone are the
days of ethnic hospitality and identification, of strong identification and support also by the Roman Catholic church and its
clergy. Second, individualism, always a strong thread of our
culture, had now become dominant: do it on your own. That
aphorism comes often from individuals who themselves rely on
organizations and political power to protect their interests.

This cultural trait, which implies that unions somehow do not
really belong in U.S. society, has made it easier for employers to
substitute nonunion labor for union workers. After President
Ronald Reagan's devastating union-busting of the air traffic con-
trollers' association, union bashing has become big business in
this country. Hundreds of consultants are hired to break unions.
In the newest evil wrinkle, they show employers how to legally
and permanently replace striking union workers. How a court
can permit an action that effectively negates both the right to a
strike and to have a bona fide union is quite beyond my com-
prehension. It is dismaying to see so many of my Church, in
particular sisters, priests, and brothers, join in union busting.

What can the union busters among us, in schools or health
organizations, make of the Church's consistent defense of the

right of workers to have unions of their own choosing? To take only one example, the U.S. Catholic bishops in the introduction to *Economic Justice for All* say: "The Church fully supports the right of workers to form unions or other associations to secure their rights to fair wages and working conditions" (*EJA* 104).

They go on to add that startling affirmation made by Pope John Paul II in his remarkable 1981 encyclical *Laborem Exercens* (On human work): "The experience of history teaches that organizations of this type are an indispensable element of social life, especially in modern industrialized societies" (*LE* 20).

Indispensable! Cannot be dispensed with. True, "indispensability" modifies "organizations of this type," and a further qualification is entered: "especially in modern industrial society." But exegesis of the text cannot be allowed to dilute its content into nothingness.

Surely, workers who, unorganized, are forced to accept whatever wages and working conditions management imposes on them, will recognize the indispensability of some form of worker organization. Labor unions arose out of the division of the labor market into powerful owners and hirers against powerless workers.

But there is a more profoundly human and societal principle indicating the legitimacy and value of labor unions: in Catholic social teaching, unions are an organizational principle and institution of society. I take this topic up more substantially toward the end of this chapter, where I introduce another organizing principle, that of subsidiarity. Subsidiarity embraces unions and many other organizations and units of society that lie between the individual and the state. These include families, neighborhoods, cooperatives, nongovernmental organizations, churches, and a host of professional associations.

Subsidiarity is a principle of action and of being. Of action: it is wrong to take from the individual and lesser societies what they can do for themselves. Still, there are roles imperative for government. Of being: government respects and supports the smallness of being of the family, community, and work group. Thus it promotes respect for the voice of the little ones—even large unions are little in comparison to the vast economic and political power they confront. The Church's option for the poor is a useful lens here: It seeks to empower the very being of the marginalized and possessionless and to validate their efforts to speak out their truth and their discovery of alternatives. It is relevant because it really only echoes society's proper understanding of the common good and of the role of the poor within it.

Clearly, to return to John Paul II's *Laborem Exercens,* this right of autonomous organization of work must allow workers to participate in some corporate business decisions. For the corporation is the only locus in the modern industrial order where workplace democracy can be achieved for vast numbers of workers. For, as John Paul puts it, "a business cannot be considered only as a society of capital goods. It is also a society of persons." To achieve the goals of some of these persons "there is still need for a broad associated workers' movement" (*LE* 30).

Some business associations trumpet the eventual total demise of labor unions. It would be a sad day for our society and culture if this vital force for subsidiarity and social living is erased.

What appears in these few paragraphs on labor unions is matter only of principles but, I believe, essential social principles, constantly reaffirmed by successive voices in Catholic social teaching. You find here no mention of abuses or failures on the part of unions. Yet, complaints against unions must be faced. There have been bad unions and corrupt union leaders. Labor unions, for their part, have at times been guilty of injustices to their employers, to the community, or to minorities. So far as women are concerned, labor leaders in the United States have been about as patriarchal as the rest of society. Some unions have been criticized for taking an adversarial approach, especially in their dealings with small employers and the public.

But I am not writing a history of the labor union movement in the United States. Indeed, I am not, since that would require entering into the many other labor questions that an adequate social ethic would have to address: the right to strike, wage justice, and ways of implementing wage justice (receiving part of one's wage in profits to permit an employer to compete against nonunion businesses that pay lower wages).

Besides working out wage justice, other features of work relations may demand flexibility to meet international competition and the pace of world industrial change. The kind of social compacts the nations of the European Economic Community are working out will have to be, *mutatis mutandis,* a feature of the wider society of nations. Many questions of unfairness about remuneration, conditions of work, and promotion for women remain.

Private Property As an Organizing Principle

The right to private property has been defended by every pope from Leo XIII's time on. However, they have also insisted on the social nature of property with ever-deepening emphasis. To illustrate the latter briefly: in his radio address commemorating the fiftieth anniversary of *Rerum Novarum* in 1941, Pius XII declared that God's universal destination of the goods of the earth to the service of all humankind is prior to private possession. That universal destination has since become deeply imbedded in papal and conciliar writing. More recently, John Paul II has used the very strong language of the social mortgage of private property.

Grateful as we must be for this insistence on universal destination, it does not attend to one aspect of property as an organizing principle, namely, whether Catholic social teaching embraces common ownership of the means of production. Most certainly it approves of the producers' cooperative, which is a form of common ownership. But what about community ownership? Is Catholic social teaching opposed to a form of holding and working of productive property that is widespread throughout the earth and honored and loved? It is my impression that Catholic social teaching has condemned only the one form of common ownership that it has consistently condemned, namely, socialist. That other types of community ownership never came under its purview illustrates its narrow focus on European experience.

The arguments in favor of private ownership are mainly pragmatic, even in Aquinas. Given original sin, private ownership is the only way to ensure orderly use and maintenance of the goods of the earth. Thomas does add that private ownership of productive property—he is thinking mainly of a plot of ground—permits its possessor to imprint herself or himself on nature. Leo XIII also had in mind a plot of land in *Rerum Novarum* (*RN* 9).

Considerations that might suggest some modification of this tradition include the following: (*a*) there are gross and pervasive abuses of private productive property; (*b*) the assumed connection between private property and original sin: if we had remained in original innocence, would the Garden of Eden have been divided into privately owned parcels? and (*c*) why could people not imprint themselves on nature communally? Is that not what people have done throughout the ages? Should not Catholic social teaching honor communal ownership at least alongside private productive property?

Still, it must be acknowledged that when Leo XIII retrieved the Thomistic conception of private property in productive goods, he had in mind an institution that would be a normal entitlement of all wage earners and not the power base of a privileged few. He says, "Clearly the essential reason why those who engage in any gainful occupation undertake labor and at the same time the end to which workers immediately look, is to procure property for themselves. . . . Therefore, if he [the worker] saves something by restricting expenditures and invests his savings in a piece of land in order to keep the fruit of his thrift more safe, a holding of this kind is certainly nothing else than his wage under a different form (*RN* 9)."

Subsidiarity As an Organizing Principle

While writing a book on the bishops' economic pastoral and its purview of welfare (taken in a very wide sense), I found myself enormously satisfied that one plank of Catholic social teaching that stood up eminently in the debate on welfare was subsidiarity. This principle is one deeply grounded in Catholic social teaching. It states two things: First, action should, wherever possible, be taken at lower levels of social or institutional structures, avoiding an overpowering, overburdening structure that controls all action. Second, the state has its legitimate and necessary role in social actions which promote the common good.

Although it is a key principle in Catholic theology, subsidiarity is not very well understood by contemporary U.S. Catholics. But its importance is evident if one seeks to solve the nation's ongoing welfare debate. My reflections on the pastoral's treatment of subsidiarity brought me to a critique by Andrew Greeley (1985). Greeley believed that, at least in the early draft he was addressing, the bishops failed to construe the principle correctly and thus formulated a wholly unacceptable statement. If I believe that this extraordinarily capable reporter on Catholic life in the United States was mistaken in his criticism, I at the same time recognize that Greeley was making a very significant contribution to our understanding of subsidiarity. I also must note that Greeley was attacking the first draft, which appeared in November 1984. But I also think that the following remarks in defense of the final document largely support that first draft.

What Greeley saw as the absence of adequate reference to the tradition of subsidiarity was evidence to him that the drafters felt that this theory really has nothing at all to contribute to the solution of contemporary problems in U.S. society. In addition, Greeley accused the bishops of believing that the way to solve problems was to throw money at them, and he charged them with failing to stress "participation in decision making."

Greeley provides us with a foundational perception that subsidiarity is a principle that has much more to say about constituting society than is acknowledged by most interpretations of Pius XI's famous dictum: Nothing should be done by a higher and larger institution that can be done by a lower and smaller one. He also is correct in shifting the proper emphasis from doing to being. Nothing should be bigger than necessary. Hence he favors local networks—familial, geographic, religious, economic, and political. Such an approach creates the environment where "people matter for who and what they are, not merely for what they can do." Greeley also wants subsidiarity to promote decision making at local levels.

To repeat the note I opened this section on, I will use the pastoral to expand on essentials of the Catholic understanding of this principle of sociopolitical balance. Does the pastoral fail to give centrality to the principle of subsidiarity and thus fall open to the charge of being statist? Does it incorporate the understanding of subsidiarity found in Pius XI's *Quadragesimo Anno* as an emphasis on "no bigger than necessary"? Does it promote an environment where people are important? Does it give due weight to decision making by smaller groups and by the poor themselves, whether at the local level or higher levels?

On all three points the pastoral fully supports Catholic social teaching on subsidiarity. Whatever may be the validity of Greeley's charges of inadequacies regarding the treatment of subsidiarity in the first draft, the subsequent drafts and especially the final document are very clear in their use of this principle.

On Respect for Smallness

The two aspects of subsidiarity—doing and being—are substantially treated in the second, third, and final drafts of the pastoral. It may even have been that Greeley's early challenge persuaded the drafters to augment explicit reference to the classic statement of subsidiarity found in *Quadragesimo Anno*. Here is the first of four appearances in the pastoral of that classic statement: "Just as it is gravely wrong to take from individuals what they can accomplish on their own initiative and industry and give it to the community, so also is it an injustice . . . to assign to a greater and higher association what lesser and subordinate organizations can do. For every social activity ought of its very nature to furnish help (*subsidium*) to the members of the body social, and never destroy or absorb them" (*EJA* 99).

The bishops, in chapter 4 of the pastoral, "The New American Experiment: Partnership for the Public Good," note that three of the four partnerships directly involve government (local or regional, national, and international). But each of these endorsements of government action is prefaced by an explicit statement of subsidiarity. For example, speaking of local or regional cooperation, the document reads: "In the principle of subsidiarity, Catholic social teaching has long stressed the importance of small and intermediate-sized communities or institutions exercising moral responsibility" (*EJA* 308). National cooperation is similarly introduced by explicit statement of the subsidiarity principle that emphasizes what the larger society must do: "The principle of subsidiarity calls for government intervention when small or intermediate groups in society are unable or unwilling to take the steps needed to promote basic justice" (*EJA* 308). The principle gets the same treatment at the international level (*EJA* 323).

In earlier chapters, the pastoral places heavy emphasis on the role of local associations in support of "institutional pluralism" as creating the common good (*EJA* 100). This perspective then is applied to problems of unemployment and poverty. Emphasis here is placed upon the individual and small group that ought to be helped. The most appropriate programs (that is, government programs) for poverty are "those that enable people to take control of their own lives" and "to help themselves" (*EJA* 188). Programs, therefore, should be "small in scale, locally based and oriented toward empowering the poor to become self-sufficient" (*EJA* 200). The section on unemployment abundantly attests that for the bishops the first line of action is to allow the private sector to do as much as possible. Only after that is there a role for the state: government policy should support private efforts (*EJA* 154).

In short, the bipolarity—individual and intermediary groups on one side and the state on the other—on which the bishops rest their call for action shows an eminently satisfactory understanding and practice of the principle of subsidiarity.

Toward an Environment That Respects People

The previous section stressed the pastoral's bipolar treatment of government as helper of individuals and small groups to empower them to do for themselves. But further attention needs to be paid to being rather than doing. Greeley rightly observes that subsidiarity is based on being small, on an environment where people matter, on networks of cooperative relations and smaller organizations—nothing bigger than necessary.

It is clearly the message of the economic pastoral that an environment must be created where people matter and can see their contributions build up a fruitful economy. Community is essential in the bishops' perspective. The very first paragraph of the pastoral says, "the economy is a human reality: men and women working together to develop and care for the whole of God's creation" (*EJA* 1). "Through hard work, self-sacrifice and cooperation, families have flourished, towns, cities and a powerful nation have been created" (*EJA* 6).

In dealing with persons and institutions working for justice, the bishops emphasize that the U.S. economy has been built by the labor of human hands and minds. The economy is not a machine and "persons are not mere objects tossed about by economic forces" (*EJA* 96). Thus the pastoral frequently focuses on the individual as incorporated in local, intermediary societies which create that environment of smallness that supports individuals. A strong example of this, of course, is the emphasis on the family (*EJA* 93).

Toward Participation in Decision Making

Participation has already been treated under the rubric of *economic democracy*. I take it up here more specifically to illustrate its possibilities as envisioned by the U.S. Catholic bishops in their economic pastoral. That the bishops strongly emphasize the decision-making dimension of subsidiarity is abundantly clear in their section "A New American Experiment: Partnership for the Public Good" (*EJA* 295–325). The bishops note, for example, the aspect of empowering people to enter the decision-making process. On workplace cooperation the document calls for "a new experiment in bringing democratic ideals to economic life" and "new patterns of partnership" (*EJA* 298). The call is made for "granting employees greater participation in determining the conditions of work" (*EJA* 300–303).

A part of "A New American Experiment" called "Partnership in Development of National Policies" is one more application of partnership with explicit or implicit share in decision making. The bishops see the need to "build new forms of effective citizenship and cooperation" (*EJA* 312). The challenge of today is to move to creative ways of enabling government and private groups to work together effectively" (*EJA* 314). As for the economic planning which will proceed under state guidance, "Effective decisions in these matters will demand greater cooperation among all citizens" (*EJA* 317). Several other passages in this section only confirm the strong role assigned to individuals, small groups, local entities, and other intermediary groups in the decision-making process.

To suggestions of more economic democracy and its implications for a heightened role for workers in business decisions and for citizens in local governmental decision making, the objection can justly be raised that such people cannot master the complex data and balance of competing goods. The information explosion and the intertwining of almost everything in our global village predicts that the required competency will call not for widening but probably narrowing the entry into decision making.

Without exploring this question at any length, let me suggest two possible answers. First, participation in workplace decisions requires at least that workers have an effective voice in decisions that affect their work conditions, health, hours, wages, and so on. Also, many executives have finally begun to take seriously learning ways to improve workers' productivity.

My second remark is to observe that the elitist slogan "father [that is, an authority figure] knows best" often leads to disastrous policies for citizens. Elitists and bureaucrats may know little of the reality of the life and work of the people they legislate for. Every reader will have her or his personal knowledge of such. I have personally witnessed in several developing countries the sad results of failure to consult the people affected. Just one example: I once visited at Los Baños near Manila the Rockefeller experimental station that produced "miracle rice." When it was introduced in the Philippines, it predictably made the rich farmers richer, and forced the poor farmers to sell out to the rich. Why? To achieve its high yields, the miracle rice required expensive fertilizer and insecticides. Legislators never thought of a program of credit for the poor farmers.

Catholic Social Teaching 2

T he six themes in this second chapter on Catholic social
teaching complete the previous one. They are socialization, social justice as the motivating force toward achieving
the common good, other sources that flow into Catholic social
teaching, the question of whether Catholic social teaching is
organic, whether Catholic social teaching should properly be
thought of as doctrine, and finally, changes from pre–Vatican
II to post–Vatican II in ecclesiology and theological method
which have affected Catholic social teaching.

Process of Socialization

Long before Catholics in the United States were debating the
economic pastoral, conservative Catholics in Europe in the
early post–World War II period had sought to swing the pen-
dulum of subsidiarity over to the side of the individual and
individualism. They sought to diminish sharply the role of the
state. Their activities, it was widely believed during my Rome
years, persuaded John XXIII to reinforce the subsidiarity of
Pius XI's *Quadragesimo Anno* by introducing the principle of
intervention.

Chapter 2 recounts the role of Msgr. Pietro Pavan in redrafting that very encyclical. Pavan is credited with adding this

principle to the traditional ones needed for a viable sociopolitical order. His conflict with the Jesuit Gustav Gundlach, another professor of Catholic social teaching at the Jesuit-run Gregorian University of Rome, led, as related in chapter 2, to Pavan's departure. During his tenure, Pavan gradually distanced himself from Gundlach's misgivings about trade unionism, favoring, against Europe's big national unions, which bargained for all workers in a trade, the smaller unions, which sometimes seemed to be company unions.

Pavan promoted, as Gundlach did not, a stronger role for government in modern industry and commerce. (Gundlach, however, had his own brilliant, forward-looking intuitions. Many are enshrined in the seventeen Christmas Allocutions, composed in great measure by him for Pope Pius XII.)

John XXIII adopted Pavan's concern that the problems of today's economic society are so complex and interdependent that public authorities would have to assume still more responsibilities. Thus the principle of socialization addresses modern society's complexity and interdependence. Socialization in itself is not to be dismissed as evil. Quite the contrary; it is, however ambiguous, a new manifestation of the evolving social thrust of humankind (*MM* 59–67).

Socialization appears in the patterns of social life that generate new social institutions. John XXIII speaks of a "wide range of groups, associations, institutions having economic, cultural and political ends." Socialization is the "effect and cause of growing state intervention" (*MM* 60). Because of modern social problems like health care, rehabilitation of physically or mentally handicapped persons, and education, the state intervenes even more in society.

The word *socialization* in John XXIII's encyclical *Pacem in Terris* sparked a controversy because the official Vatican Latin text reads *relationum incrementa socialium,*[1] which translates as "multiplication of social relationships," and the Paulist Press edition in English opted for that literal translation. In the United States the press translated the term as "socialization," following the version used by the Vatican Press Office. The Vatican Italian text read *socializzazione;* the Spanish, *socializacion,* the French, *socialisation.* At least one German text followed with *Zocialisierung.*[2]

It has been alleged that the word *socialization* suggests to many *socialism*. This association is perhaps understandable. Some argue that the real reason why the Vatican Latinists came up with their unwieldy (and uninformative) phrase was to avoid any confusion with socialism, but there can be little doubt that the pope's helper in writing the original text had in mind—contrary to the subsequent Latinists—the meaning delineated in the encyclical itself.

Dangers of Socialization

Of course in the process of socialization, as in those of subsidiarity and intervention, the freedom of the individual may suffer. John XXIII warns that "an atmosphere develops wherein it becomes difficult to . . . do anything on one's own initiative" (*MM* 62). But he is confident that such abuse will not be common. He puts the question: "Will people perhaps cease to be personally responsible?" He answers negatively: "This socialization is the creation of free people who are so disposed to act by nature as to be responsible for what they do" (ibid.).

Perhaps a more fundamental answer is found in another of his statements: "This trend also indicates and in part follows from that human and natural inclination . . . whereby people are impelled voluntarily to enter into association in order to attain objectives which each one desires but which exceed the capacity of single individuals" (ibid.). Socialization is the process by which small children are inducted into the mores and customs of their society (Berger and Luckmann 1966). "Within these intermediary groupings individuals must be considered persons and be encouraged to participate in the affairs of the group" (*MM* 66). Yet just one paragraph later, Pope John XXIII returns to a reassuring note about the state's role in the process. "If this norm is observed socialization will enable people not only to develop . . . but [it will] also lead to an appropriate structuring of the human community" (*MM* 67).

Socialization must be recognized as a process running through subsidiarity. It begins with the impulses of human nature that confront the complexities of social life through social organization to achieve the common good. Note how it is linked to social justice, for that virtue supports these human impulses. The process then moves forward as other actors enter the picture; for example, the state in its proper role. The same bipolarity is at work in socialization as in subsidiarity. Socialization has consequences for welfare, as the bishops' economic pastoral makes evident.

Social Justice and Building the *Oikos*

In the traditional language of the Schoolmen there were three types of justice: legal, commutative, and distributive. Commutative justice referred to justice in exchanges between individuals or the justice of part to part of society. Distributive justice was justice of the state to its citizens or the justice of the whole to the part. Legal justice was justice of the individual to the state or to the good of the whole, as represented by the state. Why legal? Because it was assumed that social relationships of a right-ordered society would be reflected in law. This justice was also called general justice.

In the latter part of the nineteenth century, the term *legal* became widely unpopular because the justice enshrined in legal codes was inadequate. Legal justice now seemed synonymous with *legalistic*. The term no longer conveyed the idea of a virtue that ordered social relationships toward the common good. Hence a new name was sought.

The term *social justice* took over. First used by nineteenth-century theologians, it became enshrined in papal documents, especially Pius XI's 1931 *Quadragesimo Anno* and his 1937 *Divini Redemptoris* (Atheistic Communism). The question was whether this was a new name for legal or general justice or whether it was a new specific justice or both. Let us examine key texts: "there is also a social justice with its own set of obligations. . . . " (*DR* 51). "The distribution of created goods . . . must be effectively brought into conformity with the common good, i.e., social justice" (*QA* 57–58). Productive effort cannot yield its fruits "unless a truly organic and juridical order watches over the exercise of work" (*QA* 69). "Institutions . . . of all social life ought to be penetrated with this justice" (*QA* 88; see also 70, 110).

Several characteristics of social justice emerge. First, it is the equivalent of the earlier general or legal justice, for its object is the common good. Second, in the name of that common good it commands all specific acts of justice—at a minimum, commutative and distributive justice. Third, it organizes the institutions of a social and juridical order. From this organized and productive society benefits will be distributed. This need not be interpreted as if the state does all the distributing, but it does imply that the state oversees a just distribution in conformity with the common good. Fourth, social justice commands individuals, intermediary organizations, and the state.

One other piece of this somewhat fluid tradition needs to be entered before trying to say a final word on social justice. Scholars are aware that the first draft of what was to become John XXIII's *Mater et Magistra* attempted to resolve the debate over social justice. But the final draft manifests a serene indifference to the debate. It uses the term only twice, without any elaboration or definition. It turns with seeming indifference to such equivalents as *justice and equity* or *justice and love.*

From all this I suggest that the following are elements of a gathering consensus. First, doing justice, not naming it, is the important factor. Second, the 1971 synod's *Justitia in Mundo* uses the unmodified term *justice* to the virtual exclusion of such modifiers as *social* or *distributive.* Their usage has had a strong impact on the Catholic community. Third, the concept of social justice, worked out from the social nature of the person and the common good, has established itself at least as a replacement for legal (general) justice. Fourth, this social justice commands acts of justice from the individual, and hence in some way becomes a particular justice of the part to the whole. Fifth, in this latter function, social justice commands the organization of such institutions as the common good may call for. Sixth, social justice, as all justice, must be informed by love.

I would summarize my position on this term, which for me has strongly evocative power despite the controversy surrounding its understanding, in this way: "The concept remains fluid; where scriptural influence is strong, as in *Justitia in*

Mundo, the unmodified *justice* will be most common. Many will remain powerfully attracted to *social justice* as a symbol. Some of these will use it exclusively as substitute for legal or general justice; others will tack on another use. They will use the term, perhaps with some ambiguity, for the call to organize a just society in the name of the common good" (Land 1987). Over recent years I have ·personally inclined to the belief that social justice is only another name for the love that does justice. I noted in Land 1987 that "time-honored distinction among the virtues assigns primacy to love. Love informs all the other virtues, lives in them, is their soul force. Love transforms justice from within. More fundamentally, the doing of justice stems from the fundamental option for God who loves us and wants me to love others as God loves them, and out of this love to give them their full due in the community of social living. Another sense of the priority of love over justice is the Christian conviction that owing to human sinfulness the motive force of justice may not be adequate to the job of getting justice done; on occasion the power of love may have to reinforce the colder force of justice."[3]

Sources of Catholic Social Teaching

In this section, I want to add to the above summary statement of the noetically normative in Catholic social teaching a brief account of the types of people who influenced my personal formation in social thought. This I have approached more anecdotally in the earlier chapters.

Obviously, such a lineup will have to take into consideration the fact that the Catholic Church has consistently taught that she draws from the Scriptures and from reason, that is, human nature or the natural law. But how does the official teaching Church get those truths of reason and revelation? And are there other sources of Catholic social teaching than the official teachers?

Considerable space will be devoted elsewhere in this book to reading signs of the times. But here it must be recorded that John XXIII and Paul VI inaugurated a revolution in the way of doing theology when they opened this subject. First of all, we could no longer look for God's ongoing revelation exclusively in the Book or in official teachers. We would also seek that revelation and what God was doing in history in the trends and events of our times.

Moreover, readers of these signs would be all in the Church and also those not in the Catholic body. Theologians of Latin America, for example, would find this source of theologizing in the poor and the oppressed. These professional theologians would now be prepared to hear how the people experiencing the cross read God's call, just as feminists would turn to women's experience to fashion an anthropology that responds to women's consciousness. The faithful around the world who know the human and Christian value of communal ownership ask whether private ownership of productive property is valid.

That people contribute to Catholic social teaching from living out of the conditions of their lives is not wholly new. Pacifism and nonviolence have become a part of Catholic social teaching. Although it is remarkable that they have made such headway, the main early source of theological reflection has indisputably been laity like Dorothy Day, Gordon Zahn, Catholic Workers, and Catholic laypeople in other peace movements. Later, the pope and some bishops began to address nonviolence. Pope John Paul II advanced this theme during the United States' Gulf War with Iraq and in his last encyclical, *Centesimus Annus,* written for the hundredth anniversary of *Rerum Novarum.*

Here, surely, is the place to acknowledge the enormous influence that great French layman, Jacques Maritain, has had on my understanding of Catholic social teaching. I will name a dozen or more others in another chapter.

People of other religions have contributed to my understanding of Catholic social teaching impressively. Since I am not writing a treatise on the contributions of other religions to Catholic thinking about society, I confine myself to their contribution to my thinking. To mind spontaneously jumps the enormous contribution of Mahatma Ghandi on nonviolence, not only to me but throughout the world.

Through cultural exchange Catholic theologians are discovering riches in other religions, riches that often deepen Catholic understanding of our own deposit of faith, as I have learned by reading these theologians. Jewish exegetes have helped us to grasp the vitality ancient metaphors can have in our sociopolitical life today. Thanks to them, recent U.S. Catholic bishops' social pastorals have turned powerfully on themes of exodus, exile, confession, and covenant.

The contributions of Protestants to my understanding of Catholic social teaching have been significant. In this autobiography I limit myself to how they influenced me. The U.S. Catholic bishops' pastorals on peace and economic justice witness to their impact.

Some Protestant writers I have read with profit are Reinhold Niebuhr, John Bennett, James Gustafson, Larry Rasmussen, John Raines, Charles West, and Jim Wallis. Viewing the world scene, I think of how much very many of us were influenced by the World Council of Churches' 1966 Church and Society Convocation on social thought and current problems. Many of us read avidly the volumes that went into its preparation. I devoted a great deal of attention to such English-language sources as *The Ecumenical Review* and other publications of the WCC, latterly, the fine publications on justice, peace, and integral creation; and European theologians like John MacQuarrie on natural law, Canon Ronald Preston for his *Church and Society in the Twentieth Century,* Jurgen Moltmann, and countless others, including Protestant theologians of Africa, Latin America, and Asia. All of these have helped me frame social thought in a Roman Catholic context.

One of the most interesting Protestant contributions was a letter by a theologian of the World Council to a preparatory commission of Vatican II working on a chapter that bore strongly on Catholic social teaching. Lukas Vischer, head of the division of Faith and Order, offered a schema setting forth how the publications of Faith and Order might go about writing a chapter on the church and the contemporary world. Citing a 1955 World Council study, "Christ's Lordship over Church and World," he criticized natural law and placed the Church in an active relation to the risen Christ. "This letter made the working committee realize the need to speak of Christ's lordship and to make central the specifically paschal aspect of Christ's lordship and the need not to confuse it with natural law themes" (Moeller 1969, 21).

Organicism of Catholic Social Teaching

The term *organicism* addresses Catholic social teaching as a body, a corpus. Each new addition to Catholic social teaching is supposed to fit into an integral wholeness. I wrestled with this idea and supported it at various stages during my half century of engagement with Catholic social teaching. However, I made the following discovery early. Although the manuals of neo-scholasticism insisted on the organic character and papal encyclicals always drew attention to their predecessors' body of teaching, each encyclical has been a specific project addressed to a specific problem.

To illustrate my proposition I will take papal writings from Pius XI through Paul VI. To do full justice to our present pope would require a lengthy disquisition. John Paul writes in the tradition of organicism, for example, *Laborem Excercens*, though that document is highly idiosyncratic. He moves distinctly beyond the tradition of natural law to the biblical tradition in *Redemptor Hominis* and in *Dives in Misericordia* (Rich in mercy). His writings in the liberal tradition are typified by his *Sollicitudo Rei Socialis* (The Church's social concern). Concerning his most recent encyclical, *Centesimus Annus,* commemorating the century of social teaching since Leo XIII's 1891 *Rerum Novarum*, commentators differ. Many are bewildered that the author of *Laborem Exercens* and *Sollicitudo Rei Socialis* could have written the strong approbation of capitalism and the free market they find in that encyclical. This appears to them a singular departure from (to some, an advance in) the tradition. Others believe that the pope's approbation of capitalism is evenly balanced by the questions about capitalism and its free market that John Paul, following the tradition, raises about free market capitalism, even while noting its good points.

I do not depict the specific projects of Pope John Paul's social writings here because several of them figure in other chapters of this book, especially chapter 9. I end this section with an exploration of our present pope's differing approaches to the question, Is there a social doctrine? for this question follows on that of organicism.

At this point I would like to get on to the problems prompting the popes to write. The English title of the 1931 social encyclical of Pius XI, *Quadragesimo Anno,* explicitly calls for reorganization of the social order. Social justice prompted the reorganization. The proposed instrument of reorganization was the Vocational Order. This concept did not appear in Leo XIII's *Rerum Novarum,* written before the Great Depression that pervaded the industrial countries in the early thirties, a depression that called for some new thinking about social and economic order.

The 1961 *Mater et Magistra* pursued a project similar to *Quadragesimo Anno.* But, while nodding to organicism and continuity, it made several departures from the traditional body of natural law. Justice, for instance, was generalized into love and justice. Socialization instead of the Vocational Order became the key to the encyclical's organizational structure, thus introducing new language into Catholic social teaching. Socialization was not a call for socialism, but it was so interpreted in conservative circles. It simply reinforced the already existing principle of intervention by the state—one of the two poles of the principle of subsidiarity—against opposition. The heavily sociological content of the newly stated principle had no continuity with past teaching.

Although the 1963 encyclical of the same pope is named *Pacem in Terris,* its project was human rights. While it is true that human rights had been defended in previous documents, they had never received such a systemic and thorough treatment. The encyclical was heralded, not for its continuity, but as a breakthrough.

In 1965 *Gaudium et Spes* was much more than a more satisfactory theological statement about the Church. It put the Christian and the Church in the world as a human‚project belonging to the reign of God. Following chapters reflect at length on this remarkable document.

Populorum Progressio in 1967 addressed the notion of development for the peoples of the world as a humane ideal. Some paragraphs are devoted to development in *Mater et Magistra* but development was not the project of that earlier encyclical. Since a major obstacle to development was the rapacity of the Western world, the encyclical exhorted the rich nations at length to share with developing peoples.

In 1971 two influential documents, *Octogesima Adveniens* and an apostolic letter, *Justitia in Mundo,* appeared. The first, published in the spring, celebrated the eightieth anniversary of Leo XIII's *Rerum Novarum*. In it, two projects stand out: first, the universalization of the social problem to include the whole world; and second, the invitation to local communities of Christians to shape their culture and social order with creative imagination (*OA* 4).

That invitation appears in several passages of *Justitia in Mundo*. The most crucial is this: "In the face of such widely varying situations it is difficult for us to utter a unified message and to put forward a solution which has universal validity. Such is not our ambition, nor is it our mission. It is up to the Christian community to analyze with objectivity the situation which is proper to their own country, to shed on it the light of the gospel's unalterable words and to draw principles of reflection, norms of judgment and directives for action from the social teaching of the Church."

Where can one look for this social teaching of the Church? The letter goes on: "This social teaching has been worked out in the course of history and notably in this industrial era, since the historic date of Pope Leo XIII's message" on the condition of workers, *Rerum Novarum*.

Two different readings have emerged from this passage. One, focused on "social teaching has been worked out," asserts that for Paul VI there is indeed a corpus of social teaching, needing, surely, to be reshaped as it addresses different situations or problems, but nevertheless a true body of social teaching. The other focuses on the invitation to Christian communities to reflect on their differing situations and to draw from them principles of reflection. Newly discovered principles of reflection based on historical situations suggest that the eternal verities of natural law are being repudiated. Still it must be recognized that the pope who utters these words follows them up immediately by the words quoted above that recognize principles of social teaching formed in an earlier epoch.

Corroboration for this latter view is discovered in a passage (*JM* 48) in the conclusion of *Justitia in Mundo*. Paul there distinguishes a task of the Church as teacher and a task of the laity in social action. The Church will "enlighten minds in order to assist them to discover the truth and to find the right path to follow amid the different teachings that call for their attention. . . ." Again, in the same paragraph, "If the role of the hierarchy is to teach and to interpret authentically the norms of morality . . . it belongs to the laity without waiting passively for orders and directives, to take the initiative. . . ." The paragraphs that follow delineate these initiatives: infusing a Christian spirit in the structures of society and effective social action, in which there will be "a legitimate variety of possible options."

In the fall, Paul VI published the conclusions of the synod of bishops. Therein the project of development was honed down to the precise enterprise of the "doing of justice" as "a constitutive dimension of the preaching of the gospel." That document, too, occupies our attention later on.

Paul VI, toward the end of his pontificate, produced another remarkable apostolic letter, his 1975 *Evangelii Nuntiandi*. While its project was a call to the whole Church to renewed preaching of the gospel, that project, in line with so much of Vatican II, recognized that the gospel is a message about doing justice in this world (the 1971 synod's "constitutive dimension"). Paragraphs 29–39 are entirely devoted to this: "But evangelization would not be complete if it did not take account of the unceasing interplay of the gospel and of man's concrete life, both personal and social." This is why "evangelization involves an explicit message about rights and duties. . . life in society . . . international life . . . peace, justice and development [and] liberation."

Paul in these eleven paragraphs uses the word *liberation* as if he had invented it. His uses of it are owing to a singular conversion, which I can testify to from personal experience. In my eight years of half-time work for the Pontifical Commission Justice and Peace I had a number of occasions to introduce into documents I was preparing for the commission the word *liberation*. But in every such document that underwent scrutiny by the secretary of state, that word was stricken out.

Two hemisphere-wide conferences of the bishops of Latin America, in Medellin, Colombia (1968), and Puebla, Mexico (1979), affirmed the project of just development as the preferential option for the poor. This became a project also for John Paul II, as his many messages and his encyclical *Laborem Exercens* clearly demonstrate.

Thus we see that the official teaching instruments are largely project oriented. To be sure, these sources did intend to maintain and contribute to a truly organic corpus of teaching, even though their focus was on a specific project. But the projects made their own breaks with continuity, which is not the same as contradiction of the past.

Is Catholic Social Teaching a Doctrine?

In the previous section I consider organicism. Here I would like to reflect on an analogous term—*corpus,* or body. A body of truths implies an organic corpus of truths. As used in Catholic social teaching the concept of *corpus* is usually conveyed by the English word *doctrine;* for example, Catholic social doctrine. Beyond organicism, *doctrine* connotes systematization, completeness, and authoritativeness.

As such, the notion has widely been rejected. Hence, the word *doctrine* with all the baggage just described, has gradually been abandoned. The term *teaching,* as in Catholic social teaching, has replaced *doctrine* as more palatable, less rigid, and less oppressively authoritative.

I find the many social writings of John Paul II interesting in this regard. On the one hand, he seems not to want to exacerbate the dispute by insisting too heavily on the doctrinal. Thus alongside the phrase "social doctrine" he will frequently use the alternative, "social teaching." Yet because of the challenge from Latin America to Catholic social teaching he has seemed more likely to insist on doctrine. At least when speaking in Latin America, as in his address to the Puebla conference in 1979, he seemed to be determined to insist on doctrine and its binding character. More recently he has reverted to using the two labels in the same document, as in his recent *Sollicitudo Rei Socialis.*

Changes in Doing Catholic Social Teaching

While changes in doing Catholic social teaching are the heart of this entire volume, it seems appropriate to make some preliminary comments here as rounding out the topic of influences in the shaping of Catholic social teaching, for the shaping of Catholic social teaching was intrinsic to the movements and changes going on within the life of the Catholic church and its ways of thinking and doing.

Occasionally throughout this study we explore the shift in methodology in Catholic social teaching from pre–Vatican to post–Vatican. The terms are symbolic rather than historical. The former was largely the fashioning of abstract universals, drawn only from deduction about human nature. It was a degenerate neo-scholasticism. In its beginnings in the early 1800s, the new Scholasticism was inspired by Saint Thomas Aquinas's Scholasticism. It also hewed closely to Aristotelian realism, which, in contrast to idealism, derived ideas from the senses. That insight Aquinas had long before formulated as *nihil est in intellectu quod non fuit prius in sensibus* ("there is nothing in the intellect that was not first in the sense order"). Over time, for much of neo-scholasticism that vision was lost to idealism.

The post–Vatican II method of theologizing about society shifted dramatically to emphasize the historical, the concrete, the individual, together with stress on creativity in making social order.

But, as observed above, this change was intrinsic to a shift in the life of the Church and its way of doing theology. I present this in tabular form, warning that the contrasts will, at times, appear excessive. They even may give the impression that one must totally discard an item in column A in favor of its opposite. It may well be only a matter of emphasis.

I. Church Looking Inward

A	B
Hierarchical	Participatory
Church as mystical body (Vine and branches)	Church as body of people
World for the Church	Church for the world
Church embodies the reign of God	People of God serve the reign
Power at center	Power as service
Domination	Equality
Patriarchal	Males share as females
Elitist	Inclusivist
Bureaucratic	Prophetic *Sacramentum Mundi*
Church leads	Church accompanies
Church assigns roles	Church dialogues over roles
Jesus as epiphany of God	Jesus the Way, risk, search
Descending Christology	Ascending Christology

II. Church Looking Outward

Dualism	Integration
Center decides	More decisions made by local church
Ideas have power to move	Heart guides ideas to move
Social doctrine deduced	Social doctrine derived historically as well
Revelation only in original deposit	Revelation also in reading signs of times
Flight from world	Join and respect world
Primacy of reason	Primacy of love
Faith as assent of intellect	Faith also as commitment
Orthodoxy	*Orthopraxis*
Total rejection of Enlightenment	Good in world recognized

This may not be very helpful, though it has meaning for me. If not read as overly stark contrasts, it fits my experience of the pre– and post–Vatican Church with regard to its impact on Catholic social teaching.

As I remarked, the emphases should not be read as totally dichotomous, as if in choosing column B you must totally reject its opposite in column A. Obviously, there is a deposit of faith; *orthopraxis* does not dismiss orthodoxy, but complements it with another way of reaching truth. Faith, while receiving much more emphasis as a committed relationship with God, remains intellectual assent.

I have mentioned the impact of some items in *The Church Looking Inward* on social teaching. As an illustration, let us look at the last one, descending versus ascending Christology. The first rejects the historical. All of Christ is deduced simply from his being God. He lives the carrying out of a prefixed divine mandate. Apart from stultifying the life of Jesus, the danger for social thought is that, if Jesus did nothing but carry out the divine mandate and did not or could not affect history in any way not dictated by that fixed mandate, then neither may we affect history. If there are sins of injustice in this world, that is a matter of God's acceptance, and we must likewise accept them passively.

A Christology that ascends starts with the historical Jesus. What did he do? What did he preach? Did he count for anything in his society, in his day? Only answering those questions will we know Jesus. One remarkable fact stands out: Jesus was always on the side of the poor and the despised. Jesus did challenge the powers that controlled and the institutions that contributed to oppression of the people. A conclusion, so different from that of a descending Christology, is that I should be on the side of the poor. I should challenge unjust institutions of my world.

This chapter introduces three themes. First, ways of formulating Catholic social teaching: I chose one that for me has more centrality than others. Then I developed a body of social teaching within that framework. The body of social teaching presented here is entirely noetic or intellectual norms. Other chapters will add responses other than the noetic. Second, I took up other sources for the development of Catholic social teaching. Third, I have imbedded the noetic that makes up the first part of this chapter in the historical forces that directed the shift in the Church's life and theology from the pre- to post–Vatican II approach.

Moral Making in the Social Order

M oral making in the social order is not different from moral making in individual decisions. Cocreativity with God is fundamental in this realm. We make ourselves and our society moral. In the language of Thomas Aquinas, when making a final practical judgment the moral actor works like an artist. This image is a far cry from a conception of natural law as dictated by God into our individual and social natures, thereby requiring only obedience to the dictation.

Moral making in the social order, however, does differ from that of individual morality in two respects. First, social moral making is more complex. Second, it more powerfully announces the interpersonal or structural dimension of the love of God which is love of neighbor. As that love reaches out to create community and to build structures which ensure rights to the whole community, especially to the marginalized, it underscores the profoundly structural dimension of love of God and love of neighbor. Think only of the transformation of mind-sets and institutions needed if women are to have their rightful place in society and in the society which is the Church.

My Moral Making in the Social Order

My own moral making in the social order originally focused on applying a narrowly conceived natural law to changing circumstances that were always contained within the universal norm. Once one had the proper assemblage of relevant norms and a well-defined situation, the norm automatically fit the case. It was the approach of the manualists.

Challenged

As my autobiography also reveals, at times I resisted the manual approach. The first corrective was discovering in the mid-forties Aquinas's treatment of the virtue of prudence. Specifically addressing social order, Aquinas elaborated his lengthy and eminently pertinent section on political prudence. To his discussion of natural law, which precedes his treatment of prudence, Aquinas devoted very little text compared with the text he devoted to the prudential or final practical moral judgment. With this discovery, moral making could no longer be the simple application of universal norms (retaining, nevertheless, their appositeness) to cases somehow contained squarely in the universal. One does not need to go back to Aquinas to formulate a proper social *praxis* for the individual, for society, or for the Church. But because this book is autobiographical I will record in the final chapter the debt I owe Thomas Aquinas (alongside the theologian who dominates this chapter, Karl Rahner) for helping me to understand moral making. I go further in that chapter to state my belief that the retrieval of Aquinas in moral making could strengthen the rooting of the turn to the subject.

The motive and circumstances of the action contemplated clearly affect moral making. Christian attitudes also affect moral conduct. But some attitudes, even social attitudes, arise instinctually in a person experiencing love: benevolence, neighborliness, solidarity, and cooperation. In this historical order of grace these attitudes are elevated to become acts of charity. Also, God can and does call in individual ways and unique instances.

Love Discovered

The second corrective to a manualist approach was discovering that love is the true foundation of human and Christian morality. Aquinas had already taught me that love, not law, is the foundation of moral making. Love, he affirmed, is the form of all the virtues. Love informs justice. The full truth of the latter reality escaped me until my reading of the Belgian Jesuit Gerard Gilleman's *The Primacy of Charity in Moral Theology* (1959).[1]

William Ryan, the Canadian Jesuit who founded Center of Concern, coauthored the English translation of the Belgian Jesuit's seminal study of the role of charity in social teaching. Ryan arrived in Louvain for theological studies just as the Catholic faculties of that city were becoming one of the fountainheads of the new theology that would undergird the changes that Vatican II promoted.

Gilleman, I learned from Ryan, was bothered by moral theology manuals of recent centuries which emphasized transgressions, sins, and how to confess them. This approach obscured the moral life, the love of God, and our response in love to God, which is identified with love of our neighbor. The manualist approach was minimalist moral theology: keep the commandments. In Gilleman's words, "Moral treatises had become divorced from theology and become an ethic" (ibid., 346–47). Although there were chapters on love and other virtues, love lost the central position Aquinas had given it with his statement that love is the form and "spiritual sense of the other virtues" (ibid., 347).

Gilleman also reflects Joseph Marechal's turn to the subject: "love is nothing if not personalizing," and more pertinently, "Moral doctrine with charity restored to centrality now appears as more intimately related to Christian dogma" (ibid.).[2]

Gilleman links Marechal to Thomas Aquinas: "The work of Marechal, S.J., had already made explicit the notion of the dynamism of the intelligence, which was latent in Thomism. . . ." (ibid, xxxv).[3] Gilleman also connects the turn to the person to moral life: "In the course of this study we have fixed our attention primarily on the interior pole of our being in order to discover there the sense of our moral life at its root." He also links this stress on the subject to love as would Rahner following him: "This returning to oneself—for that is what this interiorization of charity really is . . ." (ibid., 344).

With Gilleman, the virtue of social justice took on new meaning for me. Gilleman describes justice as "one of the more exterior mediations of charity" (ibid.). Where before this time I had accepted the familiar Catholic social teaching pairing of love and justice as quite separate virtues, I now conceived social justice as justice under the informing power of love. Does not the doing of justice, that is, giving to another what is his or her due, also give to society its due, beginning with the love of that one to whom something is owed in justice? Does not informing love impregnate the act of justice, so that it is hard to separate giving what is due from giving the love that is commanded? Does not informing love end by contributing to the *debitum* not just motivation but content?

Karl Rahner's Turning to the Subject

In my student days in philosophy and then theology, Karl Rahner was only beginning to write his magisterial theological reflections.[4] Since none of his works had yet been translated, I was through philosophy and theology without any introduction to his new thinking in theology and morality. I did not notice Rahner until he appeared at Vatican Council II as *peritus* (expert), indeed one of the most influential experts.

Rahner's moral system builds on the natural law tradition, but is founded on other components of the human person as well. This German explicitly acknowledges the role of his fellow Jesuit of Louvain, Joseph Marechal. Marechal helped Rahner to build resistance against all idealism with his idea of turning to the subject implicitly present to all reflection.

In *Foundations of the Christian Faith,* Rahner succinctly summarizes the anthropological and philosophical structure of his moral being. To this he adds a Christian anthropology or "orientation [of the person] toward incomprehensible mystery," described also as holy mystery (1978, 57–66, especially 60 and 66, n. 9). This anthropology begins with a fundamental option in love for God and for the neighbor; the two are one love. This constitutes our fundamental moral attitude (ibid., chapter 2). Rahner explains: "In the fact that man raises analytical questions about himself and opens himself to the unlimited horizon of such questionings, he has already transcended himself and every conceivable element of such an analysis or of an empirical reconstruction of himself" (ibid., 29).

In the same section Rahner further elucidates subjectivity: "[Man] is experienced as the subjectivity of these multiple objectivities (the various ways human empirical sciences name the human)" (ibid.). Furthermore, "Man's ability to be related to himself, his 'having to do with himself' is not and cannot be one element in him alongside of other elements" (ibid.). No, "Being a person means the self-possession of a subject as such in a conscious and free relationship to the totality of itself" (ibid., 30).

Other language may be helpful: the person (subject) as an autonomous and transcendental being, not as an object, even an object of reflection. As subject, the human person is self-conscious and self-directing. The person has self-experience or, rather, the human person *is* self-experience (ibid., 30–31).

The I is not the sum of all the anthropologies that can be predicated of the subject. It rather transcends all biological, chemical, organic, psychological, and anthropological statements about the I (ibid., 27–28). As it transcends these statements, so it transcends history and earth time. The person (subject) is self-maintaining in continuity through all that conditions it, whether those are interior or exterior conditions, including culture.[5]

This self-conscious, self-directing, self-experiencing, and self-maintaining I prompts us to call the person a subject. We recognize that although this autonomous power is influenced by forces acting within and without, it transcends all.

This person (subject) is essentially social. "His subjectivity and his free personal self-interpretation take place precisely in and through his being in the world, in time, and in history, or, better, in and through world, time, and history. The question of salvation cannot be answered by bypassing man's historicity and his social nature" (ibid., 40). Since that aspect of the person is extensively explored in another chapter I will not here elaborate on it, except to make one point. This transcendent subject grounds all moral making, even though the normative remains important. Consequently my conception of Catholic Social Teaching must accord preeminence to this person (subject) also in the social order.

The Fundamental Option

"By its very nature subjectivity is always a transcendence which listens, which does not control, which is overwhelmed by mystery and opened up by mystery" (ibid., 58, 131–32). The entirety of the human subject is at stake in the fundamental option. Our moral being rests on this option for our God who is love, ground of our being, and incomprehensible mystery (ibid., 60). Responsiveness is the grounding act of moral life. The fundamental option shapes the self. All particular moral acts reflect this characteristic of personal response to the call from a personal Being, sharing life with us as a gift. This option, this "response with a 'yes' or 'no' is subjectivity actualized in a posteriori and historical encounter with the world of persons and of things [actualized] in his [a person's] encounter with a human Thou in whom history and transcendence find their one actualization together and in unity and there he finds his encounter with God as the absolute Thou" (ibid., 133).

The preceding paragraph has the phrase "world of persons" to which is added "things." Earlier, Rahner had phrased this relationship exclusively in terms of things. It was in colloquy with Johann Baptist Metz that Rahner changed the language. Later he wrote: "Man experiences himself by experiencing the other *person* (his emphasis) and not the other *thing*. . . . Self-experience is achieved in the unity between it and the experiences of other persons. . . . He who has not discovered his neighbor has not truly achieved realization of himself either" (Vorgrimler 1986, 126).

A challenge to this characterization of the fundamental option was on the score of its transcendence excluding the social situation of the human with all its devastating manifestations of inhumanity. Here again, Metz led the charge (Metz 1980; see also Lamb 1982).

Once again Rahner was capable of generously acknowledging a contribution to theology made by his former student. Thus: "If Christianity is love of God and the neighbor, if love of God can only be realized in a mysticism of the experience of the nearness of God, and if love of neighbor can only be realized by perceiving a social and political task which everyone has, then what Metz says is, I think, clear: Christianity particularly today has a mystical and social component" (Vorgrimler 1986, 127).

Gregory Baum formulates the challenge as follows: "*Fides caritate informata* does not include *fides iustitia informata:* faith informed by charity is not faith informed by justice" (Baum 1987).

Rahner has repeatedly responded to critics who fault him for lacking something or other (such as not enough exegesis of Scripture) by saying that he did not pretend to cover the whole frontier of theological speculation, and that, if he had, he could not do so anyway. However, especially with regard to Metz, he has avowed his great admiration for Metz's contributions: "To a certain degree theology today must also become political theology. It wasn't I but my student, Johann Baptist Metz, who developed political theology" (Imhof and Biallowons 1990).

I find these criticisms troublesome, since I rely so profoundly on the anthropology of Rahner's moral system. I would certainly prefer that Rahner's transcendentalism would more explicitly and specifically include building the social order in which the one opting for God must concretely carry out the option.

But, I believe that the social aspect is contained implicitly: first, in Rahner's insistence that the encounter with God is in the encounter with the human Thou, and, second, in his union of love of God with love of neighbor. For Rahner can say with the apostle John, if you cannot love your neighbor whom you see, how can you love God whom you cannot see? Loving God is the fundamental option of one's moral life; so, *eo ipso* and essentially, the fundamental option is love of neighbor in some fashion, in one's discovery of God as Thou in my neighbor as Thou.

And surely the record of our Scriptures is of a God calling us to communal, social life. Rahner fails to spell out the consequences, but for me he profoundly lays the groundwork for our emphasis on social good. Rahner was a major *peritus* in the theology of Vatican II's *Gaudium et Spes,* which surely tells us that the doing of the kingdom is very much a matter of social living and the doing of social justice. In an interview by Ton

Oostveen in Amsterdam in September 1978, Rahner says: "My insights go along with the spirit of Vatican II especially in *Gaudium et Spes* on the mission of the Church in society and politics" (ibid., 61). Having said all this, I would have to agree with political theologians that Rahner's transcendentalism is not a method that, as they demand, starts with the suffering subject as the interrogator. This point is developed in chapter 9.

The Free Subject

Among students of Rahner who helped me at this point, I am especially indebted to James Bresnahan, S.J. (1980, 169–84). Several paragraphs of the next section draw deeply upon his commentary.

Bresnahan's commentary attracts me because it appears to be grounded in that school of theologians who, taking their lead from the second Vatican council's *Dei Verbum* (Divine Revelation), have abandoned an older propositional approach to revelation in favor of one that makes Christ the fullness of revelation. In the words of the constitution, "Jesus perfected Revelation by fulfilling it through his whole work of making himself present and manifesting himself: through his words and deeds, his signs and wonders, but especially through his death and resurrection from the dead and final sending of the Spirit of truth" (*DV* 4). The ramifications of this approach for natural law receive due notice later on. The fundamental option for God, if made in love, is the core act of the person and as such commits the person wholly to that choice in a way that is true of no later moral act. The fundamental option, as we have discussed it, is a dimension of the self in action, because it is immediately aware of the self, but also because it is accessible to reflection only through personal acts of free choice. Yet, all acts of free choice possess moral meaning only as embodiments of the fundamental option, our free surrender into incomprehensible mystery.

The incomprehensible mystery creates our world and us as an expression of the inner reality of holy mystery. The Creator thus offers creation a share of divine being and invites a response of cocreativity. We, expressions of holy mystery, are to create ourselves, our moral being. We begin by saying yes to the structures of our being, and in particular to our grounding freedom (Rahner 1978, 81–86).

That freedom is not merely the sum of our free acts of choice, but the freedom of our fundamental option which accepts and affirms holy mystery's gift of the free, responsible self. Freedom, so understood, is a risk-taking that participates in God's own risk-taking in creating a world of persons able to respond to God. Freedom, so understood, is a risk-taking which participates with the divine creativity in shaping the self as someone new.

The free subject is a far cry from an understanding of human nature as the mere execution of a divinely dictated destiny according to the norms of nature. In the latter, freedom was seen as those many pitfalls which the norms rendered less dangerous (ibid., 38).

Although many moralists, turning to the subject, seem to have expunged from their description of the moral act any and all norms deriving from nature, Rahner's description is thoroughly dialogical, embracing both. His concept of the free subject does not do away with natural law but modifies it. Attention to the subject, with its newness of vision, does not require dismissing that source of objectivity which is channelled through human nature.

Thus, even when Rahner extols loving freedom as primary to a revision of natural law, the essentiality side of natural law retains its place, albeit a complementary one. In this dialogical relationship, the natural, instead of being sought totally in abstract reason, is now sought more in structures imbedded in direct experience (ibid., 410).

The newness is decidedly there in this dialectic or dialogical relationship. For the search for nature as normative in morality begins—I stress *begins*—by searching within the human person's "immediate experience of the self acting morally within subjectivity" (ibid., 35–39). Says Bresnahan, "Since the fundamental option of freedom realizes itself in conditions of bodiliness, acts must be examined as to whether they express loving creative option for the ground of my being."

Concomitantly, the old Scholastic adage, significant for moral making, that "doing follows being" (*agere sequitur esse*) shifts a little. Although an older tradition discovered that *esse* that must be followed to act morally by looking at only what was presumed to be essentiality, even imposed from outside, Rahner attaches greatest importance to what dialogically grounds and empowers, alongside what in human nature channels the uniqueness of human creativity, the being of the autonomous human self which is grounded in the nature of the human (ibid.). This is also indicated since not all norms of the older natural law were essential to the human person and consequentially immutable.[6]

Rahner (1963a, 228) makes much of another limitation of objective norms, this time not from the side of essential ethics but from that which he calls an existential ethic: "God is interested in history not only insofar as it is the carrying out of norms, but insofar as it is a history which consists in the harmony of unique events. . . . The fact that this divine binding force, which regards the individual as such, cannot be expressed in a general proposition, is no proof of its nonexistence. . . . The perception of this individual norm . . . cannot come about in the same way as the perception of a universal norm. . . ."[7] In his system of the moral experience of the self in action, Rahner is far from dismissing reason and ethical reflection.

In conclusion, for the free subject, freedom is the drive toward the incomprehensible mystery for whom we fundamentally opt. Later in the development of theology, freedom is focused on moral choice in accord with the fundamental structures of nature which encompass and channel freedom.

My procedure in this analysis of the various namings of the self as free person (subject), fundamentally opting for incomprehensible mystery, obviously divides what is a whole, a living unity. I do think this dissection is helpful and does not sacrifice the essential whole. Likewise the sections to follow on the unity of love of God and love of neighbor as well as on graced world and history separately address aspects of essentially unified wholes.

Love of God and Love of Neighbor

The article of Rahner's from which most of this material is drawn is a sustained meditation on the creativity of love and its essential thrust to social order (1978, 410).[8]

If one understood that love of God mandates love of neighbor, no further comment on the connection would be required. When Rahner enunciates this truth, however, he means something very profound, with pivotal consequences for moral making in the social order. In keeping with the Scholastic tradition, Rahner holds that the two loves are one. From this unity, he explicitly draws social implications. In an interview on the social and political order, Rahner commented: "My insights . . . emerge from a concept of love of neighbor as *bearer* of the love of God" (Imhof and Biallowons 1990, 61, emphasis added).

Hans Urs von Balthasar took exception to Rahner's point.[9] The eminent Swiss theologian believed that Rahner's approach made the love of God altogether secondary. Rahner (ibid., 26) answers: "As a primary occurrence, prior to reflection, radical love of neighbor always attains and must attain God. But obviously, the opposite is also true [because love of God always attains love of neighbor]. I must love God who loves me and my neighbor. With respect to the specific fulfillment of love of God and love of neighbor we have from the outset a *perichoresis,* that is, a mutual conditioning of both elements. But here I must also say, at least theoretically, that God's love is more important than love of neighbor. I have never disputed that."[10]

Rahner's core emphasis on the unity of love of God and neighbor has also led to criticism that he is guilty of horizontalism. To this critique from some theologians and bishops, he responded: "At every turn I have fought against a primitive horizontalism . . . the unique heresy of our time. . . ." (ibid.).

Social Side of Rahner's Anthropology of Love

Rahner (1974, 231) begins his anthropology of love by highlighting the social impact of love, "which is not merely an organized effort of sociopolitical organization, but which in truth remains love." A love that truly supports the social efforts because it is flowing out of love "is not the function of secular society but itself constitutes a completely new society. . . ." Moreover, "it allows the eternal Kingdom of God to begin in secret. . . ."

Rahner also addresses the implications of love for social living this way: "If Christianity is to say something to the man of *tomorrow* who must understand himself *where* and *in the manner* in which he exists, then it must be made comprehensible to him that the *whole* truth of the gospel is still hidden in germ in what he finds most easily as a deed . . . viz. in the love of one's neighbor" (ibid.).

The powerful social significance of this unity of love can be seen from another reflection. The key here is that ours is a graced world. It is the one reality of faith, hope, and love which constitutes that depth into which God has immersed the world. How did God effect this? By offer of the divine reality which God is.

Rahner roots this radical unity of love of God and love of neighbor first in the Scriptures. Matthew understands unity as an eschatological criteria for judgments of the nations: "What you did to the least of these little ones, you did unto me" (Mt 25ff.). In Romans, Paul maintains that Christian existence is discovered in love of the neighbor as fulfillment of the law (Rom 13:8).

In a different vein, John reflects that love of neighbor constitutes the totality of human existence: "God has loved us not that we might love him in return but that we might love one another" (1 Jn 4:7, 11). Hence, "Anyone who does not love the brother whom he can see, cannot love the God whom he has never seen" (1 Jn 4:20). For Rahner the Johannine passages are saying that the God in us is really the one loved above all else and who is reached precisely in the love of our brethren.[11] Rahner thinks that the Johannine texts, coupled with other scriptural passages, give us a first approximation to his own thesis of unicity.

Christian Anthropology

Starting by identifying the love of God with the infused virtue of charity, Rahner proposes that such love is a love of God for God's own sake. What we call love is at least an act of total surrender to God. When this supernatural love is addressed to the neighbor, the neighbor is loved for the sake of God. Love of neighbor is an act of this love. In Rahner's own words: "Wherever a genuine love of the human attains its proper nature and moral depth, it is in addition always so heightened by God's saving grace that it is also love of God, whether the subject explicitly considers it such" (ibid., 237).

But is the converse true? Is every act of explicit love of God truly and formally love of neighbor? Before answering this question, some assumptions must be clarified.

Love of Neighbor Is the Basic Morality for the Human Person. Love of neighbor is not just one of many moral acts of the human subject; it is the basis and total of human morality. Human morality can be divided into categories of family morality, business morality, political morality, and so forth. All these categories describe the objective world in and through which human persons dispose of themselves toward their final end. In so doing human persons impose on the multiplicity of things a unifying law, which in love systematizes the multiplicity.

Love of Neighbor Manifests the Wholeness and Essence of the Human Person. For Rahner, even apart from the supernatural, love of neighbor has a quality of mystery. The free self-determination toward one's final end takes place in loving the neighbor so that all else is a concrete instance of this free self-determination. This is the mystery of the human person. All of the previous anthropological statements address a love which is not sectorial but the whole in which the subject possesses the self completely. Such love is achieved in history and in human experiences, including suffering.

It follows, therefore, first, that the concrete love of another Thou—the neighbor—is not just something that exists in us alongside many other things; rather it is the I in total achievement. Second, given the actual economy of salvation, as mentioned, love of this Thou comes in the form of supernatural charity, hence love of neighbor remains radically open to the immediacy of the God who communicates the self in grace.

The Encounter with the World Is the Medium of the Original Experience of God. To say that we experience God through the world raises an objection, that the religious act directed toward God must be basic and not ranked alongside encounter with the world. Rahner dismisses this as a misunderstanding. God is not an object—albeit superior—alongside other objects. We do not direct ourselves intentionally toward God in the fragmentary way we do when addressing creatures. Rather, God is the ground of this world of all our experiencing (ibid., 244–48).

But God who is origin and destination of my encounter with the world is nevertheless mediated through my loving encounter with the Thou (neighbor) in that world. To put the same truth in other language, grace and the revealed Word always happen through the human in the world. God's self-communication in grace always happens through entering into love in the world and through communication with the Thou of intramundane experience.

Thus, Rahner asks: Is every act of explicit love of God truly and formally love of neighbor? Or is love of neighbor, as supernatural love, only a secondary moral act among many others, that proceeds as a command from a loving God? Is love of neighbor secondary only because one who loves God must be well disposed toward one's neighbor?

Rahner answers, "Our love of God always intends God in supernatural transcendentality in the love of neighbor. Even the explicit love of God is still carried by that opening in trusting love to the whole of reality which takes place in love of neighbor. . . . It is radically true . . . (ontologically and not merely morally) that whoever does not love the brother whom one 'sees' also cannot love God whom one does not see. . . . One can love God whom one does not see only by loving one's visible brother lovingly" (ibid., 247).

Meaning of the Unified Love for Society

I have dwelt at length on this component of Rahner's moral system because it has explosive significance for social living. Rahner (ibid.) lists three specific implications: First, "Today, when by reason of its enormous numbers, its concrete unity and its necessity of new social forms, mankind must learn to love completely anew or go under" (ibid., 248–49). Second, "God opens out anew as silent incomprehensibility so much so that man is tempted to honor him by silence" (ibid.). Rahner means that humans, for whom God is incomprehensible, will find God again revealed in love of neighbor. Third, Rahner turns to a subject he has written on with freshness, namely, the human invention of new worlds: "When an extremely worldly world is coming into being, a world which man creates for himself and which ought not be sacralized but which must be experienced and acted in the depth *sanctified,* i.e., opened toward him, at this dawn love of neighbor might easily be the root-word [instead of faith or conversion] to move people and be the key today" (ibid.).

To say it more simply: "Whenever someone loves someone else truly and to the end, the whole of Christian salvation and of Christianity is already grasped" (ibid.).

Graced World and History

A World of Grace is the title of a volume which explores Rahner's theology. The editor, Leo O'Donovan, S.J. (1980, vii–viii), comments on the title: "Can we really speak of . . . a *gracious* world? For Rahner, the answer is: 'We can only seek God as we seek true humanity, and we can only find truth about ourselves as we find truth about God.'" O'Donovan adds: "this good news, that God and humanity can only be found together, has guided Karl Rahner's life and thought from the beginning."

Rahner (1974, 248–49) reflected in an interview on the significance of grace for him: "At one time, grace, assisting grace, and the outward circumstances shaped by God's grace in human affairs were conceived extrinsically as distinct realities occurring now and then. . . . My basic theological conviction is . . . in opposition. . . ." What is his opposing conviction? Rahner answers: "What we call grace is obviously a reality which is God-given, unmerited, free, dialogical—in other words supernatural. But for me grace is at the same time a reality which is so very much the inner core of human existence in decision and freedom, *always* and above all given in the form of an offer . . . a transcendental peculiarity of his being at all" (Imhof and Biallowons 1990, 21).

In his *Foundations of Christian Faith* Rahner rejects the notion that the supernatural can be spoken of only in conjunction with God as "basically false" (ibid, 151). His reason: "For if man's transcendentality is really mediated to itself by all the categorical material of his a posteriori existence, then, presupposing that a free subject in his transcendentality is acting, the only correct understanding is that supernaturally elevated transcendentality is also mediated to itself by any and every categorical reality in which and through which the subject becomes present to itself" (ibid.). That categorical reality includes our world. Rahner continues his thought: "It is not the case that we have nothing to do with God until we make God conceptual and thematic" (ibid.).

So that, just as there is an unreflected experience of God whenever subjectivity is realized, so also, through grace, our supernatural transcendentality is "mediated to itself . . . whenever a person appropriates himself as a free subject in the transcendentality of his knowledge and his freedom. . . . The world is our mediation to God in his self-communication in grace and in this sense there is . . . no *separate and sacred realm where alone God is to be found.* . . . Even though a categorical objectivity is in the first instance explicitly profane, it can be adequate for the mediation of our supernaturally elevated experience. . . ." (ibid., my emphasis).

Rahner's anthropology is theological and Christian because salvation history is a fundamental of the human person or another transcendental. Anne Carr maintains that for Rahner, salvation is "not a future 'something' that happens to us from the outside after life is over. . . . Salvation means precisely the ultimate validity of our real self-understanding and free self-realization before God. It is the confirmation of our way of understanding ourselves and what we have chosen to be . . . in our selves. . . . Salvation always refers to this transcendental essence of the human person" (O'Donovan 1980, 26ff.).[12]

I owe to Joseph Komonchak (1990) the reminder that the French Jesuit Henri de Lubac was immensely influential in the time before Vatican II to this understanding of salvation as a transcendental of the human. Komonchak notes how de Lubac, against a liberal positivist theology that postulated and pushed a state of pure nature with an end appropriate to this naturalness, retrieved especially from the fathers of the Church a Christian anthropology of humans constituted by gift with a desire for the vision of God.[13] De Lubac and the emerging school of *nouvelle theologiè* put an end to the centuries-old portrayal of the supernatural as the second of a two-tiered structure, a superstructure imposed on nature. To de Lubac, nature carried on, pursuing natural ends through natural human activities and natural virtues. Grace ran a parallel course, pursuing its higher end with its appropriate supernatural means.

Thus salvation history, to return to our main theme, ramifies out into the social order in a dozen different directions: sinful and graced social structures, the reign of God over the structures of society, the mystical body as paradigmatic for society, the people of God as a metaphor for social participation, the Trinity as model of social living, supernatural charity as operative in society, the Christian ideal energizing the philosophical norms of a just war, reading signs of the times for God's call, Jesus as historically joined to the world's sufferers, Jesus as paradigm of social living, Christian equality in love requiring justice toward women, and the eschatological destination of the whole of creation, which invites respect and communion with the totality of creation. It has also implications for whether Christian ethics has a content not found in natural law or in other faiths (Chirico 1991).[14]

Christological Implications

As we have seen, there is much of the philosophical in Rahner's ethical system. Since, however, we are in the historical order of revelation and grace, Rahner concludes that faith dominates in our ethic.[15] Consequently Christology influences his moral system in several ways. From his anthropological understandings, Christ becomes the quintessential exemplification of the moral life. Christ is also the source of moral life. The grace of Christ in persons flows out into societal structures, so that there are graced social structures.

Finally, Christ is Lord over social structures, gracing them with his presence. Consequently we should go eagerly to the encounter with Christ in social movements, culture, and structures. In the words of Monika Hellwig (1980): "The claims made by Christians for Jesus as Christ and Lord are seen as essentially and directly, and not accidentally or indirectly, concerned with the social structures and systems of the world."

Some of these concepts need further development. We have said that Christ is the source of the moral ideal. Rahner's depiction of the human person and freedom finds its fullest expression in Jesus Christ. The basic moral ideal of love of God and love of neighbor in unity finds both its exemplification and its historical origin in Jesus, who lives out his moral life in love, gives his life up for his friends, and in his resurrection confirms the absolute, final value of the moral ideal.

Jesus exemplifies the unity of love of God and love of neighbor. The life of Jesus identifies with greater accuracy what love really implies. It shows concretely what is at stake in the risk and venture of freedom. In Jesus, we see the power of human love, triumphing through the cross. With Jesus as exemplar, Christian faith offers both newness of vision to a natural ethic and an awareness of the deficiencies of love in the moral experience.

Bresnahan (1980) summarizes the notion of Christ as source and origin of the basic moral ideal: "This demands a theory of freedom under grace, a theory of grace as the grace of Christ, and above all an understanding of grace as a dimension of immediate self-consciousness. Rahner's theory of the supernatural existential supplies this need. If all humanity can be understood as moving toward the full truth about itself in Christ, then the consciousness of freedom and of the basic moral ideal is part of that movement in the grace of Christ."[16]

Social Grace

A second concept emerging from Rahner's Christology is social grace. To my knowledge, Rahner himself has never given extensive attention to social grace. But Rahner's interpretation of grace as the vocation of the human person to the supernatural life has societal implications.[17]

Thomas Clarke, S.J., (1974) offers these considerations about social grace. Whereas traditional theologies of grace have confined themselves to intrapersonal grace, Clarke's starting point is Romans 5:20: "Where sin increased, grace has abounded all the more." On that basis, Clarke complains that "inter-personal grace in the relationship of two persons has only recently come to theological awareness. And a grace beyond the inter-personal, that is societal, has been almost totally neglected."

Similarly God's revelation has traditionally been conceived as an I-and-Thou relationship between God and an individual person or between God and God's Church. Traditionally revelation is not understood as the I-and-Thou relationship between God and persons related in public societies. But God has been revealing God and giving the Godhead to humans through the public institutions of our lives. We encounter God in those institutions; they are revelatory; they can be graced. Clarke (ibid.) comments: "The world of public structures and institutions, instead of being conceived as a mere neutral setting for the drama of God's search for us and our search for God, now becomes the locus of revelation, and in this sense sacred."[18]

But to return, as we conclude this chapter, to the German theologian, Rahner has another christological implication. This concerns the lordship of Christ. The lord of this grace has his own special relationship to the structures of social living, that is, one of lordship. Rahner, along with Vatican II, maintains that this lordship over the structures of human living is an invitation to Christians and to their churches to follow the political Jesus in his engagement in the political order. This point, how-ever, is the subject of the next chapter.

The Reign of God over Social Structures

8

T his chapter brings us to Vatican II and its contribution to understanding the moral act performed in the world. For our present purposes we can confine our attention to two chapters of the first part of *Gaudium et Spes*, namely chapter 3, "Human Activity Throughout the World," and chapter 4, "The Role of the Church in the Modern World."

But first, why am I not talking about the reign of God over culture? Am I saying that the reign of God is not equally, even more importantly, over culture—specifically, U.S. culture? After all, this chapter will have much to say about the Second Vatican Council's *Gaudium et Spes*. That constitution has an innovative chapter on culture.

Bringing Christ to U.S. culture was undoubtedly a project of early U.S. Protestants, notably Calvinists. These believed they were called to bring Christ to the North American culture abuilding. Later, much of Protestantism rejected any such direct influence of religion on culture. In its place it chose the virtues of civic life that a more deist band of forebears insisted on. These virtues, derivable from human nature, have historically been known as *republicanism*.

Vatican II cut loose from any religious hegemony of the Church over society. As the following chapters show, the Church at the council cut loose definitively from any Christendom, any rule of Church over civil society. It opposed any theocratic state and any monopoly by one religion. It decisively supported religious pluralism.

Still, as Vatican II is equally clear on, this world is God's. God created this cosmos of goodness and beauty. God has a purpose for it and a salvific will. The instrument for achieving this purpose is humankind exercising responsible steward-ship. Jesus entered it to save it both as a whole and as a per-sonal enterprise of individual people.

If, then, Jesus is active in this world, is he not as active in culture as in social structures? Perhaps even more? First, let us make some preliminary remarks about these two rivals for Christ's and our attention.

First, social structures: I have in mind not just economic structures, but family structures (both nuclear and extended) and all levels of education. Beyond economic structures in the free market are government agencies that, for example, con-trol the money supply (the Federal Reserve Board), regulate employment and collective bargaining (the National Labor Relations Board and the Department of Labor), and, as more people choose barter to avoid taxes or to pursue alternative life-styles, attempt to regulate the informal economy.

Second, culture: For our purpose we may define culture simply as the public mores of a people. It is their imbedded values, their national character, their consensus. It was once thought that culture was unitary. Now diversity and multiplic-ity are recognized. We have African-American, Latino, and Asian-American culture, and remnants of earlier immigrations. Cultural differences among all these are significant. Some minority religions (Amish and Mennonites, for example) carry their religion explicitly into their whole way of life and work.

Others, not for religious reasons, seek to live their shared human values in (and despite) the dominant culture. Thus the Greens, the alternative movements, the groups who proclaim "small is beautiful" or preach appropriate technology.

Lastly, of relevance for our reflection is hegemonic culture. That is a culture which dominates other cultures. The hege-monic culture in the United States is the culture of money and power. It exists in its own stratosphere subordinating all other cultures in U.S. society. We are, though many would find it hard to accept, a plutocracy. Holders of money and power can manipulate education, media, and government to serve their culture and, at times, to draw the Church into supporting its values.

U.S. Cultural Traits

Individualism

To proceed more concretely, let us name some U.S. cultural traits. We need not be exhaustive. Most cultural anthropologists would include individualism, the me-too-ism that propels us in the mad rush to get ahead, to climb up the ladder, indifferent to those we trample. Our individualism holds a creed of upward mobility for all who have any drive, those who believe in the American dream and are willing to take risks, work hard, and sacrifice present pleasures for the longer range goal.

Technologism

We demand ever more efficient tools of work, communications, and transportation. We are enamored of machines. The conquest of outer space allures. We hold to the creed that whatever is technologically feasible we are honor-bound to do. Technologism carries over into how we approach social or political problems; for instance, the persuasion of the media may guide national policy. Many social scientists subscribe to this technological mentality when they imitate the seventeenth-century economists who turned Newtonian physics to the task of guiding economic life scientifically. The methodology of Newtonian physics, the technologically minded social scientist believes, is just as applicable to social behavior.

Consumerism

Consumer culture is much more than thirst for more. That aspect of consumption is too familiar to need further elaboration. It is symbolized by our shopping malls, which we have made a new temple of worship. In addition, consumption is a means to achieve recognition. Consider the display of fashionable brand labels, the statement a powerful imported car makes, or what a reserve box at sports events says about its occupants.

Certain exponents of consumer culture maintain that consumers are simply victims of the powerful advertising industry, which sells consumption as the way of life in the United States. Consumers are presumed utterly powerless, condoned by society. "Victims" is at least an exaggeration. Many consumers have freely bought into the ethos. They connive in building the power of attraction exercised by advertising media.

The Free Market

The business of the United States is business. That business is served by a free market, guided by open competition.That the market is subject to many controls—monopoly power, political influence, collective bargaining, environmental regulation, powerful farm interests—does not erode the hold this cultural metaphor of an unfettered free market has on people in the United States.

The business of the United States, that is, what its people are about, is not concern for civic virtue, public enterprise, better education for its citizenry, more holistic health care, the arts, or religion. To be sure, this nation is not wholly indifferent to these other purposes of national life, but it is predominantly interested in buying and selling in the free market, delivering an ever-growing gross national product. Without exaggerating, we do recognize that business somehow stamps our culture. We admire our business system. We metaphorize it: "Let's get down to business. There's no business like show business. That's my business." And even our pets do their business. Our business leaders are glorified. We overlook their shortcomings. We want government to be more businesslike, to be run like a business.

As we esteem business, so, in principle, we esteem the free market presumably guiding business choices. We take pride as a nation in the falling command economies of Eastern Europe. The free market has triumphed. Capitalism has won out.

These four cultural traits have their disturbing aspects. They are indeed at times presented as irredeemably evil, as totally secularist, mechanistic, as wholly self-serving. But such is not an adequate appraisal. Take technology and the drive to improve ways of doing. Who does not want a microwave oven? Who does not count an automatic dishwasher a blessing? Indoor plumbing? The TV—yes, a mixed blessing. But how many of those who condemn it as an unmitigated disaster do not occasionally find it entertaining? I am writing this book on a personal computer and, though I curse it from time to time, count it an enormous blessing.

Or, take business markets. Here is how two authoritative voices, one, a U.S. bishop, the other, a pope, treat the culture of business markets. All quotations and points made below are drawn from either the 1986 pastoral, *Economic Justice for All: Catholic Social Teaching and the U.S. Economy,* or from John Paul II's encyclical, *Centesimus Annus,* which commemorated the hundredth anniversary of *Rerum Novarum.*

The pastoral says: "There are many signs of hope in the U.S. economy today" (*EJA* 5). "The market contributes" (*EJA* 8). There are benefits of specialization (*EJA* 22). The roles of investment and of business leaders are extolled (*EJA* 110). Private property as an instrument of business activity is "important to the economy," and "creative," [and] "effective" (*EJA* 114). "We encourage a sense of vocation in the business community" (*EJA* 117). "The great venture of our founders" in the political order needs only to be carried forward, "completing the business of the American experiment" (*EJA* 296). The call here is to give social and economic rights their rightful place alongside civil and political rights.

True, the bishops point out and urge vigorous action against the defects and failures of the U.S. economic system. Indeed, the pastoral abounds in such. But my point here is that the pastoral has none of that moralistic tone which in other critics gives way to hyperbole and to demonization of the four cultural traits treated here.

The parallel language of John Paul II has astonished many observers around the world. One had grown accustomed to John Paul's severe indictments of capitalism and the market. But now, writing in May 1991, the pope uses language about capitalism that evoked from conservatives in the United States rhapsodic praise for the encyclical. The same language shocked liberation theology to its roots.

Ours here is not to weigh the pros and cons of the pope's critique. Our present point is to note the generous praise that John Paul accords the system of which U.S. culture is recognized as the epitomization.

Examples of the language of *Centesimus Annus* follow: "The free market is the most efficient instrument for utilizing resources and effectively responding to needs." The business leader and investor is extolled (*CA* 63). "Initiative and entrepreneurial ability become increasingly evident and decisive" (*CA* 32). "The modern business economy has positive aspects. Its basis is human freedom exercised in the economic field" (*CA* 32).

Shifting to the poorer countries, the pope deplores "the erroneous path often chosen by their leaders of isolating themselves from the world market." Hence the "chief problem is that of gaining fair access to the international market" (*CA* 33). The pope follows up on this statement. He poses the question: should "capitalism be the goal of the countries now making efforts to rebuild their economies and society?" (*CA* 42). His answer distinguishes. If you are thinking of unreformed capitalism, the answer is no. But "if by *capitalism* is meant an economic system which recognizes the fundamental and positive role of business, the market, private property, and the resulting responsibility for the means of production, as well as free human creativity in the economic sector, then the answer is certainly in the affirmative." Rather than name these economic attributes *capitalism,* John Paul would prefer *business economy* or *market economy* (*CA* 42). True, the pope is cautious. He does point out the failures of capitalism. But these need not occupy us here. Our point is that the present pontiff has strongly endorsed central components of a preeminently U.S. culture. The pope says in language of his own that there is much in this culture which must still be subject to the reign of God. But, at the same time, much, in his view, already bears that stamp of a humane social order in harmony with human nature, ethical reasoning, and the gospel.

With this brief sketch of culture we can now respond to the question: why are you not addressing God and culture—the reign of God over culture? We can now point out that very much of this book does address that culture and the reign of God in it. Very much of this book is as relevant to culture as to social structures. First, in my approach to Catholic social teaching, I address human and Christian values and attitudes quite as relevant to culture as to social structures. Chapters 5 and 6 address the more noetical (derived from social ethics) values, principles, and attitudes that shape our search in justice for the *oikos*. That *oikos* will represent much of the reign of God in the present. It is analogous to the republicanism, drawn largely from human nature, with which our Calvinist forebears tried to shape U.S. culture.

Second, this chapter, as those to follow, is more specifically derived from the gospel, either directly or indirectly through the council's reading of our Scriptures and tradition. The council's procedure was to ask: what is God calling us to as we try to live morally in our secular order, in the here and now, where the reign of God is establishing itself *in signo* and inchoatively in the *oikos,* the city of Shalom?

Let me illustrate with the danger of technological mentality. Noetic Catholic social teaching (social ethics) shows that the human vocation is to seek humanization of life. Surely this is decisive for any culture. Indeed, the challenge of the counter-culturalists is precisely that U.S. culture has been at war with our humanity. That is corrected by Catholic social teaching. Its biblical component here only confirms reason: God in the creation story calls us to responsible stewardship. However one proceeds to shape cultural ways of doing, he or she must exercise responsible stewardship.

Take individualism: Catholic social teaching teaches us that our nature is of its very essence social, made for living with others, working with them, and sharing in solidarity. That human indicator is supported by Jesus' constant appeal to table-fellowship. In many places of, say, Luke's gospel, Jesus appeals to the fellowship of table to announce the reign: "I will not drink of the vine again until I drink it with you in the kingdom." At table Jesus tells the story of the prodigal son and the father's mercy, replicating that of God. He ends that narrative by having the father celebrate the sinner's return with a banquet, symbol of the banquet we sinners are called eventually to share with our God. The council affirms that the sociability of human life is founded on the sociability of the life of the most holy Trinity.

And consumption: Catholic social teaching asks first, on its noetic side, how does this serve the human? All our acts are to be measured by whether they add to our human stature or diminish it; so with what we eat, drink, and wear; our homes, cars, vacations, and leisure time; and whether we make an idol of consumption, replacing the true God with that god.

The value of the common good will enter to modify my consumption, indeed, perhaps demand that I sacrifice some of it in favor of others who are in need. This value is reinforced, too, by the example of Christ who "emptied Himself" and who proclaimed the lilies of the field "clothed as was not Solomon in all his glory." The rich man who, on the occasion of an unexpectedly rich harvest, tore down his barns to build bigger ones, was condemned: "Thou fool, this day thy soul will be required of thee."

According to the concept of an *international* common good, in the name of global solidarity the richer peoples of the earth must share with the poorer peoples. On this theme, John Paul II, after giving social reasoning, frequently appeals to the biblical symbols of the rich man's table of abundance and the poor Lazarus hoping for crumbs from it.

I do not in this book address a program that some would say embodies the best of the reign of God in our world. This is alternative society. Such a social ordering would challenge the values set forth in the two chapters on noetic Catholic social teaching. It would question whether social nature and solidarity adequately embody biblical (or even humanitarian) communitarianism. It would call for more unequivocal rejection of private productive property than I contemplate in those two chapters. It would challenge market economics and competition more decisively than I have in these pages. It would go beyond my admiration of the slogan "small is beautiful" and "appropriate technology" to assert that nothing short of these embodies human or Christian society. It would on biblical or secular grounds call more categorically for a simpler life-style. "Consider the lilies of the field." That would suggest a starker communal living, based on basic needs.

It would be extremely attractive to reflect on whether these are categorical imperatives of the reign of God. I do not do so mainly because I may already have overloaded this book. I also believe that these chapters lay the ground for any future wrestling with the question of whether these are biblical imperatives or options.

Now, back to the opening paragraph of this chapter: what contribution has Vatican II made to Catholic social teaching? The pastoral constitution *Gaudium et Spes* is preeminently a chapter in Catholic social teaching. The second part of the document is a review of the body of Catholic social teaching, focused on four areas: family, culture, economic society, and peace. I believe this is the first time in the Church's official teaching that culture has been so specifically treated.

But it is part 1 that so richly contributes to Catholic social teaching. It opens with a chapter on the questions raised by human beings today. Chapter 2 is on the social nature of the human. Chapters 3 and 4 are on our supernatural vocation which, if it is indeed to be fully realized only in the beyond time, is nevertheless deeply bound up with the creation of a better world now. Chapter 5, while named "the Church's vocation," treats the vocation of the Church's members. It continues chapter 4 and deepens the eschatological vision realized if only inchoately and *in signo* in efforts of Christians and others as instruments of God's lordship to bring about in the here and now a kingdom of justice and love and peace.

Kingdom? Reign? Lord? At the outset of our inquiry we encounter a problem of language. We pray, "Thy kingdom come, thy will be done on earth as it is in heaven." Jesus' language and teachings focused on establishing the kingdom of his Father. *Gaudium et Spes* uses this language: "For though the same God is Savior and Creator, Lord of human history as well as of salvation history. . ." (*GS* 41). Elsewhere, the decree speaks of Jesus as "appointed Lord by His resurrection and given all power in heaven and on earth. . ." (ibid., 38).

Our contemporary discourse resists the metaphors both of king and lord and of power and reign. To avoid the sexist terms *king* or *lord,* some fall back on the term *reign.* But *reign* suggests lording it over people. Is that what Jesus does? Does he not rather walk with us? Many Latin Americans have adopted the term *acompañaremos*. Micah exhorts us "to walk humbly with our God." If we are walking with our God, our God is walking with us as companion. The Jesuits like to call themselves the Company of Jesus, not in the sense of a business company but of companions on the road. If my preface suggests that I will in this chapter avoid these traditional ways of speaking about Jesus' presence among us, I confess that I have not thought this through enough to follow my own suggestion.

Another subsidiary question can stand in the way of an unobstructed look at the significance of Jesus' reign in society. The title to this chapter may suggest that our inquiry will be about Jesus' direct action on the structures of society. I do believe, and have already noted this, that Jesus is present not just to hearts but to the structures of society, not just to husband and wife but to their matrimony, not just to individual citizens but to the object of citizenry. Elsewhere in these chapters is a good deal of questioning where God is calling us in our culture and society. But here the main emphasis is on Jesus working through us to change structures to those of justice. To sum up, Jesus does work to establish his reign over the structures of society (as also over culture). This, however, he effects largely through our human instrumentality. This chapter, accordingly, is mainly concerned with our instrumentality: instruments in the hands of our God, working for the kingdom in our time and beyond time.

Directly after their publication, the chapters I now quote extensively became central to my thought about Catholic social teaching. In the summer following the council I lectured on *Gaudium et Spes* at Ottawa for the Canadian Catholic Conference and the University of Ottawa. (The talks were published by the conference. Other lectures on the same theme, but linked to the spiritual exercises of Saint Ignatius, appeared in Land 1976.)

One source for the Canadian lectures was the history of the successive drafts, over many months, of that pastoral constitution (and the other documents) that G. Caprile, S.J., was developing in the pages of *La Civiltá Cattolica*. There, he noted the shift from the earliest draft, which had relied heavily on natural law. Alfons Auer (1969, 182ff.), a well-known *peritus* and another chronicler of the pastoral, tells us: "This chapter gradually developed from its beginnings in social philosophy via two intermediate forms, one theological and systematic, the other biblical and expressed in redemptive history, into the ultimate pastoral form in which it was finally adopted by the council." The first two versions were in the style of classical Catholic social metaphysics and social ethics, the style "of the social teaching of the Church in the papal social encyclicals" (ibid., 183).

Part 1 focused on human history making, considered both as a purely natural phenomenon and as a process possessing a christological dimension. The Christian dimension was initiated by the Incarnation, which linked all of created materiality eventually to the order of grace through Christ's body. The world is graced. Anthropology is Christian, and hope is transcendent. The complete anthropology of the human is not expressed unless it includes the eschatological gift. Anthropologically I am eschatological.

In the process of formulating this document, the council fathers asked themselves grave questions. What must we think about earthly realities? What value does the Church assign them? What about their autonomy? What about the world's progressive evolution? How does the world fit into the reign of God?

World as it is used in *Gaudium et Spes* connotes the totality of human activity on earth. Thus it is the whole economic system, including productivity and just distribution. It is a nation coming to grips with just-war theory. It is rich nations versus poor nations. It is protecting the environment and extending the common good to creatures other than human. It is debate over national health insurance and then making it work. It is urban planning. It is allocating resources from research for ever-more sophisticated weapons to research on systemic changes to end poverty.

When we ask ourselves whether solutions can be found to these seemingly impenetrable issues, we ask ourselves whether this world is only that world of evil for which Jesus did not pray. We ask whether corruption in banking and business is everlasting, and whether we will never end racial injustice or stop denying women their proper place in society. Theologically, we are asking if the reign of God is of this world or only of the world beyond time. Should we give up and retire into the sanctuary of our own hearts to encounter the Lord of history?

The council addressed these questions and came up with a surprising and to some observers distressing optimism. Although the optimism may have been excessive, undoubtedly the theology of the council with respect to the world was on the right road to newness of vision.

Gaudium et Spes Chapter 3: Human Activity throughout the World

The third chapter begins with a consideration of human activity in light of the mystery of creation (*GS* 34–36). Then it proceeds to a consideration of human activity in light of the mystery of sin (*GS* 37), next it moves to human activity in light of the mystery of Christ (*GS* 38), and finally it develops the proof that the world along with the human will have fulfillment beyond time.

Paragraph 34 sets forth the full program to be developed in successive paragraphs: "To believers, this point is settled: considered in itself, this human activity accords with God's will. For men and women, created to God's image, received a mandate to subject to themselves the earth and all it contains, and to govern the world with justice and holiness." This mandate is further specified: "to relate self and the totality of things to Him who was to be acknowledged as the Lord and Creator of all." Consequently, "Christians are convinced that the triumphs of the human race are a sign of God's grace and the flowering of His own mysterious design" (*GS* 34–36).

Since this is true, it is impossible to separate work for the world from preaching the gospel: "Thus we are witnesses to the birth of a new humanism, one in which man is defined first of all by this responsibility to his sisters and brothers and to history" (*GS* 55). The fathers of the council therefore urge that "there be no false opposition between professional and social activities on the one hand, and religious life on the other" (*GS* 43). Indeed, professional and social together with religious life make up the human "total vocation" (*GS* 35).

One can conclude from the above that professional and social obligations possess *intrinsic* value from their Creator. In the words of chapter 3, "By the very circumstances of having been created all things are endowed with their own stability, truth, goodness, proper laws and order" (ibid.).

It is noteworthy that the council fathers were not afraid to describe humans collaborating with God or completing the work of the Creator; they did not fear that collaboration would attribute too much independence and creativity to human effort and diminish God's omnipotence. On the contrary, human accomplishments only render more homage to the Creator.

In his commentary on paragraph 36, Auer (1969, 190) observes that the regulation of human activity in the world must aim at developing the person, at integration into social life, and at shaping material things. "More important than things and the technical progress in mastering them is man himself and the universal fraternity of all men."

In the words of the *Gaudium et Spes:* "The norm of human activity is therefore that, in accord with the divine plan and will, it should harmonize with the genuine good of the human race and allow men as individuals and as members of society to pursue their total vocation and to fulfill it" (*GS* 35). Although the distinction between moral worth and religious value seems clear in the passages quoted, let us clarify that moral worth is achieved when the person is developed, when social life is enhanced, and material things are creatively employed.

The council also addressed the rightful autonomy of earthly affairs. The specific issue which they addressed was how earthly affairs could maintain any rightful independence in view of the religious orientation of earthly affairs to God. The pastoral constitution is explicit: "If by the autonomy of earthly affairs we mean that created things and societies themselves enjoy their own laws and values . . . then it is entirely right to demand that autonomy." The council, however, notes the religious value of earthly activity: "Whoever labors to penetrate the secrets of reality . . . is being led by the hand of God. . ." (ibid., 36).

To sum up: there are significant values, norms, and direction in the active transformation of this world, but only after that is there religious meaning to this transformation. In other words, there is intrinsic value before religious finality, and there is ontological goodness in human endeavor. The things of this world are not merely material for moral making and for religious orientation.

Yves Congar (1969, 217) encapsulates what chapter 3 has said thus far: "God's saving plan . . . includes the well-being and final success of the world and cannot be reduced to a decree of salvation in regard to some individual persons as such, taking no account of the world."

Gaudium et Spes Chapter 4: The Role of the Church in the Modern World

Paragraphs 40–45 treat the function of the Church in relation to earthly pursuits. First and foremost the Church recognizes the autonomy of human history. What follows from recognizing this autonomy? Congar (ibid., 208) points out that recognizing the autonomy of human history effectively ends the subordination of secular and bodily to the religious and spiritual. From the perspective of history, "the Middle Ages dealt with the question of the spiritual and the temporal in the framework of the distinction between two authorities, the *sacerdotium* with its summit in the pope on the one hand, and the princes on the other."

Congar also observes that the relation between spiritual and temporal existed on the juridic level. On the grounds therefore that there could be only one head and that the spiritual was superior to the corporal, the secular was subordinated to the religious. Kings ruled over persons' bodies; monks over their souls. Princes were to enact laws in harmony with the law of God, as expounded by the priests. Subordinating the earthly led to disregarding earthly activity.

The perspective of *Gaudium et Spes* is different both in that it recognizes earthly autonomy and in the descriptive language it uses about the Church. As generally used, *Church* denotes the organized society which originated from the Incarnation and was entrusted with faithful preservation of the gospel and its mission. In its mission, the *ecclesia* speaks through Christians. But in effecting relations between the spiritual and the temporal, it is the Church as people of God who act: "The people of God believes that it is led by the Lord's spirit. . . . Motivated by this faith, it labors to decipher authentic signs of God's presence and purpose in the happenings, needs and desires in which this People has a part along with other men of our age. For faith throws a new light on everything, manifests God's design for man's total vocation and thus directs the mind to solutions which are fully human" (*GS* 11).

As the question indicates, the people of God do not live separated from the rest of humankind. Rather, the discussion has shifted from secular authority versus religious authority to relations between the *ecclesia* or ecclesial community and the human family (ibid., 44). What had been a problem of relationship between spiritual and temporal has become the relationship between "faith and history, gospel and civilization."

What about sanctification or even consecration of the world? Congar (1969, 208) maintains that the Church does sanctify, but not by removing elements from their place in the structures of the world or from secular use. Rather, it respects their true nature and "sanctifies them through the actual use made of them in harmony with the transcendental purpose of salvation." According to Congar, the Church's magisterium certainly is competent to declare what constitutes these transcendent purposes. But the Middle Ages are over. It is no longer a question of subordinating the temporal domain to the Church; rather, the Church relates the secular to the Last Things, to its salvation. We will pursue this relationship further in the following section.

Eschatology of Vatican II

John Paul II, as I have noted in the preface, enthusiastically introduces into one of his encyclicals on Catholic social teaching, *Centesimus Annus*, that is, since Leo XIII's encyclical *Rerum Novarum*), the council's rich approach to the Bible and theology. But as to the council's immanent eschatology he has been somewhat ambivalent. In his earlier (1979) encyclical, *Redemptor Hominis,* he opposed it. Later, in his *Laborem Exercens* and *Sollicitudo Rei Socialis,* he endorsed the council's position.

Paragraph 39 in *Gaudium et Spes* is a remarkable eschatological statement, which links the present world to a future and a beyond-time future: "We do not know the time for the consummation of the earth and of humanity, nor how all things will be transformed. . . . We are taught that God is preparing a new dwelling place and a new earth. . . ."

In the new heavens and the new earth the works of our hands will have transcendental fulfillment: "Enduring with charity and its fruits, all that creation which God made on man's account will be unchained from its bondage. . . . For after we have . . . nurtured on earth the values of human dignity, brotherhood and freedom, and indeed all the good fruits of our nature and enterprise, we will find them again . . . transfigured. . ." (ibid.).

Yet here on earth the works of charity are abuilding: "Here grows the body of a new human family, a body which even now is able to give some foreshadowing of the new age" (ibid.). This number is a remarkable retrieval of the communal aspect of eschatology.

We will find the fruits of our charity again. One cannot forget that salvation has also to do with this time. It is not a salvation of a pure essence of the human or of naked subjectivity, but a salvation of humans becoming more human as architects of their own history. The subject together with his or her decisions and actions in this world is saved. This is what the pastoral constitution *Gaudium et Spes* means in paragraph 39 when it speaks of finding the fruits of our charity once again, transfigured.

Vatican II's theology of beyond time (*tunc*) relates to now time (*nunc*). It succinctly summarizes the relationship in *Gaudium et Spes* paragraph 38: "Christ is now at work in the hearts of men . . . arousing not only a desire for the age to come, but by that very fact animating those noble longings by which the human family makes its life more human. . . ."

A few paragraphs earlier we see that Congar (1969), while asserting a sanctifying role for the Church in earthly things and earthly tasks and progress, insists that this role does not rob these earthly realities of their genuinely earthy natures. Relating the secular eschatologically does not diminish the secular. Why not? Congar has a threefold answer. First, the *eschata* or Last Things are the meaning of the earthly things and historical activities themselves. Although they come from above as a gift, they will not come as a breach in earthly things or life, because they will come about precisely with the attainment of the goal.

Second, "The *eschata,* or salvation, are inclusive in regard to history and nature. They mean fulfillment and transfiguration. They are not something external and foreign" (Congar 1969, 211). Consequently, if Christians direct their actions and life towards the *eschata,* they do not renounce earthly activity, nor may they betray it; rather, they give it its ultimate integrity and realize their integral vocation as human beings. This point is central to our chapter.

Congar's third argument concerns the relation between nature and grace. Although little can be added to what we have already said on this subject, it is worth noting it in the council's pastoral constitution. As Rahner does, Congar asserts that, despite the absolute gratuitousness of our vocation to become children of God, we must recognize that this vocation was intended by God from the beginning as the goal of human-kind created in God's image and likeness. This involves for human nature a capacity, openness, and vocation which is what the pastoral constitution calls our total vocation. Neither humankind at work nor the world are juxtaposed to the Church. Humankind at work is capable of becoming Church. It is marked by the hidden presence of Christ, or his Holy Spirit.[1]

On the one side, human accomplishment in this life is not the plenitude of our vocation. All accomplishments here are penultimate. Our hope moves beyond. The idea of plenitude within this temporality and this history contradicts Christian hope, for that would place the primacy of salvation in human hands. Moreover, the radical capacity of the human to receive the free gift of ultimate salvation will surpass all earthly achievements. So history itself will be saved, that is, will be freed of its fallen state, freed of temporality, "and be integrated into the metaphysical duration of humankind that has been raised and glorified with Christ and will share God's eternal life" (Alfaro 1989, 505–13).

But within history human achievement is already participating in its metahistorical plenitude, a plenitude not possessed by history itself but received through the risen Jesus. It is grace inserted into human transformative efforts. Because Christ's grace operates in human history, this history is on the road to the plenitude of the beyond time.

This destiny of history is not known to reason, but it is a truth of revelation. This has great importance for Catholic social teaching, for it reminds us that Catholic social teaching must rely on other sources for its truth and not merely human nature and the natural law.

This transcendental gift of graced history does not spell identity between the history of humankind and the history of salvation. There is not identity but "existential inseparability." The two are not parallel, standing side by side. Rather, as Rahner insists, the history of salvation unfolds within the history of humankind or, vice versa, the order of salvation exists within the order of creation.

Commenting on the eschatology of Vatican II, Juan Alfaro (ibid., 508) makes the following points. First, every fragment of history will be integrated into the final salvation to come: "The mastery of nature . . . will be assumed and advanced through the new link between the world and glorified humanity." The whole of creation will be saved, brought to its metahistorical consummation beyond its hope as intrahistorical reality. To put this in still other words, far from an earlier day's belief that the earth would end up in smoke (*solvet mundum in favilla* we used to sing), the improvement of the human condition, living in the *shalom* of the common good, will reach ultimate fulfillment in the communion of saints, the hope which will not be deprived of concrete achievement.

Second, Alfaro notes an emphasis on salvation for the whole of humanity, which, as one brotherhood and sisterhood, is heading toward its promised homeland. Christian hope cannot be hidden within the individual person. It has to express itself through the structures of common life in society. To contribute to setting up the kingdom of God is to foster a world of love and justice "and so to arouse in others hope" (ibid., 510). Since this is true, Christian life is not only the time for individuals to determine their salvation to come, but also the time for the whole Church to establish the reign of God in this life. This reign is one of *shalom,* of just and amicable relations. It is one of sharing in common the creation put at our disposal. This commitment is covenantal in both testaments (ibid.).

Finally, Alfaro links hope to love as our pillar of Catholic social living: "Mere promise of a good life beyond does not suffice. We need the tangible reality of a society dedicated in love to justice in order to have a hint of a better life promised beyond" (ibid.).[2] Thus hope now is the beginning already of future salvation.

In a nutshell, because Christ took up our world as his body, our working with Christ to create a good earth builds up the body of Christ (*GS* 38).[3] One draft of the pastoral read, "The work of humankind constitutes an integral part of the economy of salvation because by our work we prepare that consummation by which God transforms the world" (Auer 1969, 187).

Rahner's Unity of Redemption and Creation

The previous chapter dwells at some length on the unity of love of God and of neighbor and its implications for social living in Catholic social teaching. We have similarly reflected on the contribution of eschatological hope. Let us now turn to the significance of the unity between the orders of salvation and of creation for Christian social life. Here I rely on the celebrated article of Karl Rahner entitled "The Order of Redemption Within the Order of Creation."[4]

For Rahner, the order of redemption and the order of creation are clearly distinct. The order of redemption and grace includes everything which pertains to concrete existence and to practical execution of grace. Since the order of redemption includes the order of creation, the two orders, while not identical, do not remain adequately distinguishable in practice. "The supernatural order is that order established by the gracious will of God in which God's Creation exists as a necessary factor and presupposition, so that the supernatural order is related to the natural as whole to part. The autonomy of the created is relative. The world cannot achieve even the significance which is its own and immanent, except through the grace of God in Jesus. A profound need arises from this" (Rahner 1963b, 50).

If fully experienced and realized in what it is, namely, necessarily supernatural in its goal, everything natural is actually always more than purely natural. If one tries to achieve the purely natural in this concrete order, what results is not the

purely natural but the guilt-laden merely natural. As a consequence, we can say that whenever natural moral law is being
observed, the healing grace of God is de facto present.

Because the incarnation of the Word has already happened,
this unity of grace and nature exists even more so. In the
Incarnation God has taken the world definitively into his own
life and has made the world personally his very own. "Within
God's creation there is not only existence constituted as created; within this world takes place the miracle of divine love,
the self-communication of God to what God has created. This
takes place when God, coming forth from himself in person
takes a created reality to himself as his own in the hypostatic
union. . ." (ibid., 48).

The unity of grace and nature, working itself out as the
redemption of nature, is irreversibly achieved. But this unity
remains unconsummated in us. Christians can therefore expect
that God's redemptive act will be realized if they themselves
make their own contribution to saving and healing the world,
to establishing its internal structures, and to a fragmentary
beginning of the hope achieved in the now time. Their work
in this world realizes their own eschatological faith. This
activity will be "an act of positive healing toward the world,
an act of protection toward the world despite the doom of
death put upon it . . . an act of faith in that glory which God
confers upon the world and has already imparted in Christ"
(ibid., 57).

Rahner specifies this point in his treatment of the secular
life and the evangelical counsels: "It is not permissible for the
secular status to involve either a degree of indifference toward
the redemptive order or a practical identification of the two
orders without distinction or qualification. Nor is it permissible for the status of the counsels to be regarded as committed
to the redemptive order as to have no further task in the
world. For each of the states the unity of the two orders as
distinct from each other and . . . unconsummated remains a
permanent task" (ibid., 62).

In further explanation, Rahner says that the secular Christian
cannot attend to the world as if he or she had found God
when all he or she has done is be true to the world. Otherwise
the created order would simply be identical with the redemp-

tive. Even the Christian in the world must always be something more than a human person working at the immanent tasks of the world.

One's relationship with God cannot be adequately mediated simply through the world: "A man acting competently in the world and the affairs of life is not, so far, simply a Christian, true though it be that human competence in these matters is indeed an element of being Christian. As Christian, even living a secular life ('in the world'), a Christian must seek realization of the redemptive order as something which, even though it integrates the created order into itself, nevertheless surpasses it. But it is equally true that the followers of the evangelical counsels must, if they seek to realize the redemptive order, carry out that descent of grace into the world which has been accomplished in the incarnation and resurrection of Christ. Such a Christian, too, must heal and sanctify the world" (ibid., 6ff.).

From the preceding, we can now say what the sanctification of the world means. Sanctification does not begin where we take a sound, well-developed world and then impose upon it a supernatural structure. Rather, we must relate secular affairs to supernatural salvation in Christ; secular and explicitly religious matters must unite. In Rahner's words: "Christian life must come into action in that same sphere of the external material world in which the secular, profane life of this world has its activity" (ibid., 67).

In this light, natural law requires the grace of Christ. Natural law is to be respected as God's will. "A right relation, consequently, to persons and to reality in general, is materially identical with the norms" (ibid., 68). This statement might seem to imply that the hallowing of this world by grace begins when it would seem that nothing is happening except genuine respect for the real order of things.

This leads Rahner to conclude: "Wherever in this world . . . in the whole length and breadth of individual and social life, right actions are performed according to reality and decency and humanity, there Christianity is achieved . . . and hence the strictly Christian task of Christians . . . is fulfilled" (ibid.).

This is not all God demands of Christians, but it is the most "essential element of the healing and sanctification of the world" (ibid., 69). Consequently, for Christians in the world, the experience they have of the world's need for healing is a summons to their Christian task. Rahner makes clear that this does not mean that Christians have a supernatural blueprint of life, nor that Christians do everything from supernatural impulses and guiding rules. Since Christians rarely love others as an actualization of their love of God, we are brought face to face with the importance of the unity of the orders of redemption and creation.

The Christian has two designs for living, earthly and heavenly, neither of which can be deduced from the other. But if they believe in the unity of the two orders they will believe in the ultimate congruity between them. The grace which is active in nature arouses in the world a demand for a fulfillment which completes all that is positive in the world and yet goes beyond its possibilities. But the far more powerful call from the earth is its experience of the need for salvation which this earthly and sinful world bears in itself. Christianity here shows the created order the way towards the higher order of redemption.

Rahner ends his discussion of the unity of the two orders with two conclusions. First, the life of the world, if experienced in its wholeness, is itself a part of the spiritual life. Second, the Christian should regard the world, precisely in its worldliness, which is distinct from grace and redemption, as a presupposition of the redemptive order and a factor within the redemptive process. This is because "the higher order itself established the lower as its own presupposition, different from and lower than itself, in such fashion that the lower, while fully retaining its real and abiding difference, has no need to fall away from unity with the higher order" (ibid., 72).

Reign of God over Social Structures

We conclude this chapter with another component of the Christian reality, namely, the reign of God over social structures. I will continue to follow Karl Rahner along with the ideas from a group of theologians with whom I collaborated in a book on this subject (Clarke 1980).[5]

Rahner in his *Foundations of the Christian Faith* (1978, 178–322) devotes nearly 150 pages to a treatment of Christology. Therein he maintains that the whole theology of Jesus can be read as "political theology," that everything we do has social relevance even when it is not intended as such.

The theme of intentional relevance is treated by Monika Hellwig, Thomas Clarke, S.J., J. P. M. Walsh, S.J., and Otto Hentz, S.J., in Clarke 1980. This question first highlights the significance which Christology has for all *praxis* theologies, including political theology, liberation theology, and Catholic social teaching, for they all seek the transformation of social structures and culture. Second, it reminds us that the politics of Jesus is mediated through free choices in human activity, including imagining social structures that will serve justice better. We dwelt on this in an earlier chapter.

Rahner divides Christology into Christology from above (descending) and Christology from below (ascending). Descending Christology is speculative and deductive. It treats of Christ as coming forth from the Father. Thus its starting point is the dogmas of Jesus' divinity and God's lifting him up to be the savior of his people. This theological stance moves from the essence of the Word and election to reflect on Jesus' life on earth and its consequences for us. In this approach, Jesus could not be ascribed the humanness, exercised in full power of creative freedom, which Rahner depicts in a Christology from below.

In contrast, an ascending Christology starts with the historical person Jesus. Its concrete inductive approach asks, how did Jesus understand himself, how did others see him, and why did he suffer and die? This Christology begins the Christian reading of Jesus' life from the perspective of the Christian faith community.

Ascending Christology is obviously congenial to liberation theology and political theology. In my estimation it is also an inspiring basis for Catholic social teaching. This does not mean that choosing ascending Christology over descending Christology commits one to totally reject the other. But ascending Christology is a powerful remedy to an abstract and deductive Christology that minimizes the incarnation and the human personality of Jesus.

Hellwig (1980, 17) raises one grave reservation on extreme forms of decending Christology: "What is here important precedes history; the ultimately significant events are programmed or blueprinted in Heaven." The history of Jesus, his crucifixion and death, "simply had to be that way because eternally foreordained. The vision of the Christian dispensation offered here is one in which creative or constitutive decision making is seen as a divine function. The human correlate is to obey."

The danger Hellwig sees here is that perfection of "the human will be acceptance of the status quo as if it were divinely willed. Surely this would or could lead to passivity and acceptance of the status quo even when it represents injustice, even when it victimizes. Given the proclivity of many highly placed hierarchs to support the existing order, provided it supports the privileges of the upper clergy and the Church, this turns members of the hierarchy into supporters of privilege. The reason for calling Jesus Lord would be the elimination of human creativity" (ibid.). Jesus would be lord only as incarnating that foreordaining will of God.

By contrast, an ascending Christology is more likely to align itself with the marginalized, with Jesus and the dispossessed, who confront the status quo. For this reason, says Hellwig: "An ascending Christology tends to a view of salvation as a truly historical dynamic in that it involves the interplay of human freedoms and decisions. . ." (ibid., 18). This Christology is historical too in that it allows for "ultimately significant events that are not seen as blueprinted in heaven but as the outcome of human struggle of creative and constitutive decision-making by Jesus and others aligned with him . . .", a truly historical interplay of "structuring and restructuring of human societies. . ." (ibid.).

The claims made by Christians that Jesus is Christ and lord are seen as essentially and directly, not accidentally and indirectly, concerned with social structures of the world. Ascending Christology seeks a future transformation of social structures through human cooperation to eliminate all exclusion, oppression, and contempt (ibid., 20). Such a conclusion obviously could not be reached on a theology which views the creation of the world by God outside time but with a history simply unrolled by the divine hand.

In this approach, Christian living would be an imitation of Christ's passivity and an execution only of God's preordained plan. Christians would patiently suffer under structures of injustice since God would have ordained such structures as the framework for human existence. On the contrary, the Jesus of the Gospels "is to be understood from studying the difference he has made, is making and can make to the course of human affairs throughout history" (ibid., 21).

The reign of God challenges oppressive structures. In following Jesus, Christians are called to exercise creative freedom and imagination under empowerment of the Holy Spirit.[6] Creativity of personal initiative does not compete with God, in even the most remote sense. Nor is it elective, that is, something optional for activists who do not appreciate contemplation.

Earlier in this chapter we make the point that lordship is relational. That of course is implied in the very term; one is lord over someone or something. In the scriptural reality, lordship is covenantal, two-way. "If you will be my people, I will be your God." In exchange for your fidelity I will be faithful to my promises. The transcendent God emerges as the lord who brings us out of a contemporary slavery, like Egypt. God is named the lord who does battle with the powers and principalities which shape or misshape cultures and societal structures. Even though not all structures have been freed, we hope in the reign of the now time as it becomes ever more fully realized.

Walsh (1980, 35–65), in his essay, "Lordship of Yahweh, Lordship of Jesus" makes the convincing case that the Israelite tradition always refers to what we call here social systems. Consequently "the terms in which the New Testament writers proclaimed the good news of salvation in Christ have direct—not secondary or adventitious or illative—political reference" (ibid., 35).

He says: "Yahweh's Lordship is nowhere envisioned apart from the context of the life of the nation, of economic and political relationships. Even the Deuteronomic theology, which seems to be the most 'interior' or 'spiritual' or 'religious' . . . in the Old Testament, represents a meditation on the causes of political collapse, and on the conditions of the possibility of peace, abundance, and comity" (ibid., 55). Walsh shows how an Old Testament reading of God's lordship is equally true of Jesus' lordship.

In a long footnote, Walsh questions one point in Hellwig's essay which could also be raised about my viewpoint. "To insist on the centrality of human creativity and human freedom—the capacity to make history—can easily lead to a kind of 'works righteousness' which sees our human dignity and fulfillment as consisting in the capacity always to be in control, to achieve maximum predictability in all aspects of our life, to shape nature and events according to what we freely choose as the good. It is not this capacity to be in control that constitutes our humanity but the capacity for reverence, appreciation, wonder, 'thanksgiving'" (ibid., 63, n. 38).[7]

As I remember seminar discussions with Walsh, we had the same problem. Do we stress the Suffering Servant image of our role in bringing about the reign of God, or do we stress more active capacity under and in the lordship of Christ to remake our world in peace, justice, and community? Walsh warned against those who would exaggerate the active capacity, a warning always to be heeded. But I do think, however, that the sections from the conciliar documents which I have quoted in this chapter sustain my position, namely, I do not here succumb to the temptation of works righteousness, nor of assuming capacity always to be in control, nor of shaping the events according to what I freely choose as good. I would also hope that I am open to the Suffering Servant and to reverence, wonder, and thanksgiving (Rahner 1963c, 32; see also Hentz 1980, 147).

North American Political Theology

A revised Catholic social teaching, my version, at least, has strong affinity with a group of post–Vatican II theologies. These are called *praxis* theologies or contextual theologies. Some of them are indexed under another rubric, political theology.

This chapter will reflect, first, on three contextual theologies that, if not appearing under the rubric of political theology, are certainly in that genre. Affinities between these theologies and Catholic social teaching will be noted. Second, the last half of this chapter will consider the challenge political theology mounts against Catholic social teaching, as well as one statement from the United States specifically designated as political theology, that of Matthew Lamb. Affinities will again be noted. The chapter concludes with feminism as a form of political (or liberation) theology.

Chapter 10 takes up one European statement of political theology, that of Johann Baptist Metz, followed by a reflection on Latin America's political theology, known more familiarly as liberation theology. Here again affinities with Catholic social teaching will be noted.

In this chapter I make no pretense of providing a thoroughgoing exposition of either *praxis* (contextual theology) or of political theology. I propose to treat those topics by discussing the following questions.

First, I ask myself what is attractive in *praxis* or contextual theologies and in what is referred to more specifically as political theology. That question is followed by asking whether the same is missing, either absolutely or relatively, or is, on the contrary, essentially present in a retrieved—I do have to insist on this word—Catholic social teaching. Then, from the perspective of a retrieved Catholic social teaching, I will point out certain inadequacies in some of the theological statements on which we are reflecting. But, first some definitions.

Contextual theology (broadest of the three) starts its theological inquiry with experience and a problematic involved in that experience. This problematic can be one of oppression (including racism and sexism), or of poverty (such as the feminization of poverty), or of environmental destruction, of war, and so on.

Praxis theology is a contextual theology focused more narrowly on structural change to right injustice. Over against traditional orthodoxy it calls for *orthopraxis,* a right way of *doing* theology.

Political theology is contextual theology and *praxis* theology that takes as its object the salvation of the political order in contrast to individual salvation. Its ground of reflection is sufferers. It calls for solidarity with the sufferers and with Christ, who in the midst of the sufferers hangs on the cross.

Three Prominent Theological Statements

American Strategic Theology

An American Strategic Theology is the title of a work by Jesuit religious sociologist John Coleman (1982a). It is, first, a most impressive survey of many, if not all, facets of *praxis* theology, with political theology in the front line. It is, secondly, a very thoughtful setting forth of what his strategic theology has to contribute to a political theology for the United States.

Coleman's strategic theology is "primarily a lay prerogative," that is, one that empowers the laity to assume their rightful role in the Church as sacrament of the world, and it is "oriented to action or *praxis*." It is "concerned with the social-izing preconditions for a creative impact of religion on society (ibid., 4, 247)."

Coleman describes his strategic theology for the United States as an amalgam of theology and social ethics in "dialog with European political and Latin American liberation theology" (ibid., 4). Coleman's "practical" theology is in effect a political theology or at least a theology of politics, but it is decidedly a political theology for the United States and is sharply critical of significant aspects of both European political theology and Latin American political theology (liberation theology). Among several points, Coleman shares the conviction of European political theologians that privatization of theology calls for rectification by a political theology.

Coleman addresses the "ways in which the social question is worldwide . . . the Catholic sense of internationalism, and [the link to] voluntarism" (ibid., 283). *American* in the title concerns itself with civic community, civility, communication, and simplicity of life as the foundations for republican virtue, that is, the ideals of the Founding Fathers. More specifically, U.S. Catholics share these ideals of a participatory, democratic society, based on trust in the native wisdom of common people (ibid., 81, 277).

Coleman names John A. Ryan, Dom Virgil Michel, Jacques Maritain, and John Courtney Murray, S.J., as Catholic contributors to social theology. Coleman comments, "Murray stands as the major interpreter of the Thomist position on politics and state" (ibid., 98), and ranks Maritain beside Murray as a highly influential revivalist of Aquinas in the political arena" (ibid.).

Finally Coleman notes that for his method of theological reflection he has adopted the pastoral circle, which he describes in several pages (ibid., 247). That pastoral circle is described later in this chapter.

Theology of Culture

Another *praxis* theology is one that focuses less on political structures and more on culture. Langdon Gilkey's *Society and the Sacred: Toward a Theology of Culture in Decline* (1981) admirably exemplifies this focus. Gilkey had previously written a notable exploration of political theology, *Reaping the*

Whirlwind (1976). In *Society and the Sacred,* the professor from the University of Chicago Divinity School describes his approach as religious reflection looking at society, seeking to understand the latter much as economic, sociological, and political theorists might do with the same shared object (1981, ix–xii).

Gilkey strongly believes that religion, but a very particular religious lens, is needed if we are rightly to examine cultures. "And just as it would be difficult for any of them—economic, sociological and political theorists—to analyze society without presupposing and using a particular interpretation of human community, without some fundamental social theory or other, so it is hard to view society from the standpoint of religious reflection without representing in one's thought a particular viewpoint *in* religion (ibid., 15–25)." Gilkey elsewhere calls this viewpoint in religion an ideology, a particular stance vis-a-vis religion, its relation to human beings, and its implication for reality as a whole—in short, a theology of culture.

Gilkey in this book has two points I do not find in other *praxis* theologies. First, his object of study is culture with its imbedded social structures. I would pause to observe that very many practitioners of Catholic social teaching have largely focused on structural transformation to the neglect of the culture from which they stem. In keeping with that, they have relied less on cultural transformation to change unjust structures and more on personal behavioral change. Until quite recently, official Catholic social teaching has not shown much interest in culture.

Second, in his effort to shed light on that culture, Gilkey utilizes a very specific religious viewpoint which he calls an ideology. That viewpoint can be encapsulated (my interpretation) in the symbol of the kingdom as portrayed in the two testaments. Of that symbol in the Old Testament Gilkey says: "As the Old Testament makes clear, [hope for a new covenant] also represents a historical and social hope, a confidence in God's creative action in the political and economic orders of secular society" (ibid., 54). Gilkey shows that the kingdom in the New Testament, while surely one over the hearts of women and men, is, as the covenant in the Old Testament, equally one of reign over political structures. He shows this not only by critiquing the symbol of the kingdom in both testaments but also by providing the promise and the appearance of new possibilities of social existence.

Canadian Gregory Baum's Theology

A theological statement that could be characterized as contextual or *praxis* or political is that of the eminent Canadian Catholic, Gregory Baum. His *Theology and Society* (1987) ranges widely. The first third of the book describes the evolution of Catholic social thought. Although the other two-thirds largely address liberation theology and political theology, these chapters make considerable use of three documents associated with Catholic social teaching. These are two apostolic letters and one encyclical of John Paul II, namely *Redemptor Hominis, Laborem Exercens,* and *Sollicitudo Rei Socialis.* Baum's contextual theology does move beyond Catholic social teaching; still it relies heavily upon official Catholic social teaching.[1] I consider this point of Baum's essential to my study: New approaches in Catholic social teaching do not thereby make it cease to be Catholic social teaching.

This point is perhaps made even more specifically in another book of Baum's, *The Priority of Labor* (1982), a commentary on John Paul II's *Laborem Exercens.* In the introduction, Baum makes the point that "while the encyclical remains in continuity with the Church's social teaching, it introduces new ideas derived from a critical and creative dialogue with Marxism" (ibid.).[2] In that dialogue Baum makes much of the pope's adaptation of Marx's alienation by the market of workers from their products.[3]

Affinities with Catholic Social Teaching

I turn now to some affinities between Catholic social teaching and the above contextual theologies, limiting my survey to Coleman as standing also for Gilkey and Baum. Coleman's American strategic theology is concerned with social conditions for a creative impact of religion on society. It is also an amalgam of theology and social ethics (1982a, 278–82). Surely the same can be said of the scope of Catholic social teaching.

Coleman astutely indicates the role played in social ethics in the United States by the civil ideals of the Founding Fathers, such as participatory democracy, civic community, simplicity of life, and native wisdom of the common people. This is surely of great importance. While it is true that some of the Founding Fathers were Lockean in their philosophy, they were nevertheless also listening to such ancient proponents of civic virtue as Aristotle and Cicero. The founders of our republic stood in the tradition of eminent early contributors to Catholic social teaching: Grotius, Pufendorf, Soto, Vitoria, and Aquinas.

Another affinity is discoverable with the pastoral circle. John Coleman relies heavily on it. Noting first the work on this as a tool of social analysis for Catholic social teaching by two former Center of Concern associates, Joe Holland and Peter Henriot, Coleman comments, "All four steps in the pastoral circle are necessary components of a strategic theology" (ibid., 283).

What then is perceived by John Coleman as necessary to strategic theology the Center of Concern had already recognized as essential to Catholic social teaching but revised to fully recognize with *praxis* or contextual theology that the starting place for theologizing about the world is the concrete reality of suffering and the questioning it raises. That pastoral circle has four moments of reflection which embody faith and build upon empirical observation. For our purpose, we can use an abridged description from a chapter Peter Henriot, S.J., and I wrote for a recent commentary on John Paul II's *Sollicitudo Rei Socialis*. Our chapter, "Toward A New Methodology in Catholic Social Teaching," built specifically on the four moments of our pastoral circle (Land and Henriot 1989, 68; see also Holland and Henriot 1983, 8).

We wrote that a brief overview shows these stages: (1) Replacing an earlier reliance on speculation and deduction, we now proceed more inductively, more experientially—out of an insertion into living history.[4] (2) To become the matrix of reflection, this experience must next be subjected to an analysis that defines and clarifies the experience (one should here adduce the full social and cultural analysis provided in the writings of all the authors briefly characterized above). (3) On reality thus analyzed we proceed next to reflect in the light of a Christian anthropology and cosmology. This reflection draws on reason and natural law as well as on Scripture and theological tradition. (For instance, if Gilkey is standing for the rest of our authors, this is his particular viewpoint of religion.) (4) The range of options we have for an action, we concluded, could now be made through pastoral planning, in light of this reflection on socially analyzed experience.

I note elsewhere in these pages that Coleman on this fourth point rightly criticizes Metz's political theology for being steeped in an all-inclusive eschatological proviso, one that critiques any and all efforts at the political ordering of society. This circle, finally, is an operation that stems from practical reason coupled with imagination, both operating under the virtues of faith, hope and love. This circle seems to be *praxis,* both agapeic and noetic in the language of Lamb (1982, 13).

The Challenge of Political Theology to Catholic Social Teaching

In the rest of this chapter, I first set out the challenge political theology makes to Catholic social teaching, which is explored from a different perspective in the next chapter, where I take up Metz and then liberation theology. I will draw considerably upon Matthew Lamb for that chapter's interpretation of Metz. I want to acknowledge that much of the following remarks on the nature of political theology also draws upon Lamb. One of Lamb's own statements on political theology will be the subject of the next to last section in this chapter.

Chapter 3 discusses the revelation discoverable by reading signs of the times. While an earlier Catholic social teaching perceived revelation only in the norms discoverable in our God-given nature, contemporary Catholic social teaching attends to God revealed in the events and crises of our times. Having said that, it is worth recalling that Christian social living is the accomplishment of the reign of God in our now time, one to be more fully achieved in the reign of the beyond time.

Political theology and liberation theology, however, challenge Catholic social teaching on its failure to make the oppression and suffering in the Third World of Africa, Asia, and Latin America the problematic of Catholic social teaching. Catholic social teaching, they charge, has confined its vision to the working class of industrial Europe and North America and ignored the plight of those seeking liberation and the means available to them.[5]

These theologians raise questions of method and content. Who is the interlocutor? With whom are theologians in dialogue? To what questions are they giving answers? With which problematic of moral social living does one choose to engage Catholic social teaching?

Political theology and liberation theology do address certain themes hitherto not found or rarely found in Catholic social writing, as discussed in the next section.

Rahner and Lamb

At a deeper level, political and liberation theologians challenge Rahner's transcendental Thomism. Notable challengers are his former student and friend Johann Baptist Metz and Matthew Lamb. Their challenge is that Rahner focuses all his transcendental theologizing on God as God and the human as related to that God. For Metz, Rahner shows inadequate attention to the concept of God in the world (Metz 1980, 55, 59, and chapter 9). Consequently Rahner's Christology fails because it lacks a theology of the suffering Christ in his solidarity with the world's sufferers.

If Metz criticizes Rahner's transcendentalism as being too idealist, he at the same time affirms Rahner's method for its intellectual and religious strength. He asks of it only a more concrete historicity, a more critical questioning of institutionalized Christian practices from the perspective of the contradictions in contemporary cultures and societies. Matthew Lamb (1982, 118) says of the suspicion that Rahner's method raises for Metz: "Such a metaphysical conceptuality, unable to thematize the concrete origins of ideas and concepts, too easily spills over into a somewhat romanticist idealization of originating, prethematic experience as unifying and unproblematic, thereby downplaying the concretely contradictory and problematic character of human experience in history and society."

Perhaps more concretely, says Lamb, "the social sins of racism, sexism, ecological destruction, political and economic oppression, cannot be adequately counteracted within the churches and society at large by pious or indignant moralisms, nor by cleverly conceived techniques. They require profound conversions of personal, social, cultural, economic and political conduct or *praxis*" (ibid., 120). Rahner has recognized the legitimacy of political theology (ibid., 29–30).

What, then, is this political theology which Rahner came to recognize as complementary to his own transcendentalism? We have already had an introduction to it. Lamb describes political and liberation theology as initiating a new framework for understanding the task of theology. This judgment rests on *praxis* being foundationally significant for the way theology should be done. Moreover, it is not merely a matter of pastoral or ethical applications of theology, but foundational to theological understanding itself. Says Lamb, epitomizing what I have just written: "I call 'political' all those theologies which acknowledge that human action, *praxis,* is not only the goal but the foundation of theory" (ibid., 103).

Political theology emphasizes how faith transforms human action. Its concern is the transformative character of religious truth. Thus, political theology contrasts with those theological methods focusing primarily on the disclosive nature of religious symbols. This does not mean these methods have no contribution to make, or, as we shall see in a moment, that the disclosive is not to be encountered in political theology. But these disclosive methods cannot do full justice either to human experience or to Church doctrine. "Disclosure provides us with different interpretations, contradictory historical analyses, opposed ontologies. It is against this limitation that neoorthodoxy argues on the score that their continuously revised hypotheses are not life-giving. Human experience has to be linked to religious faith. The merely disclosive minimizes the transformative effect of religious and doctrinal symbols on human experience" (ibid., 104). It also may disclose only "the alienating falsehood of biased theories, techniques, and human conduct (*praxis*) in repressive social structures" (ibid.).

Political theology, on the contrary, attends to the transformative import of religious symbol on human experience as well as to the transformative structures or dynamics of human experience itself. Lamb sees the transformation *praxis* of political theology in contrast to a materialistic emphasis on human production, for the transformation is effected in the subject's performance or doing. The subject is also the community in which the disclosure of truth is effected. For such transformative *praxis*—a *praxis* with imperative orientations to freedom which can be disclosed only through transformative actions in accord with those imperatives—is the ultimate arbiter among conflicting theories. Theology, according to political theology, will have partners in fashioning its disclosures, that is, other sciences, scholarly disciplines, and pastoral and social ministries. Together they seek to disclose and transform the concrete personal, communal, social, political, and cultural life forms within which Christians live out, or fail to live out, the transformative memories and values of their tradition. This is *orthopraxy*—doing the truth (ibid., 105–7). Dogmas have their foundation in and are "expressive of a knowledge born of transformative religious love—a love that is not to be just words or mere talk, but something real and active, a love by which we can be certain that we belong to the realm of the truth" (ibid., 112; 1 Jn 3:18ff.).

More Affinities between Catholic Social Teaching and Political Theology

My confidence that Catholic social teaching, as I am now framing it, has affinity with what is foundational in political theology grows as I reflect on the two disciplines. That is to say, Catholic social teaching accords with political theology's insistence on the transformative import of religious symbol on human experience and on the transformative structures of human experience itself. Go back to the striking theological passages from John Paul II's *Centesimus Annus* I introduced in the preface. Add to that the theological themes from Vatican II appearing in these pages. All equally with political theology affirm that the truth about social living has its foundation in knowledge begotten of transformative religious love.

Note, too, the affinity of this theme of political theology with the pastoral circle—which is, as I have shown, strongly rooted in the *praxis* of the Center of Concern—a pastoral circle that builds its social truths very much out of experience and reading signs of the times, both of which are drawn from and analyzed through cultural and social instruments.

Although liberation theology will be taken up in the next chapter, we need to introduce here one theme. After Vatican II, liberation theology joined European political theologians in their critique of Catholic social teaching. Both charge Catholic social teaching with failing to respond to the problematic of sufferers. Liberation theology's call has come for solidarity with a wide variety of victims, for it is in the *kairos* of the suffering that we will find God, who is calling to conversion.[6]

This chapter in several ways addresses this challenge to Catholic social teaching. Has Catholic social teaching failed in this regard? We see some ways in which Catholic social teaching surely has not failed, and we now look at other ways in which the Church's social teaching has not failed.

But before proceeding to that amplification, let me address another question many political theologians (as well as liberation theologians) bring up. This is the failure, as they perceive it, of Catholic social teaching to meet or even to understand the legitimacy of conflict, of violent struggle for justice as a last resort. Catholic social teaching, so they argue, has been too "harmony-minded" to admit conflict as, arguably, the only means for the masses to liberate themselves from oppression by the powerful elite who control their lives.

These theologians point to the thirteen families who allegedly control the productive land of El Salvador, which generates the wealth to maintain armies to keep down the landless masses. Their power generates, too, the prestige that at least in the past has allured many churchmen into identifying with the oppressing class.

Hence liberation theologians appeal to the New Testament, where Jesus is depicted as often in conflict with the teachers in the temple, the Scribes and Pharisees. Scripture recounts Jesus using such language as "I have come to bring not peace but a sword." Did he not say, "I pray not for this world"? Perhaps more cogent: "Do you think that I have come to give peace on earth? No, I tell you but rather division; for henceforth in one house there will be five divided, three against two and two against three . . ." (Lk 12:51).

Official Catholic social teaching—led much earlier by unofficial voices, those of the Catholic Worker movement and other pacifist groups, such as the more pacifist wing of Pax Christi USA—rejects the argument from last resort or that of the sayings of Jesus. Once only, to my knowledge, did a pope admit the possibility of using violence. This was Paul VI in his 1967 encyclical, *Populorum Progressio*.[7]

The papal tradition of nonviolence has been strongly reinforced by John Paul II in his encyclical, *Centesimus Annus*. Addressing himself precisely to a situation that, if any, might justify violent conflict, he argues that "the masses won by eschewing violence in favor of winning their oppressors over with love" (*CA* 23).

Addressing the dramatic fall of Marxist socialism in his native Poland, but also generally throughout Eastern Europe, he says, "Worthy of emphasis is the fact that the fall of this kind of 'bloc' or empire was accomplished almost everywhere by means of peaceful protest, using only the weapons of truth and justice, while Marxism held that only by exacerbating social conflicts was it possible to resolve them through violent confrontation. The protests which led to the collapse of Marxism tenaciously insisted on trying every avenue of negotiation, dialogue, and witness to the truth." The pope continues, "They appealed to the conscience of the adversary, seeking to awaken in him a sense of shared human dignity" (*CA* 23).

This papal analysis observes that nonviolence was successful because, as it ended totalitarianism in Poland, so did it generally in East Europe. "While always refusing to yield to the force of power [they] succeeded time and again in finding effective ways of bearing witness to the truth. This disarmed the adversary, since violence always needs to justify itself through deceit, and to appear, however falsely, to be defending a right or responding to a threat posed by others." The pope concludes: "May people learn to fight injustice without violence, renouncing class struggle in their internal disputes and war in international ones" (*CA* 23). John Paul has in this document other strong statements repudiating violence.

Now let us return to the charge made by political and by liberation theology against Catholic social teaching, namely, of not responding to the sufferers of this world. The charge which we have just taken up of failing to acknowledge validity to one way many liberation and political theologians would suggest for effective response—their liberation of themselves by conflict, violent if need be—has been the burden of the last few paragraphs.

Metz—a most significant figure with whom to resume the discourse about failure— charges Catholic social teaching with failure to be concerned about the mass of the world's poor and oppressed.

This surely cannot be said of Vatican II's *Gaudium et Spes*. "The griefs and anxieties of the men of this age, especially those who are poor or in any way afflicted, these too are . . . the griefs and anxieties of the followers of Christ" (*GS* 1). Nor is it true of the 1971 synod's *Justitia in Mundo:* "We have nevertheless been able to perceive the serious injustices which are building around the world of men a network of domination, oppression and abuses which stifle freedom and keep the greater part of humanity from sharing the building up of a more just and more fraternal world" (JW 3).

Paul VI's encyclical *Populorum Progressio* is surely not devoid of concern for suffering humanity. His powerful, prophetic voice called for true human development in the name of suffering humanity. Admittedly, his prescriptions for achieving human development were inadequate. Paul VI in his pastoral *Octogesima Adveniens* declared that the social question had become worldwide.

John Paul II's three great social letters, *Redemptor Hominis, Laborem Exercens,* and *Sollicitudo Rei Socialis* have all been powerful cries for the liberation of suffering humanity. John Paul has on more than one occasion invoked the New Testament image of the banquet at which Lazarus, representing the poor and abandoned of the world, seeks to have some share with the rich banqueter, representing the rich nations. John Paul surely here demands that we address decisively this abuse that calls to heaven for vengeance. The two recent pastorals of the U.S. bishops on peace and on the economy are equally determined to represent the suffering victims of war and the poor. (It is true that some classes of victims are virtually neglected by Catholic social teaching, most notably women and the environment.) In all these calls, the need to respond by pressing for structural reform is evident. Our work in this field has always been done under the aegis of Catholic social teaching. (For one example, see Holland and Henriot 1983.)

As I weigh all of these documents, and there are several more, I find in them ample evidence to answer one conceivable challenge to me. This challenge is that I have no warrant to borrow—from political and liberation theologies—ideas that have not traditionally belonged to Catholic social teaching. But these documents establish the legitimacy of my claim that Catholic social teaching has been concerned about the problematic of political theology: my effort is not a tour de force. More of this will develop in the following section and chapter 10.

Lamb Again on Political Theology

Lamb[8] has two expositions of political theology that I would like to explore further. The first is an article on this topic in a dictionary of theology (Lamb 1987). The second reworks fundamental themes as referred to by Metz (ibid.).

Lamb's dictionary article introduces the reader to a number of themes characteristic of political theology's contribution to theological development. Since many, if not all, have appeared in the paragraphs above, I choose to pull out other themes I want to compare with Catholic social teaching.

First, political theology condemns "eighteenth century capitalist individualism enthronement." Second, political theology calls for "discernment of genuine values and alienating values" and a lament over "setting ourselves up as Lords of history." Third, Lamb cites Augustine's point that "Christian faith can fulfill the narrative,"[9] metaphysical, and political civil functions required for concrete human living better than the other school of thought at that time, namely, the school favoring absorption of Christian faith into Roman culture and the heresy of Pelagianism, which maintained unbounded faith in the capacity of the human community through its own God-given powers to create a good society exclusively out of human resources. Fourth, political theology laments that "past and present histories of suffering are ignored." Fifth, concern about alienation and contrasting solidarity is addressed as a major target of political theology's critique. Sixth, privatization is another major concern of political theology. Lamb holds that "modern theologies tended to concentrate upon the significance of religious teaching and practice for individuals" and "religion is portrayed as very private." Consequently, "for Political Theology the social and political mediations of Christian faith are [not] genuinely dialectical." Seventh, "not only fundamental orientations of Christian faith and theology, but the very possibility of establishing more just and good societies and cultures" are at stake in the choice of theological approaches. Eighth, Lamb reports that the goal of political theology is "to show how a faith-enlightened understanding and *praxis* can heal and transform social and political living." For Lamb, political theology is decidedly not simply another form of social ethics (Lamb 1987, 772–79).

Catholic Social Teaching Parallels Lamb

What strikes me on reading this explanation of political theology is the extraordinary likeness to what I conceive to be Catholic social teaching. Let me illustrate this point by point. Political theology, says Lamb, condemns capitalism and is value-oriented. But papal encyclicals have consistently been highly critical of capitalism. And even if they have never explicitly condemned capitalism, they have—at least up to John Paul II's *Centesimus Annus*—found very much to question and condemn. Political theology's theme of value discernment pervades Catholic social teaching.

Lamb notes in his third point that Christian faith better fulfills the social functions. I have learned this (the narrative component aside) through Catholic social teaching. As a corrective Lamb calls for creative collaboration between Christian theology and contemporary natural and human science. Toward that project I acquired a doctorate in political economics to complement my licentiate in theology. Other practitioners of Catholic social teaching have followed similar paths in their work.

The charge that theology has ignored suffering I have dealt with above. There is truth in this, yet Catholic social teaching has surely not been completely derelict in this duty, as we see just above.

If political theology urges solidarity, so has Catholic social teaching consistently. Lamb links to solidarity in his fifth point political theology's dialogue with Marx on alienation of the worker. I reserve comment on that for my treatment of liberation theology below. In his sixth point, Lamb has political theology charging Christian faith with failing to enter into genuine dialogue with the political order. Political theology may do a better job than Catholic social teaching in initiating that dialogue, but Catholic social teaching has led a strong attack against spiritualities that privatize.

In his seventh point, Lamb says that the very possibility of establishing more just and good societies and cultures is at stake in the choice of theological approaches. That is surely right. But that, equally surely, is precisely what my four colleagues in the Gregorian's social science faculty who concentrated on Catholic social teaching were trying to do. We, as other practitioners of Catholic social teaching, were keenly aware of the implications of theological method for our task.

Lamb's eighth and final point is that the goal of political theology is to provide vision and *praxis* for sociopolitical change. Once again that is surely the goal of all exponents of Catholic social teaching. Lamb ends with an intriguing statement to the effect that political theology is not just "another form of social ethic." Neither is Catholic social teaching only a social ethic. But in their social ethic, analogies between the two approaches are discoverable. They are also discoverable in the components of political theology and Catholic social teaching that are not ethics. We will have occasion to push this inquiry further when we come to Johann Baptist Metz.

Feminist Theology and Catholic Social Teaching

It is incumbent on me, given the task I have outlined of considering the relationship between Catholic social teaching and political and liberation theologies, to recognize feminist theology (perhaps "feminist theologies" would be better) and to consider its relationship to Catholic social teaching.[10] I find myself uncertain whether to treat this in this chapter or in the next chapter. In favor of the latter is that the next chapter treats of liberation theology, and feminist theologians rightly consider their movement a liberation movement. On the other hand, in favor of treating the topic here is that the feminist theologians I am familiar with are North Americans. Hence the topic is appropriately treated in this chapter on North American contextual and political theology (which is also considered to be liberative). I have opted finally for treating the subject here. But whether treated here or in the next chapter, the movement addresses one of the most egregious lacunae in Catholic social teaching.

I consider myself a feminist. But I can make no pretense to being a feminist theologian. However, I do read feminist theologians. Indeed, I have had the very good fortune at the Center of Concern to have been associated with several as colleagues. Three early feminist spokespersons of the Center of Concern were Betty Carroll, R.S.M. (who retired to take up missionary work in Peru), Mary Burke (author of *Reaching for Justice: The Women's Movement,* published by the Center of Concern in 1980), and Jane Blewett, now director of the Earth Community Center. Jane took in hand the correcting of my sexist language. She would return a draft of some paper of mine apparently dripping with blood from her circling in red every blessed place I had used *man* to stand for both sexes. My present colleague, Jo Marie Griesgraber, has equally helped in my growing understanding of what is at stake. But I owe most to Maria Riley, O.P., whose writings in the field are very influential. On her thinking I rely very much in the paragraphs that follow.

This chapter has been very much about contextual and *praxis* theologies. As women have articulated their concept of themselves in their contexts, not just one feminist theology but several have emerged. Their differing experiences become embodied in different self-statements. Thus, there are womanist theology (emerging from experience of black women), *mujerista* theology (experience of Latina women), and feminist theology (emerging from European and American experience), and still others are on the horizon.[11]

But whatever the differences among these varieties of feminism, one thing unites them. This is their drive for liberation from patriarchy and its manifestation in society, whether that be civil or religious. For Catholic feminists a prime target here is Catholic social teaching.

Maria Riley, O.P., in several forums has recognized all the important components of Catholic social teaching that support feminist liberation.[12] Several are treated in early chapters of this volume. Much of the following paragraphs draw heavily upon *Trouble and Beauty* (Riley and Sylvester 1991).

Catholic social teaching strengthens the feminist movement by several major lessons. First is the dignity of the human person. Made in the image and likeness of God, women as well as men must be accorded all that is in keeping with that dignity. If women, by God's design equal with men in dignity, are not accorded full measure of dignity, then they rightly name themselves the oppressed seeking liberation. All human persons enjoy inalienable rights: political, civil, and socioeconomic. Wherever in effect, if not in theory, the political machinery demotes women to second-class citizens, it is unjust. Wherever—and how very widespread this is—women bear undue economic burdens (alongside their nurture of the family) or are paid unequal salaries for equal productivity, they are again denied equality. This right to economic justice is furthered by another principle of Catholic social teaching— the right to a just wage. That is very generally denied women. Another plank of Catholic social teaching—we limit our consideration to this one finally—is the preferential option for the poor. Worldwide, women are among the poorest. Even in the United States after a divorce the husband's standard of living rises substantially and the wife's goes down, very often below the poverty level.

In a symposium at St. Catherine's College,[13] the participants charged Catholic social teaching also with methodological weaknesses. These include, first, its Eurocentric, male filter; and second, the influence of patriarchy on its content. (Catholic social teaching is written by men, primarily about men. It assumes man—Western man—as normative for the human. Women, where they do appear, are defined through this androcentric lens.) Third, its deductive process tends almost to reflect

exclusively upon preceding papal statements, as if they constitute the unique font of Christian wisdom. The group did, however, note that the U.S. bishops have begun listening to the
people of God as they develop pastoral letters.

Over and over, feminist literature charges that Catholic
social teaching has an androcentric bias. More familiar language speaks of its blatantly patriarchal foundation, which
validates a social order in which women are subordinate to
men. Indeed, this social order of subordination is sanctified in
that it is declared to be of God's doing. The men who shaped
the tradition project their concept onto the divine. This patriarchal structure of society assures the male domination over
the female.

Women's liberation demands that Catholic social teaching
shift to a theology which sees God as liberating from all structures of oppression, patriarchal domination as well as race
and class domination. What an abomination that God is made
responsible for the vicious injustice of patriarchy!

For the Catholic segment of the women's movement, patriarchy is formidably concretized in their church. Here, first of
all, appear the "two societies" critiqued in the Center of Concern's commentary on the third draft of the National Conference of Catholic Bishops letter, "Called to Be One in Christ
Jesus: A Pastoral Response to the Concerns of Women for the
Church and Society." The sin of sexism is condemned by the
bishops so far as the world is concerned. But while the draft
does admit to some personal sins of sexism among the clergy,
it denies structural failures. It describes the Church as "seeming" to fail to live up to its teaching on equality and women
"appearing" to be excluded from governance. Thus, women
are being told that they do not suffer exclusion or injustice,
they only think they do.

This exclusion of women from power and women's voices
from any influence upon Church teaching is only part of the
wider exclusion of all laypersons. The regnant ecclesiology is
one of a single authoritative voice in handing down God's
revelation. This voice is the pope and hierarchy. It is for the
laity to receive in dutiful submission. (In this view, the role of
theologians is not to reflect upon truths of faith and play an
active role in forming them, but to teach what Rome hands

down to them.) There is no room here for the people of God of Vatican II as a legitimate voice in the fashioning of Church beliefs, nor room for reading signs of the times (except by the hierarchy). God's Holy Spirit, in effect, is possessed only by the hierarchy. *Sensus Fidelium,* (commonly held beliefs of the Faithful) has, in effect, been wiped out.

The reign of God, our *shalom,* sought by Catholic social teaching, is a reign of two classes of citizen: the haves and the have-nots (those who have power—the patriarchy and hierarchy—and those who do not—women and other laity). The reign of God in the here and now is a reign not of equality but of built-in inequality, based on a putative ineluctable inequality between men and women stemming from their unequal sharing in human nature. According to this patriarchal anthropology, they share differently. Woman's nature is lower, for it is of the body and, through woman's reproductivity, of animal nature and of the earth.

The male, by contrast, is of spirit. His nature is to be rational as opposed to bodily. For this reason, while reproductivity is assigned to woman, productivity is man's God-given task. He is builder, maker of the political order, thinker, and carrier of the human heritage of knowledge, science, and progress. In all this, age-old dualism remains afloat: Plato's conviction that the male escapes, as the female does not, bodiliness with its limitations. But in a Christian understanding of creation, the male no less than the female is an embodied spirit.

Nor in the reign of God in the here and now are other gifts of women—not gifts of their sex but of culture—to be permitted to shape in any way the culture of that reign. To be excluded then (or confined to the privacy of the home), are the values of nurturing, compassion, equality, diversity, and cooperation. These are to be subordinated to the Enlightenment's hierarchical values of competition and male aggressivity in climbing over others on the road to success. From the nonperformers in creating the nation's wealth—women by definition—will be exacted obedience and conformity. The reign will in no way be shaped by feminine participation, compassion, cooperation, reverence, or mutuality among all peoples and with the cosmos. Absent will be women's instinct for the relational—their ability to see the web of relations which surround the object they survey.

All of this inequality and denial of gifts is abhorrent to another principle of Catholic social teaching—the common good. It is often stated exclusively in terms of participants in society possessing all the conditions needed for achieving their full humanity. But even within that narrow definition of the common good, it is clear what immeasurable contribution women could render were they not denied their proper role in effecting that common good.

But common good is in reality much more than being assured the necessary conditions. It is precisely a common *good*. It is common possessions or "commons." More, it is common *being,* or commonality. For this reason Vatican Council II likened social living to the life of the holy Trinity. Within that life there are no first- and second-class citizens. The life that constitutes the common good of society is truncated wherever women are denied the fullness of their life.

Perhaps now an objection needs to be addressed. This is that my expression of "women's gifts" seems to be the old hierarchical "complementarity," the concept that they are gifted to reproduce and nurture and that that is their nature. That is surely not my concept. The embodiment I am talking about is quite other. It is not such dichotomy, body and reproduction on the female side; spirit, reason, and productivity on the male side. No, it is simple recognition that, while having the same nature as men, the same corporality as men and *no more than men,* women have some different gifts, socially and culturally engendered. One must hope that Catholic bishops the world over will one day gain clearer understanding of this.

10 German and Latin American Political Theology

Johann Baptist Metz's Political Theology

Addressing European political theology in the forms given it by Johann Baptist Metz and by Latin American political (or liberation) theologians, I make no pretense to full exposition. As I remarked at the opening of the last chapter, I want only to treat of those aspects which bear upon Catholic social teaching in the two ways mentioned.

Matthew Lamb's book, *Solidarity with the Victims* (1982), provides an excellent entree into the political theology of Johann Baptist Metz. For our exposition of Metz we will confine ourselves to three themes: the eschatological vision, memory in suffering, and solidarity.

Metz and Eschatology

The eschatological vision of Metz is rooted in the presumption that the whole of history and of the political order is essentially oriented toward the future. That future is God calling to us from beyond history. Thus God and Christianity perform the essential function of critiquing any and all political realms. And that future judges all ideologies defending the status quo. In Metz's thought apparently any, even utopian, societal arrangements can be judged status quo, from the view of the beyond. This future particularly critiques modernism's privatization of Christianity in support of a bourgeois, middle-class morality of individualism.

The *eschaton,* as presented in Lamb's version of Metz, relativizes all social arrangements, for any conformation of political order must be prepared for eschatological critique. That God is inexorably calling to something more and beyond Metz calls the "eschatological proviso." If this means that there will never be an order of society that is the fulfillment of the ultimate reign of God, then this provision is an important principle. If, moreover, it is a warning that I cannot allow the humanly doable to stop me from seeking the desired, again it is a salutary principle. But if, on the other hand, it is taken to mean that all human effort to build a decent society is doomed, that humans can never achieve any significant degree of the reign of God on this earth, then the eschatological proviso puzzles me. One would have to conclude that our only hope is in God's calling from beyond history to God's own accomplishment from and in that beyond. There is no political hope for the here and now from us or by us—or from God in any foreseeable political order. Does God's eschatological judgment reject as wrong human society's best efforts to achieve a good society? To put the matter in other words, Metz seems to challenge the possibility that human activity can be constitutive of the reign of God in this world.[1]

On the contrary, I believe we must hold that human activity —to be sure, in cooperation with God's guidance—can bring about some part of the reign of God over culture and the structures of economic and political order. Surely we do not hold this belief on grounds of the Enlightenment's optimism that essential goodness can be inevitably arrived at along the evolutionary path of reason and science. Our belief rather affirms Vatican II's position as articulated in *Gaudium et Spes.* "To believers, this point is settled: considered in itself, this human activity accords with God's will. For humankind, created to God's image, received a mandate to bring to fulfillment the earth. . ." (*GS* 34). "When we develop the earth . . . [even] with the aid of technology . . . and when we consciously take part in the life of social groups, we carry out the design of God . . . that we . . . should perfect creation and develop ourselves" (*GS* 57). These are the activities of the Holy Spirit who is "animating . . . those noble longings by which the human family makes its life more human. . ." (*GS* 38). "For after we . . . have nurtured on earth the values of human dignity, brother- and sisterhood and freedom, and indeed all the good fruits of our nature and enterprise, we will find them again, but freed of stain . . . when Christ hands over to the Father . . . a kingdom. . ." (*GS* 39).

Karl Rahner, in his *Foundations of the Christian Faith* (1978, 86ff.), notes that Aquinas "emphasizes that God works through secondary causes." Rahner's interpretation is that "God causes the world but *is* not the world." This says that "the chain of causality has its basis in God but not that by his activity he inserts himself as a link in this chain of causes as one cause among them" because the "ground does not appear within what is grounded. . ." (ibid.).

Within this context Rahner takes up a special divine intervention, God's answer to prayer. Even that is for Rahner accomplished within the causality which God put into operation. Yes, it is special intervention, but it is within the wholeness of the creation God set afoot.

Questions for Metz

If, critical of the eschatological proviso, I turn to documents like that just quoted in confirmation of the role of the human in building the kingdom, does that mean that I minimize God's role in building the human community? Surely not. God is abundantly presented to us in the Bible as intervening in our history through the creation, the Exodus, covenantal returns, the Babylonian captivity, and subsequent return. "My Father works and I work." (Jn 10:25ff). But with the Incarnation, with Jesus representative of us, comes assurance of a role for the self-initiated humanity Christ shares with us.

Metz, then, has come under fire for pushing his eschatological proviso to the extreme of relativizing even sincere, right-minded, Christian efforts to work out politically a decent society. According to Chopp, this critique induced the German theologian to shift emphasis to suffering. In her words, the shift in Metz's thought can be designated by suffering: "the suffering of a God on a cross, the suffering of the dead who shall not be forgotten, the suffering of the aged and lonely, the suffering of the poor, the victims. . . . The eschatological function of the church places it in a position of critique against the injustices of society . . . so that the church is on the side of the poor" (Chopp 1986, 41).

In a central chapter of his *Faith in History and Society* (1980) entitled "The Future in the Memory of Suffering," Metz returns to his earlier treatment of the eschatological proviso and the political order. Now, however, there is far less emphasis than there was in earlier chapters on God calling from beyond time.

Two Shifts

Prodded by critics who pointed out his lack of political realism and, on the contrary, the possibility of practical reason guided by love and the Spirit achieving something of the city of God, Metz, so it appears, shifted his emphasis to the memory of suffering as providing ground for political hope. Within this theme of suffering there are two shifts. First, the middle-class subject of modernity and of the Enlightenment who carries no hope for the future is superseded by another subject, born of suffering and carrying the memory of suffering. Both the sufferer and those who suffer with the sufferer ground their hope in the primordial memory of the Suffering One of Golgotha. Our hope is in Jesus' death and resurrection.

Second, the eschatological hopelessness for this life gives way to the political in the memory of sufferers. In Metz's words: "What emerges from the memory of suffering is a knowledge of the future that does not point to an empty anticipation, but looks actively for *more human ways of life*. . ." (ibid., 112). Negatively, this will "shock us out of becoming prematurely reconciled to . . . our technological society" and "the controls and mechanisms of the dominant consciousness. . . ." Moreover, it "acts contra-factually in making us free to bear in mind the sufferings and hopes of the past. . ." (ibid., 113). Thus "it allows not only a revolution that will change the things of tomorrow for future generations but revolution that will decide anew the meaning of our dead and their hopes" (ibid.). The significance of this latter is that "These dead . . . have a meaning which is yet unrealized" (ibid.). Thus "faith in the Resurrection of the dead has wholly social and socially-critical significance. . . . Salvation history is . . . secular history in which a meaning is conceded to obscured and suppressed hopes and sufferings" (ibid., 114). Metz calls on Christians to make "the *memoria passionis* effective in the transformation of our political life and its structures," because "the memory of suffering . . . brings a new moral imagination into political life. . ." (ibid., 115).

But what is the content of this new "moral imagination"? I am unable to find one line from this quotation to the end of the book in which moral imagination amounts to an announcement of something humans might do for their future in this world. Instead of announcing, Metz mostly denounces. Metz has only announced that suffering can, in some undisclosed manner, be a positive force in the political order. Beyond that he makes no truly imaginative leap such as that suggested to us by Paul VI in his *Octogesima Adveniens*. Unlike Catholic social teaching he presents nothing of social norms demanding transformation and conversion in history.

Metz argues, along the same lines, that an anthropology of the suffering subject stands against the anthropology of middle-class modernity which focused on the individual subject. This anthropology brings a new subject on the stage of history, and it associates that subject with the suffering Jesus of memory. This suffering and social subject contrasts with the individualistic subject, who identifies the concerns and good of the whole society with the pursuit of his or her own good.

Political theology reveals history as the history of suffering, and it identifies Christ with the history of freedom. Chopp (1988, 42) cites "poverty, institutional rule by force, racial and cultural alienation, industrial pollution, senselessness and meaningless and psychological agony" as circles of death. Again, these are familiar themes in Catholic social teaching.

Chopp then concludes that the goal of political theology is social transformation: "No longer a mere corrective to neo-orthodoxy, political theology's purpose addresses the problem of massive public suffering that lies beyond any attempt at mere understanding—this problem of massive public suffering that demands transformation" (ibid.).

Has Catholic Social Teaching Failed Sufferers?

And so we come again to the question, has Catholic social teaching failed to address suffering? Surely its analysis and theological-philosophical reflection have been about some suffering or other resulting from inhuman treatment, deprivation, rights denied, peace thwarted, social inequity, the sacrifice of fairness, efficiency, unemployment, and growing, deepening poverty.

On the other hand, these sufferers were mainly those of the industrial North. They were not the sufferers of the South whose suffering is deeper and more widespread. The two human subjects of suffering in the North and in the South, however, may be treated together as is illustrated by the 1971 apostolic letter of Paul VI, *Octogesima Adveniens*. The early chapters open up categories of sufferers that had been largely ignored in papal encyclicals. First, the list of Northern sufferers was extended.[2] Second, when the document noted that the social question has widened to embrace the whole world, the oppressed of the South were included. The vast multitude of Third World sufferers were now embraced.

Solidarity in Political Theology

A final theme remains to be explored, namely solidarity in political theology. Solidarity is a prominent component of Catholic social teaching, for it emphasizes the social nature of the human, the common good, the movement of love and justice to achieve that common good, and the conviction that we are members of the human family before being born into any particular clan, ethnic group, or nation. Finally, Catholic social teaching establishes that solidarity in the communitarian life of the Trinity.

But for Metz solidarity essentially refers to the solidarity of the suffering Christ with all human sufferers. Its origin is God, who suffers with suffering humanity. This solidarity links with hope, not a narrowly self-oriented hope, but hope for the whole eschatological enterprise.

To sum up Metz from the perspective of Catholic social teaching, I make two points. First, I press the question of his eschatological proviso. To restate somewhat differently what I say earlier on God's role and on the human role in building the kingdom of justice: if God is beckoning us only from beyond, how is God present to our world in transformation? If God acts from the future only to critique our every effort to achieve cultural transformation, to reform structures, and to work out human alternatives, what motive do we have to reform them? Why bother if our every effort will be met by a God who in effect negates these efforts from beyond time?

Second, Metz seems to have no social or political analysis other than the mediation of suffering. This lack of mediating social norms results also in an absence of the mediation of human instrumentality for the divine operation.[3] It is my contention that Catholic social teaching avoids these weaknesses. Third, the powerful meditation of Metz on solidarity with the victims of history should be recognized. Catholic social teaching must question whether its own solidarity adequately meets that test.

Latin American Liberation Theology

As with the other *praxis* theologies, my concern here is only to relate liberation theology to Catholic social teaching. In this regard Catholic social teaching, in my opinion, shares a considerable amount of ground with liberation theology. I say this despite knowing that very many liberation theologians dismiss Catholic social teaching as an effort of Europeans to address European problems, and as totally irrelevant, if not inimical, to the concerns of peoples seeking liberation above all in the sociopolitical order.

Before showing this convergence, I must acknowledge that liberation theology has rightly challenged an older, more traditional Catholic social teaching on several points. For example, historically Church teaching on private property, at least in practical statements, often proved an excuse for property owners' abuses of workers and the poor, in part because the Church insisted on harmonization between classes and deplored class conflicts. Consequently, Catholic social teaching on private property became utterly utopian and precluded any political action by nonowners to seek their rights.

Furthermore, liberation theology has at times supported Marxist claims of alienation that in the degree to which they are stated cannot easily be dismissed. For it is true that workers have suffered very much alienation from the products of their labor. Furthermore, while religion is not the source of alienation claimed by Marx, religious forces and institutions did too easily identify with and support the propertied elites and the powerful wealthy.

What are some themes of liberation theology shared by a retrieved Catholic social teaching? Some are suffering, solidarity, and the reign of God in this world, as well as the unity of redemptive and secular history. The practical order as the beginning of theologizing is shared by a revised Catholic social teaching. The eschatological proviso of political theology is muted in both. Here lies one sharp difference between Metz's version of political theology and liberation theology. Whereas Metz's eschatological proviso seems to rule out political programs, liberation theology has a definite political program for the present sociopolitical order. According to these theologians, the Bible itself provides the hermeneutic that leads them to conclude that faithfulness to Christian revelation calls for, at a minimum, a rejection of neoliberalism (classic liberalism) and espousal of some form of socialism. In the last few years, that translated for a number of liberationists even into Marxist socialism.

Questions for Liberation Theology

From the perspective of Catholic social teaching I would like to probe with liberation theologians of my acquaintance three problematic areas. The first is language that I encounter among even the most highly reputed which would have it that socialism derives inexorably from a careful reading of the Bible. More troubling is when socialism has a Marxist-state (or even Communist-state) orientation. I have never encountered any rigorous evidence that socialism—especially but not exclusively, that socialism linked to strictly Marxist ideology—is the indisputable conclusion of biblical hermeneutics.

My criticism does not preclude that some assertion of communitarian socialism can be derived from biblical symbols. Clearly, the Bible does suggest values and social frameworks that ought to be in a vision statement of a human economy, such as the creation and dignity of work; stewardship or the alternative of companionship, that is, sharing with the rest of creation; communal sharing; service of others; proper ordering of spiritual and physical goods; trust in God; the option for the poor ("caring for the widow, orphan and stranger"); letting go; concern for productivity and productive effort (as in the parable of the talents); the Exodus; the exile; and discipleship. But to leap from this to biblical endorsement of socialism is to suppose what the Bible does not teach.

My second misgiving concerns capitalist alienation of workers from their products. Workers surely have been and are very much exploited. I think of that powerful indictment of capitalist exploitation John Paul II delivered in his 1981 encyclical, *Laborem Exercens*. For the pope, liberal (that is, conservative and exploitative) capitalism's enthroning of capital over labor inverts the order intended by God: labor should be over capital.

But as understood in Marx, alienation is systematically stealing the product from the worker and paying him or her only a subsistence wage. Here, as for a number of other allegations, liberation theology, although it professes to give priority to social analysis, is wanting. If, however, liberation theologians use this alienation less as Marx's scientific socialism and more as a metaphor for the bestiality of liberal capitalism's still very widespread exploitation of labor, and if they use the word to stand only for Marx's remarkable insight into the structural nature of that exploitation, then I have no difficulty with their proposition.

But it must first be asked: If capitalism derives its profit from hiring laborers deprived of all their product except enough to cover bare subsistence, why have capitalists over decades introduced—and increasingly—labor-saving machinery and processes, even long before labor had the protection of unions or of more social-minded governments?

Moreover, over the entire industrial world the laborer's condition of life and standard of living has, at least in those respects of concern to Marx and Marxists, improved. Henry Ford's workers eventually could afford Ford cars themselves. To take another approach, is it totally unthinkable that any conceivable capitalist free market is capable of an exchange that takes account of the worker's aspirations? I raise this question despite the menacing evidence that the international division of labor—by which investors use labor around the world—is turning more and more to hiring the cheapest labor available anyplace in the world.

We do know as an empirical fact of the 1990s that the Marxist-professing Communist states of Eastern Europe and Russia have all come round to abandoning centrally controlled economies in favor of some form of market capitalism. (I strongly believe that nations seeking to create societies that conform more to John Paul II's society, which places labor above capital, will work out some form of socialism.)

These are not themes to be explored further in this book. But I should add on the theme of market alienation that it is conceivable that a socially framed market could promote a decent human economy. Writing many decades before Adam Smith, a trio of Jesuit moralists, Molina, Vasquez, Lessius—who were headquartered in Antwerp, one of the commercial capitals of the world—worked out a theory of socially framed marketing. When I read them during my graduate program, I was impressed (and remain so) by the cogency of their reasoning. Some might say that any and all such economies are precisely socialist. Perhaps. But I leave the issue here.

The third observation I make here is that a number of liberation theologians exaggerate the dependency theory, although their numbers diminish by the day. Dependency theory describes relations between the rich North and the poor South exclusively in terms of impoverishment of the latter through dependency imposed by the former. The fact and the enormity of dependency is indisputable. But, as even some neo-Marxists point out, alongside external dependency is the internally exercised power of the dominant and powerful wealthy social class. Although this internal domination is linked to external neocolonialism, it has nevertheless its own independent and powerfully subjugating dynamism.[4]

Dependency theory is not the same as the challenge raised in Third World countries to the International Monetary Fund's structural adjustment policy, which is shared to some extent by the World Bank. The South rightly sees a neocolonialism rampant in both institutions, although much less in the bank. In challenging structural adjustment, the South and liberation theologians are on firmer ground than in supporting dependency theory.

Structural adjustment is the IMF's response to the enormous debt of the South to the North. I am not yet prepared to say that all Third World debts have already been paid. But I do respect the arguments I have seen made in support of that thesis. What I do believe is that it is impossible to go on paying interest under the rules imposed, for they seem counterproductive to true development. Moreover, they fall with atrocious weight on the already poor. Even under U.S. law, borrowers of billions are allowed to declare bankruptcy to avoid the excessive hardship of trying to pay their debts off.

The IMF's argument for structural adjustment runs this way. The debts must be paid, otherwise no further capital loans will be forthcoming. To pay interest on the loans, the borrowers must earn more foreign exchange. To earn more foreign exchange, they must export more. To make exports more attractive, the borrowers must devalue their currency, privatize nationalized industries for efficiency, take deflationary measures to cut debt burden hiked up by inflation, and cut government subsidies to the poor for food and public transportation.

The kingpin is exporting more foods, grains, cattle, hardwoods, metals, oil, and light manufactured products like textiles and shoes. A hundred exporters of these glut world markets. Prices plummet. Earnings go down. In addition, successive recessions in the United States have cut demand for imports. Moreover, the exports are built up by bringing more land—first richer acres, then marginal land—under cultivation. Forests are cut down. The poor get poorer, first as arable land is taken from their own food growing. Brazil, for example, is a huge importer of foods it once raised for itself. Then the forest habitat of native peoples is destroyed.

Military governments in Latin America—a dying species—plunged their countries into debt for military purposes, and so bear some share of the blame for the further impoverishment of the people. In addition, economic elites removed their capital to safe havens. It is also true that the South remits to the North some $50 billion a year. In effect, this transfers capital from the poor to the rich.

The governments of the South run their economies no more disastrously than those of the North. Consider the United States, once creditor to the world, now the world's biggest debtor. Consider further that structural adjustment misses the international injustices and failure of the world system underlying so much of the debt. Few governments of the rich world would care to face the cruel choices imposed by the IMF, such as drastically reducing subsidies on bare-bone essentials of already poor people. What are the prospects for such draconian measures to increase national output? Some leaders of the World Bank are realizing that the structural adjustment program is not working even on the IMF's terms.

The distinction having been drawn between dependency and structural adjustment, we can return, briefly, to the dependency theory's charge that dependency unjustly prevents the poor agricultural countries from sharing the benefits of the North's industrialization. Two observations are in order. First, although there is much to this charge, other factors enter into the industrialization of a country: availability of natural resources, technical knowledge and skills, organizational capacity, marketing ability, continued research, proper population balance, and, finally, a nurturing culture.

Second, the productive system of all the economies in consideration here is industrial, largely aspiring to the industrial, if not sociopolitical, model of the rich North. Many voices are rising in the Third World to question whether imitating the industrial development of the North is the road to take to true human development. John Paul II, as pointed out elsewhere in these pages, is confident that entry into the international investment market is the only road for the poor nations.

Third, the implicit thesis seems to be that, once liberation from dependency has been effected, the socialist millenium will have arrived; there will be no more social sin. Such a thesis suggests the Marxist utopia—of a new age of sinlessness following the final triumph of the proletariat.

I have mentioned above that, although they profess to adhere to social analysis, many liberation theologians provide scant analysis. They are strong on denouncing, weaker on announcing. Once the revolution has been won, then how will they build the future? What social, economic, cultural, and political structures do they propose? Many ferociously attack neoliberal economics. But does neoliberal market economics (as John Paul suggests and as noted in these pages) not have something to learn from?

Several of the preceding paragraphs have criticized liberation theology. None of this criticism is intended to suggest that liberation theology has failed as a powerful hermeneutic device for penetrating and reflecting on Latin American and other Third World realities.

I have two final questions to raise in the dialogue between liberàtion theology and Catholic social teaching. The first turns on what liberation theology proposes after the vanguard party has succeeded in overthrowing the imperial powers. We have already seen their prompt answer: social sin will end and a beneficent socialist era will be inaugurated.

My chapter on the themes of Catholic social teaching lays out ideas that Catholic social teaching holds and still believes are relevant to building the good society in whatever circumstances. True, the application will differ according to circumstances of culture, time, and place. But these themes do represent solid and substantial building blocks, provided they are in dialogue with the historical, with reading signs of the times, and with the truths about true humanness gleaned from other religions and cultures. This dialogue corrects an excessively Western concept of what is according to nature.

What body of social principles do liberation theologians have for building the good society once the revolution has overturned the corrupt and oppressive old order? (For that matter, despite their professed prioritizing of social analysis, what serious analysis, cultural, social, and economic, have they made of their situation?)

It used to be that any and all building blocks of Catholic social teaching were summarily dismissed as irrelevant. Not so much today. It may well be that as soon as more Latin Americans begin to reflect on how the building blocks of Catholic social teaching apply to them, they may devise enlightening, original possibilities. I do not yet hear much talk about such. But there are surely some.

One final consideration: should a social theology for the United States (whether political theology, practical theology, cultural theology, or Catholic social teaching) adopt the metaphors of liberation theology? The favored biblical symbol for much of Latin America is the Exodus, wherein God leads his people out of a bondage imposed by abusive power. Any number of statements by theologians in the United States have endorsed liberation theology for the country, including its biblical metaphors.

Ethician John Langan offers a more apt scriptural metaphor for a North American strategic theology in Nathan confronting the unjust King David: "Thou art the man." Says Langan, "American Christians need a theology that hears the call of Christ in the cry of the world's poor and sees the faces of those of other races and cultures. But in the American context this will have to be a theology of the cross, of burdens patiently shared. . . . It will have to be a theology that stresses criticism of earthly power and the service that human institutions owe to human need. It will have to be a theology of self-criticism and self-giving . . . [but] based on self-esteem and not self-hatred. . . . It must also be authentically American, acknowledging both the grandeur of American accomplishments and the misery of American racism and social blindness. It will have to be a theology that is willing to listen to the cry of the world's oppressed and needy and that is also willing to speak out on the uses and abuses of American influence and power . . . a theology of response and responsibility . . . that responds to . . . liberation theology rather than being a form of liberation theology itself" (Coleman 1982a, 293–94).

Persuasive as this is, I remain convinced that, if not precisely the Exodus metaphor, at least that of the Exile—precisely as used by the U.S. Catholic bishops in their economic pastoral—is valid for us. Because I have raised this question earlier in connection with the *kairos* moment for the United

States, I here limit myself to a few words. We do have a failing social order. In a sense we are in the exile Israel suffered after its prideful fall from glory. God is dealing with us as with the chosen people. Like them we have hung up our lyres and cannot sing. We await deliverance. Like the Israelites we must confess our sin, and much of that sin is the dependency we impose on the poor of the world. I cannot shake loose from an intuition that the Babylonian captivity is a metaphor we ought at least to put on the table for discussion.

Another question relevant to Catholic social teaching is who is the instrument of social transformation? On this question we cannot doubt that traditional Catholic social teaching comes off badly. For at least in official expressions, that tradition has all too generally turned to the elites of society or to the employer class for initiative in social change. Once the elite were transformed spiritually, they would assuredly be instruments of social peace and justice in their new-found charity. The suffering masses were the objects, the beneficiaries of this elitist beneficence. This approach is most clear in Leo XIII, but it has generally remained an implicit assumption of most official expressions of Catholic social teaching. Before the appearance of *Centesimus Annus,* I was prepared to say that John Paul II had broken from that tradition. In his 1981 *Laborem Exercens,* the pope inverted the traditional order, extolled work above capital, and thereby gave the impression that he believed working people should rightfully play a stronger role in guiding the use of capital. With this latest encyclical, however, he seems to have replaced his trust in the business class.

In contrast, liberation theology explicitly maintains that the victims must be the transformers, for they are the seed of the new theological thinking that alone can lead to cultural transformation and then to political transformation. They must, then, take their liberation into their own hands. The Brazilian Paolo Freire is paradigmatic here with his pioneering theory of education which begins with people transforming themselves and their institutions. Transformation is not something done by one person to another.

Parenthetically, does this emphasis of liberation theology in contrast to Catholic social teaching extend also to European political theology? Although political theology substitutes the sufferer in history for the bourgeois subject, are these sufferers agents of their own transformation? Metz does describe these sufferers as "the new imagination of society." These sufferers also are linked in solidarity. The new moral imagination does suggest active imagining. These elements might be supposed in combination to suggest that the sufferers are the subject of their own transformation. Similarly, solidarity seems to intend actively taking hold to transform rather than simply submitting in solidarity. But these are only conjectures in the absence of strong evidence.

Jon Sobrino's Political Theology

Jon Sobrino is another forceful voice within Latin American liberation political theology. I single him out because he talks, passionately, in the name of the eight martyrs of the campus of the Universidad Centro-Americana, six of whom were his companions on the faculty of that university. Sobrino articulates a powerfully moving and strong challenge to Catholic social teaching. This theologian of liberation, educated in Germany, challenges Western theology in general and *nominatim* the German theology he was taught. He speaks of "salvadorizing" Rahner, whose influence on his theology he acknowledges (Sobrino 1991).[5]

Sobrino's challenge is that Western theology simply has not come to grips with the vastness and centrality of poverty in the world, nor with the oppression of the poor and persecution of those who dare side with the poor by those in positions of power. Why were Sobrino's fellow Jesuits murdered in their home on the campus of their Central American University? Because they dared side with the mass of Salvadorans nailed to the cross by the oligarchy in union with the armed forces. They were murdered because they dared challenge the idols of the military oligarchy. The challenged idols had to have their victims.

To comprehend the suffering of poverty and its demand on his commitment, Sobrino underwent what he called an "awakening from the sleep of inhumanity." That awakening included his conversion from centering on the theological problems of Europe to see that theology had to address El Salvador's crucified poor. "This world is one gigantic cross for millions of innocent people who die at the hands of executioners" (1991). This fact constitutes sin, massive sin.

These people are not those Western people about which Western theology is concerned. This shift cries out for a new theology which addresses these others in humanity who are missed by traditional theology and also by Catholic social teaching. "I am appalled at the lack of sense of history in Western efforts to understand humanity, as if there were a human essence which is replicated with slight variations throughout the planet." Sobrino quickly adds, "Of course there is some truth to this" (ibid.).

On one level there are two kinds of human beings: those who take life for granted and those who take anything but life for granted. To comprehend humanity Sobrino looks to these latter: "What is truly human has been showing itself to me in the faces of the poor" (ibid.). Then Sobrino moves to challenge the problematic about which Westerners theologize: "From the perspective of the poor, we have rediscovered a new kind of civilization, a civilization of poverty or at least of austerity, rather than one of an impossible abundance for all—a civilization of work and not of capital, as Father Ellacuria would say: 'Working for that new civilization implies that sharers with the sufferers imitate the Good Samaritan in bringing mercy,' but not works of mercy." Rather, "Sharing with sufferers makes the pain of the sufferers our own pain and moves us to respond and to take them down from the cross." This means "working for justice, which is the name love acquires when it comes to entire majorities of people unjustly oppressed and employing in behalf of justice all our intellectual, religious, scientific, and technological energies" (ibid.).

Sobrino eloquently articulates what all those other voices have declared, namely, that Catholic social teaching, as other Western theology, has failed to address the vastness of the crucified world beyond our Western, industrial shores. Sobrino imperatively challenges Catholic social teaching to begin to do so. Will Catholic social teaching bring the crucified down off their cross? That is the question.

Sobrino challenges Westerners' understanding of what it is to be human: to be human, everyone else must be like us. Sobrino adds, "we say that all are equal. That's a lie" (ibid.). In a 1990 conversation at the Center of Concern, Sobrino added that Catholic social teaching must come to terms with the Eighth Commandment: thou shalt not bear false witness. In our meeting, he was referring to what he describes as the lie of equality.[6]

If Catholic social teaching seems not to hold out much promise as response to his problematic of the crucified of the world, to what does he appeal? Sobrino turns to the Beatitudes and the parable of the good Samaritan. The former calls for hungering after justice, becoming peacemakers, being meek; the latter to showing mercy and serving the poor and oppressed.

To confirm the New Testament call in the Beatitudes and the good Samaritan parable, Sobrino recalls this passage from the Hebrew Scriptures, "What does the Lord require of you but to do justice and to love kindness and to walk humbly with your God" (Mi 6:8). That translates, continues Sobrino, to this: "To reproduce love and justice in human history is the way we respond to God's love." The challenge to Catholic social teaching, however enunciated, is precisely to bring about that justice of God. Catholic social teaching, as well as the rest of theology, must meet this challenge.

In other chapters we note the extensive move of Catholic social teaching toward the truths of supernatural living in the social order. Christian attitudes, precisely those of the Beatitudes and of the good Samaritan, figure among these truths. In a large measure these truths are only a Christian naming of the human attitudes conveyed by even a more philosophical statement of Catholic social teaching. Those motivated by the appeal of the Beatitudes to be merciful will seek justice and structures of justice. Hungering after justice is also hungering after the properly ordered set of relations that I have named as the common good. In the last three decades Catholic social teaching has insisted more strongly on the global *oikos,* the global village that we are seeking to construct. That global *oikos* encompasses all of the world's poor, all of the world's dispossessed and disempowered. Toward that international common good, an international call of social justice corresponds.

A Last Word

This chapter deals with two aspects of political theology: the several affinities of Catholic social teaching with the method and themes of political theology and the questions Catholic social teaching puts to certain expressions of political theology, both in its European and Latin American form. It ended with the powerful challenge of one of its chief exponents, Jesuit Jon Sobrino.

I would like to conclude this chapter by returning to Langdon Gilkey (1981, 53–56), who figures in the preceding chapter. I draw on the concluding pages of his chapter "The Political Dimensions of Theology," and include a scattering of quotations representative of the whole. "When we look closely at the central symbolic content of our faith, and through the spectacles of that witness at the divine activity and purposes in history—as that symbolic content illumines for us that activity—we find an understanding of God, of human being, and of history that is social and political in form. From beginning to end, through covenant to people, betrayal and sin, promise, new covenant to final kingdom, the inner and outer, the personal and the communal, the moral and political are intricately but continuously intertwined."

"Throughout," Gilkey continues, "the divine redemptive is directed not only against inward sin and individual death, but also against outward fate. Throughout, the divine purpose is not only to establish an inner piety but also a just, ordered, and creative outer world. . . . The symbols expressive of the creative, transforming power of God in historical time—creation, providence, redemption, love and final end—each weaves individual and community into a new fabric, a new world of the inner spirit expressed objectively in and through a community of justice, of reunion and of love."

Gilkey describes the "central symbol of the New Testament, the kingdom" as follows: "if the Kingdom signifies the reign of God in the hearts of women and men, the opposition of God's love and justice to the historical world, the final culmination of history and of persons in history in God's eternal reality far beyond the bounds of space and time, nevertheless . . . this symbol refers also to a redeemed social order and ultimately to a redeemed history as well as to redeemed individuals."

The wonderful insights of Gilkey, expounded as political theology, appear to me equally expressible as Catholic social teaching, albeit in a retrieved form. For example, Gilkey speaks about the political order and the person of Jesus: "That Kingdom represents the perfected social community that corresponds to the personal and individual perfection of the figure of Jesus. . . . The symbol of the kingdom thus functions in relation to ongoing historical and political life as the individual perfection of Jesus as the Christ functions in relation to crises, despair, and fragmentary realizations of individual Christian existence. It establishes the ultimate aims, the bases for judgment and for policies in relation to political and communal action, much as the individual perfection of Jesus' life sets the ultimate norms for our own fragmentary good works" (ibid., 55). This aspect of the reign of God I describe in earlier chapters as the normative significance for social life of Jesus as the Way.

Moral Rightness
of Social Action

C atholic social teaching, as I have said, is divided into two
sectors: the goodness of social living and the rightness or
correctness of social living. The preceding chapters by and
large treat the goodness of social living. But living in a good
way does require acting as correctly as is possible. In social
living I must act according to the right norms. Social life must
be normative. For the most part Catholic social teaching has
been portrayed in the tradition as providing norms for social
living. Since the human person is essentially social, rights
must be respected; the common good must be sought; justice
must be done at both the individual and social level; private
property including the means of production is a right, albeit
subject to the common good; and so on.

Moreover, all these norms have been stated as universally
true because they are based on the nature of the human person or on natural law. Consequently, if they are universally
true, these propositions are implicitly exceptionless. Nature
reveals the divine will for the human person. Other actions
are prohibited because they interfere with divine right; for
example, direct killing is against God's right over life.

Increasingly over the last half century, Catholic moralists have
receded from abstract, universal norms in favor of a historical
approach to moral making, both generally and specifically in

the social field. Catholic moralists have also increasingly turned away from intrinsicism to proportionalism.[1]

I describe this shift in the introductory autobiographical chapter. In this chapter I explore what for our purposes may be called universalism versus historicity or intrinsicism versus proportionalism. We pay special attention to the social and moral arena.

Moral Goodness and Moral Rightness of Social Life

In the chapter on the person in moral making I made much of the point that understanding the nature of the person acting socially requires studying the nature of the moral agent as well as of the moral acts of the agent. This brought us into the ethics of being as contrasted with the ethics of doing. It is worth recalling here the emphasis this shift gives moral making. But the ethics of being (goodness of the moral act) does require that we do our best to act with moral correctness or moral rightness (ethics of doing).

Frequently, the situation one confronts requires facing choices that involve a good effect accompanied by a bad effect. This quandary has traditionally been resolved by applying the principle of double effect, which requires that (1) the thing done not be intrinsically evil; (2) at least one good effect would follow; (3) the evil effect should not be the cause of the good; and (4) there be a proportionate reason for allowing the evil effect.

But the conflicts which abound in the social order demand a wider and more complex approach than double effect. An approach which treats the human act as a unity is preferable. Therein the object cannot be appraised apart from the other components of a unified act, namely intention (*finis operantis*), circumstances, and consequences. These components are all imbedded in multiple relationships. Does this preclude all intrinsic morality? No, once all the relevant factors have been weighed, the action taken will have intrinsic goodness or badness, but result from the behavior and its imbedded intention, consequences, and so on.

The typical perplexity of social choices illustrates the weakness of any ethical theory based on the intrinsic badness or goodness of an act considered in itself and thereby independent of intentions, relationships affected, and possible consequences.

The issue of personal charity or structural justice is one example. Which is more moral: hands-on work for the poor or changing social structures? Or are the two options equally moral? Even if some may choose charity and others justice, to which am I called? What is concretely normative for me? How do I do my level best to be my moral best? Do I work to change attitudes and behavior or to change structures? My fellow Jesuits and other groups are split over this. Surely there is much more to ponder about personal charity than just the action in and of itself.

Private property is another example. Is the morality of private ownership of productive property (or consumptive property) learned from inspecting its essential thingness? Is the thingness the same in all cultures and all epochs? Must the many peoples in the world who reject private ownership for communal property in our day abandon this position because it does not accord with natural law? Communal ownership has many recognized advantages: responsibility for the whole community; sharing; and more assured care for a people's forests and forest products, medicinal sources, space, water supplies, fishing, and farmland and its yields. This latter advantage is contradicted by one of Aquinas's more pragmatic arguments for private property, which holds that in our present sinful state only private holdings will assure care for resources. An additional complication is the World Bank's and the International Monetary Fund's push for private ownership because it serves their industrial development model. Many would question whether their model truly serves the best interests of the poor of the world. Any answer to the moral question about ownership of production property clearly cannot be derived apart from relationships.

The just-war theory also provides an interesting example since it is a child of natural law. Unlike the previous cases this theory is not just a matter of the goodness or badness of war independent of intention or consequences. Even if we set aside any consideration of intention and consequences, what is the morality of the thing done? Just-war has two moments and two questions. The first moment is the decision to go to war (*ius ad bellum*) and the second moment is the just conduct during the war (*ius in bello*). How does one test the goodness or badness of war? Clearly one cannot look at war in one particular moment of time.

Rather, a longitudinal approach must be taken, that is, the thing being done has to be weighed over time as a series of shifting options, of changed relationships, of differing answers to new questions arising as the situation shifts.[2] This is true both in *ius ad bellum* and *ius in bello*. Consequences must be taken into account. Even strategic bombardment is not the same thing on day one as on day ten. Each air sortie may look the same, but after many sorties their character changes. "Smart bombs" that eventually lay waste the infrastructure of the enemy nation are totally different from the first day's smart bombs. Even if there were no civilian deaths, what of the many deaths of enemy troops clearly fleeing from engagement, as was the case in the U.S. war with Iraq? Even if this bombing appeared no different from the first bombings, it does differ over time.

Clearly, the morality of war must be judged in relation to the consequences for those initiating war, for those subjected to war, and for the long-term geopolitical world. It must also be judged in relation to the authority to declare war in a democracy and to the potential destruction of the human collective will to seek other solutions to international conflict.[3]

Thus it seems that in the field of social ethics proportionalism is the only road to morally right conduct.

Questions Concerning Universals and Neo-Scholasticism

As I admitted in my opening chapter, I teeter-tottered between existentialist social morality and something more historicist. In chapter 12, I will reflect on two articles written some forty years ago on Thomas Aquinas's ethical system applied to the social order. In the one on Aquinas's "practical reason" (*ratio prac-tica*), my coauthor, George Klubertanz, S.J., and I approved the strong existentialist bent in Aquinas.

But my autobiography also shows that later on, during my Roman days, I backslid from that position to a more essential-ist-universalist natural law code. Only common sense inter-vened to keep me from applying in practice the rigid and inexorable conclusions that my premises seemed to warrant. It was Karl Rahner's historicity, more than any other influence, that restored me to the more sensible moral system of Aquinas that I had once so strongly championed.

In my partial departure from Aquinas, I found myself skirt-ing the fringes of the neo-scholastic abandonment of Aquinas even while the neo-scholastics professed to be followers of Thomas. My affirmation of Aquinas even in my backsliding never quite got out of my system. Simon Deploige's attack on the abstractionism of the neo-scholastics inspired in great measure my renewed affirmation of Thomas.

Neo-scholasticism embraced more than neo-Thomism even while centering on Thomas, but it was an aberration thereof. Neo-scholasticism, pressured by modern philosophies, had by the eighteenth century lost its creativity. But, to be fair, it was in part the Roman crusade against modernism that drove the-ology into the safety of manuals (Deploige 1923).

Deploige could write of Thomas: "Sociology was not for Thomas an enemy but an ally" (ibid., 240). Deploige, who recognized the contribution of the sociologists, added: "The leaders [of the sociological movement] had and keep the praiseworthy ambition of remedying a grave defect in natural law theory. They want to know society as well as possible before prescribing laws for it. Without suspecting it, they have come back to the Thomistic conception" (ibid.).

That remark of Deploige inspired Klubertanz and myself to explore its validity. For, at the time of our writing, "Thomistic theory and practice in the field of ethics . . . appeared to many Thomists and non-Thomists to be analytico-deductive" (Land and Klubertanz 1951).[4] It was our determination to demonstrate that Aquinas's system of practical knowledge, on the contrary, fully justified Deploige's characterization of it.

But let me conclude this brief introduction to Aquinas (anticipating the longer treatment in the concluding chapter) with one quotation that gives the flavor of his ethical system.

Just as every judgment of speculative reason proceeds from a natural knowledge of the first principles, so too, every judgment of practical reason proceeds from certain naturally known principles. . . . But the processes by which we come to judge about different objects are themselves of different kinds. For there are some things in human action which are so evident that with but a modicum of reflection they can immediately be approved or disapproved by means of those common and first principles. But there are others which to be judged need a full consideration of differing circumstances. . . (*ST* I–II, q. 100, a. 1).

And so it is clear that moral precepts pertain to good morals; good morals are such as are in harmony with reason; and every judgment of human reason flows in some way from natural reason. Hence, it follows that all moral precepts belong to the law of nature, but in different ways. For there are some that are immediately judged to be done or not to be done by the natural reason of every man. . . . Others need a full consideration of reason. . . (ibid.).

We made two observations in this passage. First, we distinguished between (*a*) the first principles of the practical order, (*b*) judgments arrived at by simply applying these principles to some human actions, and (*c*) judgments that depend upon a full consideration of differing and changeable circumstances (*ST* I–II q. 94, a. 5–6 and q. 100, a. 1, 11). Our second observation was that none of these judgments are arrived at by purely deductive processes.

Vatican Council II's Treatment of Moral Correctness

In an earlier chapter we saw that Vatican Council II had no difficulty in asserting that moral life is rooted in revelation. It is a fundamental truth that God has given salvation to human subjects. Personal morality is worked out within that context.

If the council had important things to say about moral goodness, did it also contribute to ongoing discussions of moral rightness and of moral correctness? On this Josef Fuchs, S.J., professor of the Gregorian University in Rome and an eminent moralist, is affirmative. He links his affirmation to the contribution the council thereby made to the task of creating a better world order. Says Fuchs: "The council speaks on this subject (moral goodness as demanding that this be realized in a right manner) above all because of human questions raised as a result of the immense possibilities of a humanity living according to a dynamic and . . . evolutionary concept of nature . . . possibilities that affect not only issues of personal morality but in a much more important way the formation of the world. . ." (Fuchs 1989, 479, 485).[5]

And how will we solve the problems that arise in a dynamic and evolutionary world? *Gaudium et Spes* requires correct "solutions." Fuchs insists that the council, while concerned also with personal morality, is mainly preoccupied with "the problem of the rightness of the human formation of the world. . ."(ibid., 486).

Fuchs assures us that the council maintains that "the human is the measure of the correctness of social morality" (ibid., 487). In this respect, the title of the third chapter, "Man's Activity in the World," in *Gaudium et Spes* has a twofold meaning: "Human activity proceeds from man; it is also ordered to him" (*GS* 37). Fuchs (1989, 487) is amazed to see how frequently this ordering, and thus the human dimension as a practical criterion of correctness of human behavior in the modern world, is emphasized in these conciliar texts. "It no doubt occurs more frequently than the indication of stipulated norms."[6]

The Gregorian moralist adds two observations on the council's view of the human person as normative of correct moral behavior in the social field. First, the council recognizes the voice of God in "the language of creatures" as the "properly understood doctrine of the natural law" (*GS* 37).[7] Second, the council "does not exclude, but rather includes, the possibility of the existence of different cultures in which there may be life-styles and 'moralities' that are to some extent different. . . " (Fuchs 493; *DH* 43, 53, and 54).

Finally, while Fuchs stresses the human person as norm and humanness as shared by people of different religions and cultures, he nevertheless cites *Gravissimum Educationis* (Christian Education) paragraph 2 to point out that the council sees "natural values as assimilated into the full understanding of man redeemed by Christ" (Fuchs 1989, 488).[8]

Rahner's Historicity

Karl Rahner is surely a principal contributor to historicity and its application to the social field. The powerful move toward historicity in Catholic moral theology is widely attributed to the German Jesuit.[9]

What brought Rahner to write on historicity? (His word *Geschichtlichkeit* can also be rendered as *historicality*, or the historical dimension of human existence.) Simply stated, it was his reflection on the neo-scholastic aberrations on universalism. The manualist moralists argued in this way: a definitive moral imperative arises for the individual in one's concrete situation as simply applying the universal norm to the concrete. The situation gives the cue for the choice of universal norms which must be carried out. The situation is conceived tacitly and as a matter of course; it *simply preexists* (Rahner's emphasis) the discovery of the norm and the moral decision. This simply objective situation and the general norm coincide and result in the concrete imperative of the situation. Apart from these two factors, that is, the general norm and the objective situation, nothing more is required to determine the concrete imperative.

This manualist ethic provides the following syllogism:

A. The major premise states a universal norm which already contains the concrete case for application as a case within the universal. Presumably the case does happen often and is abstracted to a universal state.

B. The minor premise asserts that the suppositions are verified by inspecting the concrete situation.

C. The conclusion converts the major premise into a concrete imperative for this concrete situation.

In this operation, according to Rahner (1963a, 221), conscience is viewed exclusively as the mental moral function that applies the universal norm to the concrete *casus*. The difficulty in discovering the moral imperative is seen to lie only in the exactness and adequacy of the analysis of the situation and, under certain circumstances, in the unambiguous expression of the universal norms. However, if both are absolutely clear, the concrete moral imperative cannot be doubted. Whoever knows the universal law exactly and comprehends the case to the last detail knows what must be done.

Is this justified? Before turning to Rahner's answer, it is well to note that he here makes very explicit that his challenge is not meant "in the sense of wishing to question the fact that universal norms can and must be applied to the individual case. . ." (ibid., 222). If that were so, one would fall back into situation ethics, which is pure subjectivism resting in the one expressing the judgment about the situation. She or he is the sole measure of morality.

Rahner also adds, "in practice, in thousands of cases of every day life, [this neo-scholastic method] suffices . . . obviously" (ibid.). So it is not that "there has been no theory of morals up until now sufficiently acceptable. . ." (ibid.). Rahner's problem is not that natural law should be viewed as shifting easily (as loosely mutable), but rather that change is surely thinkable and indeed has gone on (historicity).

The issue rests not in the inability to formulate general norms, but in the kind of norms: absolute exceptionable universals or the objectively true? The issue is concerned with how concrete the resulting norms will be. Rahner asks, can there be an adequate analysis of the concrete situation into formulatable propositions? Here, several considerations are relevant for him.

"Is what we are in fact morally obliged to do in the concrete case, also basically identical with what can be deduced from the universal norms in view of a concrete situation?" Certainly as a minimum "the morally obligatory cannot contradict these norms. . . . Nothing can be done in the concrete situation which lies outside these universal norms and to that extent everything which morally ought to be done in the concrete is also the realization of the universal norm" (ibid.).

Still, if some degree of universality is realized, we must acknowledge that the human is an existential and unique in every case. Hence *the human cannot be determined by a universal norm*. Norms are relevant, but they do not determine the individual. They are relevant, for in some sense human nature enfolds the individual case. It is wrong (ethical wrongness) to go against our nature, against natural law. Still, it is an individual person with her or his constitution, exercising her or his judgment in these circumstances, who decides. How then can the concrete situation be represented by the abstract universal as a case totally embodied in it?[10] In our context one could say, just as there is no purely abstract speculative knowledge in the sciences, sacred as well as profane, so there is no purely speculative moral knowledge. The historical enters into the very matrix of correctness of moral doing as in all other knowing.

Rahner (1963a, 225) explains: "The act is a *reality* [Rahner's emphasis] which has a positive, substantial property which is basically and absolutely unique. . . . Man in his moral acts cannot be merely the appearance of the universal and of what is in this universal alone 'eternal,' and 'ever-valid.'"

Again, "Insofar as man subsists in his own spirituality his actions are always more than mere applications of the universal to the case in space and time" (ibid., 226). Rahner makes this still more dynamic and forward-thrusting: "The question is not about individuality of my being and of my already freely effected state. Rather, it is the uniqueness of something *still to be done by me and ought to be done*" (ibid., 227–30).[11]

Rahner moves to theological considerations emerging from this historicity. Since men and women are destined to eternal life as individuals, as concrete someones, their acts are not merely spatial-temporal as in the case of material things. Rather, their acts have meaning for eternity, not only morally but also ontologically. Because my moral act is on its way to a destiny beyond time, it receives further specification, that is, further meaning, the normative, from that destination. This is equally true of human society.

Rahner's fundamental option is the place of the "total, basic decision about self in which the person begins to reflect about self; in which the person, when she/he begins to reflect on self always finds himself/herself already there" (ibid., 230). From this decision Rahner's moral system emerges with its fundamental norm, namely, love of neighbor as embodying love of God.

The supernatural order also modifies concrete conclusions derived from the universal through the gifts of the Spirit, supernatural instinct, and immediacy to the personal, living God. What a far cry from law and norm! Rahner calls Paul's groaning of the spirit as "the unction that teaches us everything." Rahner also holds that the rigidity of the universal cramps and confines the deity, since the rigid universal declares an imperative that excludes any other conceivable alternative route to moral action (ibid., 225).

He concedes that we may suppose that we have thoroughly understood the situation, and we can suppose further that we have discovered all conceivable universal norms applicable to the situation, and finally we can suppose that these two will guide us to a concrete moral application so that we will not offend against either the principle or the concrete morality. About those suppositions, however, he raises this question: Could the resulting imperative, which is possibly the one and unambiguously determined action, take quite a different form "in a dimension which can no longer be adequately regulated by the universal norm?" In other words, "Can it not be that from some other source altogether only one of the possibilities lying within application of the universal should be designated as the only morally right one in the concrete?" (ibid., 224–25). As an example, Rahner suggests that universal moral principles directed to choosing one's state of life leave open whether to choose the lay state or accept the call of a religious vocation. These are neutral options so far as the universal is concerned. But this is not the case if beyond the universal there is a call from God to the religious life.

Rahner here weaves in a thread mentioned earlier, that the individual act has an ontological component which arises from God-given destiny. Thus he says, "Man is to be conceived as the binding will of God. And therefore it is absurd that God's binding will could only be directed to human actions insofar as these are simply realization of universal norms and nature" (ibid., 227). Rahner continues, "God is interested in history not only as carrying out of norms (God intended that too) but insofar as it is a history which consists in the harmony of unique events and which precisely in this way has meaning for eternity" (ibid., 228). This concept of God as active in this world, in moral choice and not only through universal norms of nature, is widely held since the Second Vatican Council.

Rahner's Historicity and Essential Ethics

In the preceding section we have seen that Rahner questioned universals on the grounds that they cannot embrace the total-ity of the individual. Rahner's fundamental challenge to uni-versalism, to a traditional natural law, and to an essentialist search for moral correctness and their applications to the social field is far more significant. In this section we will examine historicity in "turning to the subject," a central con-cept in Rahner's fundamental moral system.[12]

Rahner asks that a narrow objectivistic conception of human beings and nature yield to an interpretation of the person's own experience of structural freedom. In his search for nature and structures which provide freedom with its moral ideal, he begins by looking within the human person's immediate expe-rience of the self acting morally within subjectivity. Here is the core of nature, the most basic structure of the being of the per-son. Because this core grounds freedom, it must not be vio-lated. It is in and only through that crucible that the universal passes into human attention.

The above is very close to the language of another great contemporary of Rahner, Bernard Lonergan; for him "objectiv-ity is simply the consequence of authentic subjectivity" (Himes 1990, 56).

From the earlier discussion of Rahner's thinking, we recall that turning to the subject embraces the person and his or her freedom. Therefore natural law theorists must enlarge their concept of what the nature of a human person includes, that is, they must embrace the grounding structure which makes freedom possible. The structures of nature which encompass and channel exercise of freedom act on that grounding. Freedom operates within the structures—structures of nature as earlier conceived in natural law theory.

The fundamental structure that grounds freedom is none other than the drive toward incomprehensible mystery. That holy mystery calls us to moral life, that is, to a life of making ourselves and our world moral in responsible exercise of freedom and creativity and channelling that creativity in the encompassing structures of nature (natural law).

I find intriguing the conclusion that Bresnahan (1980, 175) feels entitled to draw from this: "When natural law absorbs this new accent on freedom and its grounding structures, it must go about essential ethics differently." If it must rightly adhere to the unchangeable in nature, to channeling by the nature of the freedom to act, still it must acknowledge the possibility that "some dimension of what has been considered in the past to be core are peripheral structures to the person" (ibid.).[13] This means that a particular form a person takes might be changed by freedom without harm to what remains unchangeable. In short, freedom can be creative and bring new being even into what was thought unchangeable nature.

The moral ideal upon which natural law morality must build is the unified love of God and of neighbor. Let us look at this core through the lens of historicity and the natural law. Love has an important role to play in fashioning the normative. For Rahner, the essential grounding for the person (the person's nature) and for freedom is the loving response to holy mystery's loving call. Love responds through love of neighbor, therein encountering and loving God. Freedom is designed for love. Love is the living fundamental option for incomprehensible holy mystery.

As such, love is the basic moral idea. The essentiality of love does not set reason aside. Reason informs Rahner's global moral instinct, but commitment in love conditions reason. Love in action guides ethical reasoning, and when such love is lacking, reasoning to the norm of ethical rightness may be deficient. Any other normative thinking within natural law must now be based on the basic moral ideal of loving option.[14]

Concrete Norm Making

Flowing from the preceding paragraph Catholic social teaching must work to produce concrete norms through this analysis of our incorporation in time, space, and essential sociality. Conscience guides the entire search from first formulations into the further moral rightness and correctness of final decision making. Throughout this operation, to return to a concept developed above, conscience seeks not the absolute but as much objectivity as possible.

Gaudium et Spes insightfully remarks on this point: "The more correct conscience holds sway, the more persons and groups . . . strive to be guided by the objective norms of morality" (*GS* 16). This paragraph continues, "In the depth of his conscience, man detects a law which he does not impose upon himself, but which holds him to obedience. . . . For man in his heart has a law written by God: to obey it is the very dignity of man. . . . Conscience is the most secret core and sanctuary of a man. There he is alone with God, whose voice echoes in his depths" (ibid.).

This language might suggest that the objectively concrete norms as well as more general norms are dictated to us by God, and we have only to receive them passively. But the council has accepted that conscience can be in error. How could one listening to God speaking in the sanctuary of the heart fall into error? The obvious sense of our quotation is that the responsible probing of conscience is listening to the voice of God, but not in the sense of God infusing knowledge, arrived at quite independently of personal search and with the guarantee of absoluteness. The same passage requires a personal search to come to correct moral behavior. This does not preclude—for the council is also attentive to this—the Spirit of God being at work in the depths of our conscience. Neither does it preclude the Spirit's address to my conscience through the Church teaching, for God's spirit has been promised in Church teaching.

Indeed, the Church accepts social encyclicals as Spirit-led. Some are tempted to distort that truth by supposing that what the Holy Spirit had not done in scriptural revelation the Spirit now does in Church teaching, namely, to lay out for the

believer a whole array of universal norms. Quite the contrary
is true. Even with the Spirit's guidance the Church arrives at
most of its statements in the social field slowly, painfully, and
with an intermix of error or of very contingent changeable
judgments. The role of the believing community as well as the
hierarchy is a further reception of revelation through reading
signs of the times.[15]

Another temptation is to be convinced that past centuries of
Catholic ecclesiastical reflection have arrived at possession of
all the norms required for moral life in any age or culture.
The present task is therefore to transfer these norms to posterity. Thus the sole task of posterity is to adhere to the rules,
accepted as universally normative, absolute, and quite
unquestionably applicable to social, political, and cultural situations never before envisioned.

Conscience, as I interpret it under the guidance especially
of Thomas Aquinas, functions at various levels. In particular
conscience guides the normative search (Aquinas's *recta ratio,*
or right reason) and then delivers the intellect's final moral
judgment to the will, that is, the command "this must be
done" (Aquinas's prudential judgment). These paired functions of the spirit, as Aquinas develops them, will be our concern in the next chapter. Thus, that chapter will divide into a
first half, on *recta ratio,* and a second, on how the ultimate
practical moral judgment is made, how the command that this
must be done, the final act of practical wisdom, is achieved.

The council referred moral problems that arise in living
together in society to the conscience functioning as guide to
the search for norms. The normative is, in large part, the work
of our own hands, of human moral creativity. In Rahner's
thought the normative of human nature is the normative of
the human person. The normative must pass through the person and personal conscious experience.

Fuchs (1990, 115) similarly holds that there is "an obligation
to lay down the path to the correct solution 'creatively' in a
responsible search that takes into consideration all the available realities, knowledge and known evaluations (including
those of the ecclesial people of God and of the Church's magisterium)." He also (in the spirit of Aquinas) recognizes that
the need to avoid putting off decision making interminably

dictates that one exercise responsibility also in ending this process "once it has been sufficient."[16]

This approach delineated in several steps constitutes a concretization of *recta ratio* in norm building. It represents a realization of the council's requirement of objectivity perceived as being achieved with God in one's inner sanctuary. In that sense, conscience participates in the divine wisdom, in God's eternal law.

What conscience seeks, then, is not exceptionless universals, but normative objectivity, an absoluteness derived from a freedom from purely personal considerations.[17] Objective norms move beyond the more limited self-evident truisms. The more concrete the normative—recall the U.S. Catholic bishops' economic pastoral with its many concrete guiding principles—the more heavily one must lean upon experience. All things being equal, those of longer and more varied experience can be expected to better weigh alternatives and consequences which will enter into moral decisions. This truth has, however, its limitations. For example, the forefathers, the tribal elders, and the bureaucracy can let their experience or their way of seeing things substitute for the new look that may be required, one that is open to the unexperienced.

Such openness—Paul VI's encyclical *Octogesima Adveniens,* which celebrates *Rerum Novarum,* calls for "utopian Christian vision"—is a thing of the spirit. This openness will be shaped by the critical spirit's taking account of the reality presented to the contemplating conscience. Undoubtedly reality will take on different complexions as the world moves on. My conscience must be prepared for the changes, even though it may have to make policy within the present shape of society.[18]

Scholars in the search for moral rightness and correctness are prepared to go even further in pressing the historicity of moral doing. Starting with the core of historicity found in the person, it is reasonable, at least in different cultures, to anticipate different personal readings. Culturally based human self-evaluation could postulate different behaviors. These scholars believe that this only reflects the conditionality that is the warp and woof of being human.

Proportionalism

How can we arrive at objective moral rightness? How do we decide the fit of concrete norms that conflict? How can we decide whether we may permit evil? If the answers to these questions have relevance for individual moral decisions, the answers are doubly important for social morality, where the abundance of norms and possibly tolerable evils are much more in evidence. Our earlier example of war illustrates the complexity typical in social morality.

A growing school of moralists called proportionalists and revisionists argue that "commensurate reason" can provide a way of resolution. Proportionalists build on the distinction between premoral values and moral values. They argue that effecting premoral evil or disvalue may not make an action wrong. The act becomes morally incorrect only when, upon due consideration, I cannot discover a commensurate or proportionate reason for permitting the premoral evil.[19] Killing is surely a premoral evil, but society could have a proportionate reason for permitting this evil. Similarly, according to just-war theory I may not directly intend the killing of the innocent; however, the indirect and unintended killing of noncombatants may be permitted for a proportionate reason.

Proportionalism has moved beyond double effect as a means of conflict resolution. Double effect determined the morality inscribed in the act as intrinsically good or evil quite apart from intention, circumstances, and so on. Hence some actions in and of themselves were universally prohibited. Proportionalism considers all the complexity set forth in the immediately preceding paragraphs to seek objectivity through the manifold relationships and consequences involved in a human act.[20] As it is set forth here, proportionalism cannot be dismissed as mere consequentialism. Proportionalism involves much more than consequences. The total moral good is weighed in a way that seeks the *proportio debita* (due or proper proportion) of *recta ratio* (right reason) in the light of faith. Weighing does not mean some mathematical balancing of components in ethical judgment or of all premoral values and disvalues.[21]

Long before I ever heard the word *proportionalist,* I was one. In the writings of Thomas Aquinas, I first encountered

the language of *recta ratio agibilium* (right reason in doing).
Normative to right reason in doing was the search for *id quod
convenit,* or that which is appropriate. In weighing this appropriateness, Aquinas bids us consider that "on account of the
different conditions of men it happens that some acts are virtuous for some, being *proportioned* [my emphasis] which,
however, are evil for other men because disproportionate"
(*ST* I–II, q. 94, a. 3, ad. 3).[22]

Summing Up

We can sum up this chapter by observing that moral making
is not fulfilling norms as if our social and individual life
existed solely to be the ground for actualizing norms. Quite
the contrary is true. In Rahner's thought the moral task is to
create and to humanize life. The social task is not to observe
natural law, but rather to use natural law, the gospel, and
human creativity to create a better world for human loving
and sharing. The current bent of theology and of the *sensus
fidei* seeks to reduce reliance on a plethora of general norms.
The recent pastoral letter of the U.S. bishops on the economy
has shown great leadership in this regard. Its guidelines to
policies, stated as contingent and open to discussion and
debate, are more prominent than its principles.

Practical Reason, Practical Wisdom, and the Retrieval of Thomas Aquinas

12

As we begin this chapter, the reader might be asking: Why retrieve Aquinas? Has theology not turned away from him? Can he really have anything useful to say to men and women of today? Certainly, women, for their part, may be repelled at the outset—and justly so—as they recall that the Divine Doctor says of females that they are misbegotten males.

But Aquinas's occasional slip into patriarchy does not prevent him from making crucial contributions to moral making (my immediate concern) and particularly, as we will see, in the political order. Johann Baptist Metz has made a similar observation about Thomas's contribution but was referring to Aquinas's broad contributions to theology. Says Matthew Lamb: "Metz's earlier work with Karl Rahner in a transcendent recovery of Thomas Aquinas had convinced him that the premodern Christian and Catholic past had intellectual, moral and religious achievements crucially important to our own discernment of what is genuine and what is false in modernity. In *Christliche Anthropozentrik*, Metz showed how an appropriation of Aquinas would enable a transposition of his treatments of being, God, grace, freedom, and the world from medieval, classical, cosmocentric to modern historical, anthropocentric thought patterns (*Denkformen*)" (Lamb 1987, 774).

Second, it is fitting that this book end with practical wisdom—that power or virtue which guides to the finality of an act of goodness, and, in this book, goodness in the social and political order. For that practical wisdom this chapter draws exclusively on the thirteenth-century theologian Thomas Aquinas.

In his very lengthy treatise, Aquinas (*ST* II–II, q. 47–56) uses the language of practical wisdom only rarely. His name for this wisdom is prudence. (I will, however, quote below one instance of his use of practical wisdom.) But prudence builds upon the previous contribution to the final moral act made by practical reason. In slightly different language, the precise determination and command of a specific action to be taken is the work of the practical (moral) virtue of prudence. But that precise determination will have been advanced through the crucible of the intellectual virtue of practical reason. Practical reason, working on universals, primary or derivative, hones these into ends of action.

Unfortunately, the word *prudence* conveys to modern readers, especially English-speaking ones, the notion "don't rock the boat" or "let's not be too hasty," which often implies "better do nothing rather than make a mistake." *Prudence* translates into "cautiousness." Actually, the word as used by Aquinas derives from the Latin *providere*. In English the noun form is "providence." It suggests foresight and looking over the field of proposed action to catch sight of the right course.

Practical wisdom (prudence) is still much an act of reason. Its scope is to formulate the final command to the will: This must be done. *Practical wisdom* accurately translates the sense of Aquinas's prudence while avoiding the misunderstanding the latter may induce.

In preceding chapters, I dwell at length with the contemporary concern to ground social thinking in its social context. There is much of that, I submit, in Aquinas. It might be well to recall here that I devote an earlier section to Rahner's turn to the subject. I also attempted to show that, although he has been criticized for failing to elaborate the sociality of the subject, Rahner made an important contribution to this topic, particularly in his notion of the unity of love of God and of neighbor. What certainly can be said of Aquinas is that his concept of political prudence could well provide us with a model for how to get to practical wisdom in the social order.

In Thomas, that practical wisdom (or prudence) is preceded by an act of the intellect, guided by the will and practical reason. That act of practical reason was the operative virtue of the last chapter, where we asked how we can get to concrete norms of moral rightness or moral correctness. If practical reason has already been treated, why do I return to it in this chapter? I would answer that here we have a more formal treatment of that virtue of the intellect, one I discovered on reading, decades ago: Aquinas. In addition, I do not know any modern treatment of the content of the preceding chapter that is more perceptive than the treatment of the thirteenth-century Dominican. For that reason I want to resurrect Aquinas's cogent explanation for today's readers in Catholic social teaching.

Readers here may be puzzled. I write so much in the preceding chapters of the renewal in method of doing Catholic social teaching which I have personally undergone. Yet in this chapter, I now endorse totally my early encounter with Catholic social teaching. But that is the point. I am retrieving Aquinas—the proto-Aquinas—from the neo-Thomism or neo-scholasticism rampant in my earlier days.

Consequently, in this chapter I have a second objective besides explaining what good methodology in Catholic social teaching now looks like to me. This is to urge readers not to neglect Aquinas's remarkable accounting of practical reason and practical wisdom.

I have one other preliminary remark—even warning—to make. I use Aquinas's own language extensively. This risks turning off readers untuned to a language not of our day. But I am rejecting the other option, namely, stating Aquinas's ideas in today's language and referring readers to Aquinas's texts in the notes. Readers can, of course, skim these texts.

Practical Reason (*Ratio Practica*)

In 1951 I wrote an article with George Klubertanz, S.J., then editor of *The Modern Schoolman,* a journal aimed at retrieving a true Scholasticism from the distortions wrought by neo-scholasticism (Land and Klubertanz 1951).[1] Our article attacked the abstractionism in the older natural law described as purely deductive, a notional basis of definition and deduction. Acknowledging our indebtedness to a French social philosopher, Simon Deploige (1923, 261), we quoted, as I did in chapter 11, his praise of the sociologists for opposing such abstractionism in natural law.

We went on to point out that in spite of such statements both Thomistic theory and practice appear to many Thomists and non-Thomists, both in the field of ethics in general and of social ethics in particular, to be analytico-deductive. We challenged this concept in the following manner.

The Nature of Practical Reasoning

Practical knowledge, according to Aquinas, is such that we cannot deduce detailed, specific conclusions with certitude: "Knowledge of contingents cannot have certitude of knowledge that 'repels' all error" (*Eth* IV lect. 3; cf. *Eth* I lect. 3, 32–35). Thomas's chief reason is that the objects of human action are contingent; he writes of "the variable truth of contingent operations, which are the matter of virtue" (*Eth* II lect. 2, 256). His conclusion was that reasoning about such objects would be affected by a similar contingency: "and since this is so [contingency of the subject matter], it will be necessary to reflect carefully [*perscrutari*] to discover which of our acts are those to be done" (ibid.).[2]

Practical reasoning for Thomas is similar to taking counsel (*Eth* VI lect. 4, 1164–66). It is compositive (synthetic) rather than resolutory (analytic) (*Eth* I lect. 3, 35) and proceeds from the parts to the whole. Practical reason can and must be contrasted with analytical or speculative reasoning:

> Just as every judgment of speculative reason proceeds from a natural knowledge of first principles, so too, every judgment of practical reason proceeds from certain naturally known principles. . . . But the processes by which we come to judge about different objects are themselves of different kinds. For there are some things in human action

which are so evident that with but a modicum of reflection they can be immediately approved or disapproved by means of those common and first principles. But there are others which to be judged need a full consideration of different circumstances. . . (*ST* I–II q. 100, a. 1).

After applying this consideration of the differences of natural reason to natural law, Thomas continues:

And so it is clear that moral precepts pertain to good morals; good morals are such as are in harmony with reason; and every judgment of human reason flows in some way from natural reason. Hence, it follows that all moral precepts belong to the law of nature but in different ways. For there are some that are immediately judged to be done or not to be done by the natural reason of every man. . . . Others need a more subtle consideration of reason. . . (ibid.).

According to this analysis of Aquinas, we must distinguish among (*a*) first principles of the practical order, (*b*) judgments arrived at by simple applications of these principles to some human actions, and (*c*) the judgments made upon consideration of diverse and changeable circumstances (*ST* I–II, q. 94, a. 5, 6; q. 100, a. 1, 11). None of these is purely deductive. First principles clearly cannot be deduced, otherwise they would be conclusions, not principles. First principles are understood in experience. The second class of judgments may be thought of as deduced provided that we admit that deduction may have a minor premise drawn from experience. Judgments of the third class, those dependent on a "full consideration of different circumstances" evidently are not reached by a purely deductive process, but depend largely upon observational or experiential procedures.

In brief, Thomas's practical reason is heavily based on experience. Both secondary and tertiary principles of this reasoning are derived only after repeated and at times lengthy return to experience. These conclusions are inductive not only in their origins but throughout the reasoning process. Practical reasoning must stay close to reality.

Particular Problems of Method
in the Practical Sciences

A number of particular problems of method arise in the practical sciences. We will address four of these.

First, there is the problem of second nature. Aquinas reminds the reader: "Habit has the force of nature" (*Eth* II lect. 3; cf. *Eth* III lect. 15), that is, of a second nature. So diverse are people that one can speak of them as "so many species of animals." If habit has the force of a second nature, this is doubly true of habits acquired from youth (*vim naturae obtinet*). Whence it follows that ideas acquired in youth hold as if they were natural and per se known." This strikes me as a remarkable attenuation of rigid natural law. People hold to custom learned early in life as if *"naturaliter et per se nota"* (naturally recognized as flowing from human nature) (*CG* I, 11).

The language of Thomas at this point is not unlike that of Rahner. Human beings, constituted of two substantial principles, soul and body, live a physical life in which the formal and actuating principle is ceaselessly actuating the material and potential. There is, accordingly, a variable element in concrete facts and relationships that are to be ordered to our end.

Thomas explains the relation of second nature to first nature or the influence of social conditions upon conclusions of natural law in this way: "That which belongs to the natural law is modified according to the different states and conditions of human beings," and the "diversities of times" (*SL* IV 26, 1.1, ad. 3, 4). Finally, different forms of social and political life must be considered (*diversos modos communitatum*) (*ST* I–II, q. 100, a. 2).

Second, Thomas's treatment of the concrete situation is both Rahnerian and a key to post–Vatican moral theology. The essential point addresses the role of relationships in moral making. Aquinas says this: "On account of the different conditions of men it happens that some acts are virtuous for some men, as being proportionate and suited to them. Yet these same acts are vicious for others as not being proportioned for them" (*ST* I–II q. 94, a. 3, ad. 3).[3] For Aquinas the situation in which people stand relative to one another produces the measure of their moral responsibility.

Why, for instance, is divorce evil? Aquinas holds that "it is not a sufficient answer if one says that it is an offense against God. For God is not offended by us, except in this, that we act against our own good" (*CG* III 122). Here, too, Aquinas stands athwart all of those deontologists who argue that there is an intrinsic evil in the act considered by itself (Millar 1940).[4]

As Rahner had to face the charge that his moral making skirted near situational ethics, so Klubertanz and I recognized that some would make the same charge against these expressions of Thomas. Our answer in defense of Aquinas is the same Rahner used for himself, namely, the relational is objective; it is situational de jure, which is quite different from arbitrary acts of human wills.

What we discovered in Aquinas was an effort to reach the inner order of society that is the common good realized, but a common good that is the work of particular men and women of their time and place. We saw a further particularizing factor of these social relationships[5] in the *idèe directive* of the French institutionalists, whose thinking I had found very insightful in preparing my doctoral dissertation as narrated in my autobiographical chapter. The *idèe directive* initiate social activity, as do other cultural and even technological factors impinging on human relationships.

Following Aquinas, Klubertanz and I affirmed that the ethician should be prepared for a shifting proportioning of the common good that reflects the reordering as relations between human beings shift. This proportioning possesses a dynamic movement forward as against a purely static shifting of positions around a stable equilibrium.

Social Ordering

The third problem is social ordering. Thomas's procedure here is by way of "invention" and "composition." These are his tools for seeking "that situation in which men stand relatively to one another." This inventiveness of freely participating intelligences and wills will inevitably move down a variety of paths. In Thomas's words: "The end is fixed for man by nature. But the means to the end are not determined for us by nature: they are to be sought out by reason" (*Eth* IV lect. 2).

After having spoken of those conclusions of the natural law which are derived by deduction, Thomas gives this concrete example: "But the conclusions which are derived from the law of nature by way of particular determination belongs to the civil law, according as every state proportionately determines something for itself" (*ST* I–II, q. 95, a. 4).

The situation "in which men stand relatively to one another" is also the key idea in Saint Thomas's political theory. Therein his awareness of the need for an experiential starting point leads him to seek out what well-ruled people do and what men and women of practical wisdom propose: "The rightness of a law is expressed in relation to the common utility, to which one and the same thing is not always suited" (*Pol* II lect. 1).

Among the determinants of the ideal state are (1) the condition of the people and the objectives sought: "In the state there is need to observe the regional diversity according to the diversity of conditions of the subjects of the states and according to the diversity of the ends toward which they are ordered,"[6] (2) the virtue of the people (*ST* I–II, q. 97, a. 1), and (3) the virtue that can be expected in the available rulers (*Pol* III lect. 13; *ST* I–II, q. 105, a. 1, ad. 2).

The preceding really says nothing we do not know from our own experience. We know that people differ—they have developed different habits, outlooks, and cultural traits. There are nations of seers and nations of bridge builders. Societies, like persons, are creatures of habits both in thought and in action. Like individuals, societies grow. Accordingly, social order has temporal and spatial dimensions. In addition, the natural law as lived by a people is bound by space and time; it is situated in the concrete, and the situation of one people cannot be presumed to give an appropriate reading for another people or another culture.

Role for Ethical Insight and Experience

The place of ethical insight and experience is the fourth methodological problem Klubertanz and I considered. We concluded that the ethical judgment of Saint Thomas is a practical judgment based upon insight into a situation. For this, the appropriate method of ethical science is that of invention and composition or of the full consideration of varying circumstances. That insight must be, first, reasonable (*ST* I–II q. 90, a. 1);[7] second, unhindered by passions; third, mature (*SL* II 24 q.1, a. 1, ad. 3); fourth, informed "about the situation in which men stand relative to one another" (*Eth* I lect. 1, 4);[8] and fifth, the fruit of patient and enduring work of investigation (*Pol* II q.1, a.5; cf. *ST* I–II, q. 100, a. 1).

To these five requirements Aquinas adds an overall consideration: moral insight must be dynamic. The development of natural law prepares us to appreciate the fact that social insight advances over time. "It seems," says Aquinas, "to be natural to human reason to develop slowly from the imperfect to the perfect. . . . For the first men, who intended to discover something useful for the human community, being themselves unable to consider everything, instituted some things which were imperfect and deficient in many points. But later generations changed these institutions, setting up new institutions which could fail in fewer points from the commonweal" (*ST* I–II, q. 97, a. 1). This dynamic may sound too like evolutionary progressivism, but there is surely some kernel of truth in a heritage of insight upon which succeeding generations build.

Practical Wisdom

One of the most thrilling intellectual discoveries I ever made was learning that I could be wrong and still be right. If I did my level best to make the right decision and it turned out to be the wrong one, I still did right. Making decisions is generally a calculated risk, so if I worked as best I could at my calculation, the resulting decision, however it turned out, was a morally good decision. Although this may sound banal or only the ethic of an erroneous conscience, that is not correct.

As I began after my discovery to spread the good news in lectures, I discovered that my good news was sort of a best-kept secret for most students. It also rounded out my efforts and my preoccupation then and now to relate natural law to the historical order in which societies had to make decisions in very complex situations.

Ultimately, I owed my discovery to Saint Thomas Aquinas. More proximately, however, I owed it to an eminent Dominican commentator on Aquinas, Thomas Deman (1949, q. 47–56). Deman had written nearly three hundred pages, divided between "notes explicatives" of Aquinas's nine questions on prudence and an appendix of "notes doctrinales." With Deman to guide me, I explored the several treatises in which Aquinas treats of prudence or practical wisdom. These include, besides the long treatise in the *Summa Theologiae* II–II (q. 47–56), the commentary on the *Nichomachean Ethics* and *Quaestiones Disputatae de Veritate.*

As I am indebted to George Klubertanz, S.J., for the first part of this chapter, so I am indebted to another Jesuit, Francis Marien, with whom I collaborated in St. Louis on a series of lectures, "Prudence in the Thomistic Ethical System." (Unlike the commentaries with Klubertanz, Marien and I wrote separate commentaries on "Practical Wisdom in the Social Thought of Jacques Maritain," for the November 1955 *Social Order.*) My contribution introduced the remarkably illuminating ideas of Aquinas on what I came to regard as core to the moral life of individuals as well as of society, albeit in a roundabout way. Because few were interested in Thomism (because neo-scholasticism had corrupted it) but were deeply interested in Maritain, I decided to profit from the latter's profound analysis of Aquinas's ethical system. So I wrote a sort of Maritain reader on prudence according to Aquinas which drew on the French philosopher's many books on the subject and was based on his profound grounding in Aquinas.[9] In the following pages I treat Aquinas's practical wisdom in general and specifically with regard to the political order.

In the lectures to which I refer above, I told an audience of some two hundred fifty sisters—a witness that, while male ecclesiastics, poisoned by neo-Thomism, were unwilling to essay an effort to retrieve the true Thomism, women were open to fresh ideas—that my great saint of Thomistic practical wisdom was Teresa of Avila. I cited her decision, recounted in one of her letters, whether to close a convent in Avila. (She did not; centuries later I visited that house.) Teresa wrote that by nine o'clock of the morrow she would have to make her decision. She affirmed that however she decided, she would make a good decision.

Although it is perfectly true that a day later she and her council might believe the decision had been an unwise one because, let us say, some new information had come to light. But nevertheless the decision when made and as made was a morally good one because it furthered God's kingdom.

The decision was good because she had considered all the elements in making a good moral discernment. We turn to these considerations in a moment, but first must define the nature of this virtue in itself. Moral discernment or practical wisdom is an intellectual virtue: "For prudence it is required that one be a good reasoner (*bene ratiocinativus*) so that one can apply well universal principles to particularities which are of their nature variable and uncertain" (*ST* II–II, q. 49, a. 5, ad. 2).

Aquinas explains the need for good reasoning: "The particular operables in which prudence directs recede from the condition of being intelligibles, and only so much the more as they are less certain or determinate" (ibid.).

But this very practical knowledge (*prakticon,* that is, knowledge which makes) must proceed from a "well ordered appetite" or desire for the end of moral life (*NE* VI lect. 1). Prudence, unlike other more speculative exercises of the intellect, is not concerned with affirming or denying, but rather for pursuing and avoiding in accordance with desire. But the desire for the end requires further specification of the means that will lead to that good end. Desire (appetite) and deliberation must end in the choice of those means which are deemed best suited to achieve the end sought by our desiring.

The reasoning of practical wisdom or prudence is always directed toward an end, something to be done. But prudence depends on both desire and appetite. Aquinas endlessly insists on a "rectified appetite," about which we speak later.[10]

But it is up to practical wisdom (prudence) to determine and to direct the will on its road toward the end (although other moral virtues aid the will to elect). This direction begins with prudence's knowledge of the universal, which it uses as a major premise. But in its chief function, namely, specificity, practical wisdom issues precepts applicable here and now to the movement of the appetite. Thus prudence must know the contingency in which it makes its determination and command the will.

Such determination in the contingent order requires long deliberation, consultation, experience, and cultivation of the moral virtues which appertain to practical wisdom (*ST* II–II q. 48, a. 15 and 15 ad. 3). Thomas also suggests circumspection is needed (*ST* II–II q. 49, a. 7). By this he means that one must consider all the circumstances involved in a choice as well as exercise caution, which seeks to avoid what may be inopportune in a context.

Thomas has another operation within the cogitative of practical wisdom, which he calls intuitive reason or *ratio particularis*. (*NE* IV lect. 7; *DV* 15, a. 1). Intuitive reason affects all judgments of practical wisdom as also judgments of art. It operates with less of the rational and more of the irrational or the instinctive estimate of the good, that is, more of a feel for the situation. Differences of cultures, ways of doing, or arts cannot be reduced to reason. In the human, however, these differences are affected by reason. The way of life of a people is a summation of the means they choose. In the means chosen, which are a matter of practical wisdom, each people has taken their own route with the conviction that this particular way was their way, right for their particular character, and apt to achieve their idea of the good life.

To put this another way, intuitive reason is a faculty for infrarational generalization of contingent facts to fit new situations into that generalization as the occasion arises. It builds on Aquinas's "what is generally true" (*quod in pluribus sit verum*). Intuitive reason is the fruit of experience in which the memory of one instance is added to that of others until we feel confident that the generalization holds and can be acted on in this newest instance. According to Thomas, we do not need a philosopher's knowledge of the universals governing a particular situation to act prudently.[11]

Prudence, Aquinas insists, must know the singular, since it is action; it is the principle of acting. For action has as its object the singular. Hence, some who do not have knowledge of universals are more active in what concerns the singular than are some who possess knowledge of the universal.

This is because they are expert in some particulars. Aquinas therefore concludes: "Hence from the fact that prudence is active reason (*ratio activa*) it is necessary that the prudent one have both knowledges [of universal and of singular]. But if he can have only one of the two, it would be better to have knowledge of the particular and of the closer to action" (*NE* IV lect. 7).[12]

But all this deliberation is not the principal act of practical wisdom, of prudence. Practical wisdom, or prudence, gives the will a specific command: This must be done. John of Saint Thomas, Aquinas's most important commentator, explains: "There are in prudence two parts: the one concerned with judgment and counsel; the other concerned with command, and preceptive [*imperium et praeceptum*] or application of what was judged and counselled over" (*Log* II q.1, a. 3).

Of this latter command he goes on to say that "It is the principal act of prudence. This second act of practical wisdom does not look to the objects to be ordered, for that belongs to reason. Rather, it directly concerns itself with the applying of the will to elicit an act about the objects reasoned over" (ibid.). For the commentator the principal practical difficulty lies here: "prudence in its principal act formally looks toward the eliciting of acts of the will. . ." (ibid.). The object of this intellectual operation is the contingent, an indeterminate subject matter awaiting forming and fashioning by the determining principle of practical reason.[13]

In a parallel situation, Aquinas says: "Prudence is needed . . . [because] there is need for deliberation" (*ST* II–II q. 47, a. 2, ad. 2 and q. 47, a. 3). Aquinas does not insist upon the term *practical wisdom,* although he observes that prudence is a practical wisdom in that it is ordered to the total well-being and not to a single limited end (*ST* II–II q. 47, a. 1, ad. 1). Aquinas adds that the prudent one is not only a wise person. She or he is also an artist who considers measures and means and is skilled in seeking these means (*ST* II–II, q. 47, a. 2, ad. 1; q. 57, a. 4, ad. 3; see also *ST* I–II, q. 21, a. 2, ad. 2). "In practical knowledge, the artist [*artifex*] works out the form of his artistic work and knows by doing."[14]

Here I should address a question that may have arisen: practical wisdom, in its cognitive part, seems much like the practical reason at the beginning of this chapter. The simple answer is that practical wisdom (prudence) carries forward the cognitive operation of practical reason. Its cognitive function is to determine a unique command: This must be done. (In shaping that command it is aided by a right appetite for the end which is moral goodness.) Once the action has been so determined, practical wisdom proceeds to its most important function, that of commanding that the action be done.

Rules of Practical Wisdom

Building on our own reading of Aquinas, Francis Marien and I produced the following table of what is involved in being good in reasoning (*bene ratiocinativus*) so that one can apply universal principles to "particulars that are varied and uncertain."[15]

> A. Knowledge of the rules of prudence and comprehension of the problem and the variability and uncertainty of the contingent
>> Careful deliberation above all to penetrate into the situation and what it appears to require
>> Willingness to seek counsel
>> Resistance to impulses, to indifference about the results, and to weariness in seeking the best means
>> Flexibility to change as error is detected
>> Appreciation of compensation to help balance prudential decisions
>> Care to develop experience from which one derives one's universal, one's immediate rules of action, and one's generally true (*ut in pluribus*) rules, which usually fit the situation
>> Attention to the imaginative side of one's nature, which with the *vis cogitativa* helps provide insight into the human situation; for example, sensitivity about severe punishment or sensitivity to the impossible demands of probity we may place on politicians

> B. Right Appetite (Aquinas's *appetitus rectificatus*) to
> follow the rules and to reason
>> without prejudice
>> with honesty about one's limitations and one's
>> need to consult
>> with acceptance of the limitations implicit to the
>> contingent order
>> with readiness to admit mistakes
>> with simplicity in accepting advice even from
>> people whose opinion is not highly regarded
> C. Apply the rules (A) under guidance of right
> appetite (B) to make the prudential judgment
> D. Command the will to accept the prudential judgment

Because we are in an order of grace these four steps of practical wisdom each have its graced aspect. In the search for advice where needed, I include God's Holy Spirit. In summary, let me state the problem and solution of practical wisdom. That the problem I am judging exists in the individual, the nonrepeatable, and the obscure is reflected in Aquinas's thought that particular operations are removed from the condition of being intelligible the more uncertain and undetermined they be.

A look at the problem through the eyes of Aquinas shows the following syllogism:

MAJOR PREMISE. I must act justly.

MINOR PREMISE. Justice requires in this instance that I do this specific action.

CONCLUSION. Therefore I must do it.

Since the precise question is in the minor premise, how do I fashion that singular proposition? We have already quoted Aquinas's comment that prudent action especially requires that one be able to reason well to apply principles to particulars which are varied and uncertain.

But prudence is not just an intellectual operation. It proceeds from an *appetitus rectificatus,* a desire of the right end. The minor premise is the effort of the intellect to find appropriate means to that end, although no single means is wholly desirable. It is precisely because the prudent person is in love with the end that she or he seeks earnestly the right means to that end. A person would not be virtuous if she or he did not throw all her or his resources into the effort and did not develop skills as years go on. To paraphrase words of Thomas already seen, prudence itself seeks the end, since if we suppose the end is chosen by the will, prudence goes in quest of the means to win and keep this good.

Infallibility of Practical Wisdom

Let us turn now to the infallibility of practical wisdom. I observed earlier that when Teresa of Avila had to make a decision that could not be put off any longer than the day and hour she specified in her letter, she wrote that she was certain that it would be good before God. Thomas distinguishes between the infallibility of speculative and of practical knowledge. The infallibility of speculative knowledge lies between the intellect and its *object,* while for practical knowledge, infallibility comes from following a right or rectified appetite (*appetitus rectificatus*). But practical knowledge involves the activity of the intellect, the practical reason, working out from a right appetite to direct the final practical judgment. That rectification is embodied for me in the above rules Marien and I worked out from Aquinas.

One of the most helpful notes of Deman 1949 is several pages clarifying Aquinas's two kinds of knowledge and their respective infallibilities. He quotes one eminent early commentator on this distinction, John of Saint Thomas: "In practical virtues infallibility (*infallibilitas*) is to be taken practically, and its truth is not regulated by what is or is not in reality." No, in practical wisdom "we are dealing with contingent reality and that could be otherwise than it is." Hence, in practical knowing, the infallibility is derived from right appetite (for the end) flowing into action through the virtue of practical wisdom (prudence). "This prudential judgment makes use of a certain and correct rule, not as certain to achieve the events (*in assecurando eventu*) but in assuring proper procedure. . . . For it is certain and infallible that whoever makes use in such contingent events of counsel and is as diligent as possible proceeds correctly" (*ST* I–II; *DV* 16, a. 4).

In other words, prudence does not give us certainty about the event, but it does give us certainty that we act virtuously when we follow the rules of moral choice in a situation which allows the solution we choose, but does not call for nor command it as unique and necessary. Consequently the certitude of practical wisdom lies in Thomas's *appetitus rectificatus,* a well-ordered desire that includes working through the rules of prudence.

But Aquinas, at this point, wrestles with a problem. Is the judgment of the practical virtue of prudence devoid of objectivity? What sort of truth does it possess? Is it enough that one have a good intention to be absolved of any duty to seek in the contingent order the truth of the situation?

Here again, Thomas Deman, O.P. (1949, 459–79), thoroughly explores the background Aristotle provides to Thomas's answer together with Aquinas's own evolving understanding from one treatment of the question to another until it becomes definitive (and enduringly accepted).

The lengthy commentary by Deman comes to this: It is clear that there can be no speculative virtue pertaining to the contingent simply because the speculative reason is necessarily or infallibly conformed to the truth of its object. If there is an infallible knowing of the contingent it must be by recognizing in the intellect of another the perfection that is accommodated to this requirement. The practical intellect makes this recognition, for its truth is in the act of directing and that direction is infallibly true in the contingent provided that direction is conformed to a right appetite for the end. In other language, for Aquinas the intellectual virtue, in its knowing function (which is always true) and in its human operative function, will be infallibly true if based on a right appetite.

Deman here calls upon another eminent early commentator on Aquinas's treatise on prudence, John of Saint Thomas, who adds: "Speculative truth differs from practical truth insofar as the former is determined by what is or is not reality, whereas practical truth is not regulated by this conformity to reality but by what *ought* to be according to duty or obligation and measure of the human person."

If the truth of practical wisdom lies with the ultimate practical judgment being conformed to the appetite for the end, does this obviate working at conforming the judgment to the truth of reality, of what is? Here Aquinas answers that the prudent person will seek as much as possible of this conformity to reality. For the virtue of prudence is a habilitation of reason providing it with the capacity to adapt action as much as possible to the exigencies of reality. Were all at stake the question of right appetitive behavior, there would be no need of the intellectual virtue of prudence. Or, to state it in other words, an appetite sincerely right demands a reason fortified with all the equalities that help the action respond truly to the end proposed.

Right reason is operative in both speculative and practical reason but differently and with different infallibilities. In the latter, in the domain of things that make for the end desired (*ea quae sunt ad finem*), reason directs and appetite submits.

Now questions arise. First, if the typical situation is one in which we do not know what to do, does that not throw the moral life of individual and society into a quagmire of uncertainty? Happily, in the moral order we do have certainties, most important ones. We have the metaphysical certainties of our own existence, namely, that we can know truth and that we can reason to fundamentals. These separate us from skepticism. In addition, we have the ultimate truths of revelation, our supernatural end, and assurance of the means for getting there. In the moral life itself, besides all these truths of principle and the guide of our human nature, we have God's commandments, which shore up the certainty of natural commandments. Applying these as well as Church guidance is subject to further specification by practical wisdom with its uncertainty.

Aquinas (questions 47 and 49, among others) observes that prudent people will, especially through experience, know how to narrow the infinite possibilities that surround making a decision, reducing them to a manageable few from which finally to choose. The contingent does not rebel against rule or ordering, but the situation may be so opaque, so complicated, that one's understanding of it is limited. It may carry one into the realm of the unforeseeable.

Aiding us to work our way through these tangles will be right appetite for the end which will just as much prompt the intellect to zeal in searching for the truth of the contingent. Aiding us also is the gift of counsel (question 52). This is the gift of the Holy Spirit helping our fallibility. It is needed pre-cisely because in prudence it is not enough to have a right intention, for, as described above, prudence works to achieve indispensable objectivity. It will not do to argue that we are powerless to arrive at a more correct decision. Such an answer does not deliver us from the consequences for us and for others of the incorrectness of many of our judgments. The required objectivity is guaranteed by counsel (question 52), that is, the gift of the Holy Spirit.

Three implications of Aquinas's theological treatise on the nature of practical wisdom (prudence) should be noted. First, in the typical situation, however we decide, we could have decided otherwise. The typical situation possesses no certain scientific conclusions necessarily and universally true. As I have said perhaps too often, the prudential judgment of prac-tical wisdom is one that has to be *made*—it is a *prakticon*. I and only I (in individual morality) decide. For a community or society it is exactly the same, as we shall see shortly.

Second, is it not possible to make a decision with goodwill, therefore virtuously, even though it does not work through the rules of practical wisdom appearing here? I presume that there could be such a virtuous act. But from the nature of the rules set forth here, I would have to say that it would lack the true moral virtue of practical wisdom since it lacks the reason-ableness that the prudential seeks to educe.

Third, does the uncertainty of the prudential judgment dry up effort to get at moral truth? I would answer that it should rather help since I no longer need be harassed by the fear that I may make a mistake, and for that reason hesitate to decide. The prudent person knows well that she or he may make a mistake, but is not hampered by that knowledge. Indeed, practical wisdom may reduce the number of mistakes, for it embraces a willingness to admit errors, to change, to compensate, to seek counsel, to grow through experience, and to be flexible. Above all, it recognizes that we need divine guidance.

Practical wisdom does, however, make the following demands upon the moral person:

Responsibleness in accepting the task of working out
    prudential choices in moral decisions

Resoluteness in grappling with our lives as they are, with
their complex implications

Humility to acknowledge our limitations and errors

Effort to grow in prudential experience, to become more
fit to cope properly with our responsibilities

Effort to see the unapparent providence of God working
in and through the prudential decisions that we as
individuals and as societies make

A Cautionary Word

Here a reader of a draft of this book made this observation: to
my asserting "I could be wrong and still be right"—that, he
said, is a good point, "but I would tend to balance it with a
comment on the immense amount of human suffering and
ontic evil caused in our world by people making Thomistically
'prudent' decisions, whose unintended consequences in fact are
disastrous for themselves and/or others. Some folks make prudent decisions a lot better than other folks."

That is absolutely true, and I can only hope that I have
been adequately guarded in my exposition. Still, I am uneasy
enough about possible misunderstanding to add the following
somewhat cursory concluding remarks; most are repeats.

First of all, there are the moral certitudes we possess; for
example, the capacity to know truth, the ultimate truths of
revelation, the true end of human life, and the kernel of God's
commandments.

The crux of the problem for me (as for my readers) is that
in the typical situation, however we decide, we might have
decided otherwise. The doing of charity is accomplished in
concrete and singular situations, in a welter of indefinite, contingent circumstances. My charitable act is willed by my
incommunicable person. The resulting act does not possess
knowableness until I have posited the act. Aquinas's way of
saying that is *"in cognitione practica artifex excogitat formam
artificii et scit per modum operandi"* (In practical knowledge,
the skilled agent thinks through a work's design but recognizes its true worth only in its actual execution).

Put another way, we are in the field of means to ends. Most
means are approximations to an end. No one of them can be

demonstrated to be wholly desirable. Our experience of them manifests that all are in some aspect unsatisfactory. All this being true, the only route that can preserve our sanity is that of accepting our human fallibility. Yet act we must. We have to do something with the situations that confront us. We have to try to hit the mean of justice, of temperance, and of fortitude.

We can act in the conviction that if we have done our best to form a truly moral judgment we have done moral good. Furthermore, even persons possessing the fullness of practical wisdom will make incorrect (though morally good) decisions. We have all to allow God to write straight with our crooked lines. Still, we do have the capacity, despite the contingency out of which we make moral decisions, to arrive not only at the good but at the correct. Remember Aquinas's "a prudent man must be good in reasoning" (*bene ratiocinativus*). To demonstrate how to be good in reasoning I assembled my above rendition of Aquinas's rules of art in moral making. There, in his wondrous word, we are artists.

Practical Wisdom in the Political Order

We turn now to political prudence. Everything I have said thus far about practical wisdom, or prudence; about the prudential judgment; and about the virtue which makes it possible applies to the political order as well. Thus we encounter

the final principle of good to be done, which is the norm of political life

a desire (appetite) for that good which must be ever present to urge the practical intellect to choose only such means as bring us to the good political life

the political prudential judgment, which selects from the complexity of political life the line of action which will best lead to the good life of the citizen

We earlier noted that humans are endowed with a natural habit of knowing the end of moral action. We naturally know that good is to be done. What we now must stress is that this good to be done embraces all of our human good, not just individual good, but the *common good,* which is also necessary for the fulfillment of the human person. A widely accepted definition of the common good in Catholic social teaching is "the sum total of all those conditions of social living—economic, political and cultural—which make it possible for men and women readily and fully to achieve the perfection of their humanity. Individual rights are always experienced within the context of the promotion of the common good" (*MM*). (This definition, as I point out in the chapter on natural law, fails to include the riches of being together that also constitute the common good, but for now we can work with the more limited definition.)

Aristotle perceived the value of such civic good. For him, human goodness necessarily embraced civic good, the good of the *polis*. Hence, it could only be achieved within the order of citizenry, where alone social cooperation could be achieved.

As with the individual end, there is an appetite for the social good. This can quite properly be said to be social justice: "All institutions of public life ought to be imbued with this virtue. Succinctly, social justice is the virtue prompting to contribute to the common good" (*QA* 88). For some, social love is a virtue additional to social justice. I am inclined to believe that social justice is only a way of stating more specifically that love of neighbor, and social love of a social neighbor, which occupies us in an earlier chapter.

As with the individual prudential judgment, we come to the problem of making right decisions about the means to accomplishing the common good which are the right political means to gain the good city. Clearly, given the variety of choices, none are absolutely compelling; we must have rules for choosing. The question could also be phrased as how political author-ity (we can, for the moment, prescind from whether the regime is a monarchy, an aristocracy, or a democracy) chooses a right course of action. Political prudence, or, in my terminology, political practical wisdom is the virtue that decides, as decide a people must, in favor of the common good for all those areas of complexity and uncertainty. Political practical wisdom alone can guarantee the impress of reason on legislation. Aquinas says: "It is that virtue by which one rules the multi-tude to the accomplishment of the total good life" (*ST* II–II q. 47, a. 4).

Prudence aids the politician, the lawgiver, but, in a democracy, all citizens enter one way or another into the process of bringing about the common good. Indeed, it would be a mistake to follow Aristotle's narrowing of politics to a lawgiver, a monarch, or an oligarchy. Prudence makes those bearing responsibility for the common good seek out all the knowledge that is pertinent to achieving the common good, whether through legislation or the creation of nongovernmental institutions that promote the common good or even just individual creative efforts.

Prudence makes available at this political level the same aid given in individual discernment of means to the end. Thus the lawgiver and all others responsible for the common good are given a sense of which relationships are at once practical and fitting for society, thus deserving of legislation. Political wisdom also enables those responsible to appreciate the need for prolonged attention when the obscurity of the facts demands. It prompts them to consult with those who can supply their lack of knowledge about political theory, practical wisdom, factual knowledge, or experience.

As a wisdom specifically of action, prudence manifests itself in the wit of the politician as she or he faces decisions of often incomprehensible complexity. It shows itself as the politician skillfully lays bare the essential issues and understands the practicality of the situation.

Thomas addresses another question of political prudence, namely, the authority to make a final decision. From the very nature of the prudential, a judgment can never have that demonstrable certainty of scientific judgments. Since the need to act makes it impossible to put off the judgment any longer, all that can be expected is that a decision represents the best judgment of means under the circumstances of available knowledge at the time of decision making.

Clearly, if a community embraces such judgments, it cannot embrace them unanimously. There are always those who believe they know a better course. Consequently, for unanimity not of judgment but of action the prudential judgment arrived at must be authoritative, that is, it must bind the cooperating members of a society. Authority, in short, is needed precisely because someone must decide on an action, and all must accept it although it cannot be demonstrated with certainty to be the best action.

Although we set aside the problem of who exercises political prudence in a democracy, we hint that the virtue must reside in all who bear responsibility for the common good. Aquinas is not helpful here, for he envisioned a totally different political order. The principle, however, stands. In a democracy all should possess and exercise political prudence, or political practical wisdom. This principle obviously permits different degrees of the virtue according to the responsibilities one bears for the good of society.

A too narrow definition of *political* could obviate widespread possession and exercise of political prudence. Maritain has pointed out that for Aristotle the word *politics* is more nearly equivalent to our *sociopolitical order.* Similarly the encyclical *Quadragesimo Anno* speaks of the social and political art (*ars socialis politica*).

At minimum, all have the responsibility to vote and to exercise practical political wisdom with their vote. Beyond that, the citizenry are obliged to keep themselves informed and to exert whatever influence one can on proposed legislation. Prudence shows itself in the citizenry's ability to accept approximation to the ideal when that is all politicians can reasonably work out for the moment.

Pius XII had this to say on our subject: "When people call for a democracy and better democracy, that demand can have no other meaning than that citizens shall be increasingly placed in a position to hold their own opinions, to voice them, and to make them effective in promoting the general welfare. Further, it is not a matter of indifference whether one undertakes to hold and voice opinions and make them effective in promoting public good. It is the proper task of a person conscious of his own responsibility" (Pius XII, *Christmas Message,* 1944).

Christians and Practical Political Wisdom

Earlier chapters make clear that we actually live in the order of redemption. It is supernatural; it is an order of grace. Therefore, it has many ramifications for Catholic social teaching and for political wisdom. For a Christian, this wisdom includes revelation. We have seen expressions from the council such as that the gospel sheds light on this world's tasks. The gospel also gives a force for carrying them out. This raises the question of whether the Christian, active in the political order, acts as a Christian. To get at the answer, let us recall certain understandings growing out of Vatican II.

First, the autonomy of earthly things. "If by the autonomy of earthly affairs we mean that created things and societies enjoy their own laws and values . . . then it is entirely right to demand that autonomy. Therefore if methodical investigation . . . is carried out in a genuinely scientific manner . . . it never conflicts with faith. . . . Consequently we cannot but deplore certain habits of mind among Christians, which do not sufficiently attend to the rightful independence of science. . . ." This autonomy *Gaudium et Spes* vindicates also for culture (*GS* 36, 55).

As a corollary, the council did not fear recognizing humans as collaborators with the Creator, as if such collaboration would give too much independence to humankind and ascribe too much creativity to humans. The triumphs of the human race will only manifest the more divine goodness. It is precisely by imaging the Creator that humankind brings all things to the Creator.

Nevertheless, all such autonomy is relative, that is, the truth, goodness, meaning, and laws of earthly things are founded in the creative hand of God (Brogan 1945). The order of redemption is equally operative. "There are many links between the message of salvation and human culture"; for example, "the Gospel of Christ constantly renews the life and culture of fallen man."

This brings us to yet another question: Does the fact that the order of creation is within the order of redemption require sacralization of the secular order? Must we return to a sort of priestly benediction without which the things of earth would be of no value? Are we to wipe out the secularization that the Enlightenment rightly asserted? Surely, in great measure the council responded affirmatively to the autonomy which thinkers of the seventeenth and eighteenth centuries demanded from ecclesial control.

The clear conclusion is that, even if the order of creation is within the order of redemption, the former does not thereby lose legitimate autonomy. There are human tasks to be accomplished by all, including Christians.

To sum up our Christian cosmology: our autonomous earthly tasks are profoundly influenced by Christ's coming and taking upon himself our humanity, our bodiliness. Christ is not only the initiator of the world's sanctification but is its healer and orderer in what is natural. This incorporation in Christ, far from alienating our autonomy, our truth, only elevates and ennobles the world's truth, secularity, and autonomous value.

How, then, does a Christian proceed to a judgment of wisdom in the political order? Does one shed her or his Christianity before judging? Does one set aside the Christian norms and attitudes we discussed earlier for pure norms of nature? Curiosuly, after establishing the links between earthly reality and redemption, the scouncil seems to say that the duties of Christians toward culture are totally secular.

How to reconcile acting secularly and acting as a Christian? To begin with, a Christian acts in the political order as a Christian. She or he cannot prescind from the Christian anthropology that she or he shares, nor from the Christian cosmology of our universe. Christian political wisdom has a Christian component. As the human is eschatologically bent, so is the political order.

However, Christians may not impose on the political order their revealed beliefs. They must respect legitimate pluralism. The civic good, civic society, and the common good must admit a pluralism of approaches. Here is the clue to the council's seeming ambivalence. The Christian, even while entering ethical discourse about human reason and experience, does bring into the political order the higher meaning of understanding that the reign of God is the final meaning. Without interfering with common ethical discourse, the Christian understanding very surely establishes indicators of what cannot be a good society as well as of what an ideal social order would look like.

Unwisdom in the Political Order

Our thirteenth-century theologian Aquinas sheds more light on practical wisdom by discussing defects of prudence.

One such for him is hypermoralism. This defect holds that a Christian can have no truck with this world. To keep one's clothes clean, one has to avoid the world's mud. This ideology looks with disdain on the political axiom that politics is the art of the possible. Any resort to expediency or compromise is termed Machiavellianism.

Practical wisdom avoids this hypermoralism and refuses to hold the politician to the impossible norms of the platonic dreamer. Thus the task of the politician and of all of us who, in a democracy, share in the making of politics has been described by D. W. Brogan (1945) as that of "meet[ing] the endless, varied and unpredictable demands of situations created by human wills and working with this recalcitrant material universe to produce improvement by tolerably honest and dignified methods."[16]

A Final Word

In conclusion, this practical wisdom, which I have derived from Saint Thomas Aquinas, is the culmination of Catholic social teaching. It is the end of the long process of *ratio practica,* which works its way through principles of natural law and more specific principles garnered by repeated returns to experience. It is the fruit of Aquinas's *appetitus rectificatus,* a right and proper desire of the end. Good in the sociopolitical order is specified as the common good. The principles, further reasoning, command to will, and final willing all point to the common good and its pursuit.

In Catholic social teaching, the virtue of social justice takes command of the process and bids us make our contribution. Social justice demands contribution as well as participation in making and executing decisions. When confronted by the complexity of social life, social justice calls for accountability in following the rules of practical wisdom in this chapter.

Practical wisdom has been garnered by reflecting on our common human nature viewed in its full subjectivity and historicity. Wisdom is displayed in how humans shape their social morality and command their wills: This is to be done. But practical wisdom is also shaped supernaturally. Deuteronomy recounts for us God's contribution to the political shaping of Israel as a people. Once our country had a sense of discipleship and an understanding of the appropriateness of calling upon the deity for guidance.

If we as citizens can at all catch the vision of practical wisdom, we understand that we face responsibility and challenge. We are responsible for bringing forth the good life and the good city. But it is a responsibility for everyone. For everyone is an artist producing practical wisdom. Every person stands like Rodin, before her or his block of stone, with chisel and mallet in hand, to fashion an imaging forth of the beauty of God's truth for political order.

Now we come to a last word. This book has been fun to write despite my concern about whether it would all hold together. I hope it has been fun, at least a little bit, rather than an unrelieved labor to read. The book is not narrowly focused, but rather panoramic. I had so many avenues to explore in saying finally what Catholic social teaching is and why, despite some loathing of it, I now believe it is on the whole lovable.

The book is largely biographical. It contains four chapters of clearly identifiable biography, followed by eight chapters that biographically, if not quite so explicitly, reveal this writer's endless sweating over what methodology to let go, what new approaches to embrace, and what was retrievable of what I had learned.

In that discernment four influences have been dominant: Karl Rahner, the Second Vatican Council, the theologians of *nouvelle thèologie,* and thirteenth-century Thomas Aquinas. Imagine putting Aquinas alongside the historicity of Rahner and the council! Hidden inside my use of those four is my marriage of the philosophical and theological as foundations of society. Indeed, I read all four as pairing—in varying degrees—the two disciplines. Despite his other remarkable contributions to social and political thought, I here parted company from John Courtney Murray's exclusive reliance on philosophy for social foundations.

A problem: could I claim that Rahner's transcendentalism had for him social implications? Eminent authorities gave me a decided no. But my reflections in these pages here seem to me to prove that claim decidedly warrantable. There is so much grist for my mill in the council: reading signs of the times, the council's reach into historicity, its emphasis on establishing the reign of God in the here and now; and in particular the reign of God over social structures, to which I devote a chapter. Finally the council's remarkable enthronement of conscience—so close, it seems to me, to Aquinas's practical wisdom.

I have been so bold in these pages as to seek to show that in very good measure two foes of Catholic social teaching—political theology and liberation theology—could be (in what was right and good in them) assimilated into a reworked version of Catholic social teaching. So far as meeting the questioning of women, that reworking is mostly a thing of the future, only beginnings yet existing.

Finally, the last two chapters—in some ways my favorites—brought me back to writing I had done nearly forty years ago. Now, as I draw to a close my struggles to wed the new to the old, I discovered that I had in those writings already adumbrated the conclusions that make up the central chapters of this book, if not in the form I give them here. But my method of moral making in the social field was all right there in front of me in my writing on Aquinas's practical reasoning and practical wisdom. I celebrate, in conclusion, that retrieval.

✚ Notes

Preface

1. I use "U.S. citizen" in place of "American" to recognize the other citizens on the American continent. I have occasionally referred to "developing nations." I realize that all nations are developing. I am conscious, too, of the pejorative connotation of that term. Therefore, I sometimes use the designation South and North, even though the Southern Hemisphere includes New Zealand and Austrailia.

2. Father James Hug is director of the Center of Concern. With a doctorate in moral theology from Chicago Divinity School, he taught first at the Jesuit School of Theology in Chicago. Later he joined the staff of the Woodstock Center, Washington, D.C. That brought him to the Center of Concern. What follows here has gained much from conversations with Father Hug and from his writing.

3. I am here using *noetical* to signify that part of the normative in Catholic social teaching that derives from reasoning about nature, not about revelation. Among the latter I include the norms of social life in the Gospels, for example.

4. Another noted columnist, Charles Krauthammer (*Washington Post,* December 16, 1990), also dismissed the notion of a common good. Yet the absence of unanimity in support of an international common good, however named, accounts, in part, for the failure of the Law of the Seas to be ratified by all nations. Without such a sense of common goods shared by all nations, the attempt at global environmental protection will fail.

5. The Enlightenment's stress on the individual led popes to suspect its whole philosophy of the person, democracy, and scientific spirit. Over the years, Catholics have established a more dialogical relationship with that philosophy. First, the Church accepted emancipation of the human person from total subjection to secular authority and even from excessive ecclesial rule. Second, with Vatican II, the Church came to approve a rightful autonomy of the secular. Third, the council freely acknowledged that it learns from the world. Fourth, the Church now applauds the conquests of science.

But the Church still rejects the Enlightenment's dismissal of God, which deprived its followers of the moral basis for the progress they so heartily endorsed. Catholic social teaching was, after a necessary correction, a powerful analysis of the good and the bad in the dominant philosophy of several centuries. If, then, these pages cite ample loathing, they also cite more loving.

Chapter 1

1. This and other statements of that conference have been commented on by Gregory Baum and Duncan Cameron (1984).
2. For an absorbing account of these developments, see the "Tradition of Forging Catholic Social Thought," in Mueller 1984. This article originally appeared in Moody and Lawler 1963.
3. What Franz Mueller says about Kenkel and John Ryan (see below) is true of Nell-Bruening and Gundlach. Mueller (1984) writes: "Kenkel and Ryan . . . differed as regards the function of government in social and economic matters—a situation not unlike that in many other countries, where Catholic leaders, of one mind as to the need of social reform, disagree as to the ways and means of achieving this end. . . . This difference is not merely a matter of temperament, or a matter of the degree of intervention. In other words, we are here confronted with a difference which is not one of merely prudential judgment, but also one of principle, *depending on one's view of the nature and function of government.*"

   Nell-Bruening, called to prepare the draft of Pius XI's groundbreaking encyclical, *Quadragesimo Anno* (1931), felt confident enough of Gundlach, his fellow solidarist follower of Pesch, to invite him to write what was in effect that encyclical's third way between capitalism and socialism. (To my knowledge, Gundlach shared this understanding of his contribution.) But after that collaboration, the two were, as suggested above and verified by my contacts with them, at intellectual daggerpoints.
4. His half century of international, interrracial, and ecumenical activity has been chronicled by Frisbie (1991).
5. For a fine study, see Hooper 1986.
6. The original German title page bore also the name *Das Naturrecht.*

Chapter 2

1. Gundlach could take some consolation from the very high praise which John XXIII accorded the nineteen Christmas messages of his predecessor, Pius XII: every one a masterpiece; even more such as to merit for the author the triple title: *"doctor optimus,*

Ecclesiae sanctae lumen, divinae legis amator." Insofar as Gundlach had a strong hand in writing them, he shares some of that accolade of "highest teacher" and "light of the church" which appeared in Land 1962.

Chapter 3

1. For my paper and the workshop report, see *Churches' Role* 1970. A few months later the council held its seven-year general conference in Uppsala, Sweden. They decided to explore this issue to see if they could improve on our Beirut statement. As one prominent leader of that exploration confided to me, they came out about where the Beirut statement had.

2. Not many months after Cartigny, Gustavo Gutierrez published his famous *Theology of Liberation*. In a note accompanying the volume he sent me, the eminent theologian said he owed to Cartigny the finalizing of his ideas on liberation theology up to that time.

Chapter 4

1. Correctness of social living as well as of personal living is widely interpreted as founded exclusively in a proper reading of human nature or some form of natural law. But correctness can be learned from one's own instinctive sensitivity to the good or by observing those who have such sensitivity. I think here of one of the most extraordinary figures in the Gospels, the widow in Lk 21:1–4, who with utmost humility put two mites (which Luke assures us she could not afford) into the temple coffer. That woman knew without training, learning, or advice that this was correct (Judaic) living at that moment. Luke recounts the story to point out that such behavior ought to be emblematic of Christian living as well.

2. See, for example, chapter 3, "Does Welfare Create Poverty?"

3. While lowering interest rates may induce business investment, it can be disastrous for older people who must rely on income from interest to augment their income from pensions or social security.

Chapter 5

1. For a very readable (it received the Catholic Book Award) and comprehensive treatment of Catholic social teaching see Henriot, De Berri, and Schultheis (1992).

2. Although the bishops, in the document that I was commenting on, had their own excellent formulation of an ethic of welfare, I

felt it would be helpful for another mind, working from a somewhat different perspective, to respond to the question of how relevant Catholic social teaching is to welfare.

3. The Center of Concern's 1991 summer institute sought to promote "A Vision . . . Lest the People Perish." Its purpose was to relate Catholic social teaching to contemporary issues. James Hug, S.J., director of the center, guided the research staff in applying Catholic social teaching to these issues by seeking to reconcile conflicting interests in the topics we had chosen for discussion: healing, hunger and joblessness, Third World debt, employment for women, and destruction of the environment. Hug's perspective was that, while conflict can be an instrument of social advancement, the eschatological goal of Catholic social teaching is harmonization in a sort of win-win solution. That seems analogous to my description above of *shalom* and my other metaphors for the vocation to justice.

4. *Solidarismus* has aroused uneasiness among many Germans as well as others. Despite its unimpeachable use by Pesch, for some thinkers it smacks of Adam Mueller's organicism, which (like the Gaia hypothesis about the single organism of the cosmos) makes the human race one organ that swallows up the individual. Similarly, those who who feared Naziism and other forms of corporatism that reduce citizens to cogs in the machinery of the state suspected *Solidarismus*. But the Workers' Party and the Polish pope, John Paul II, have brought the word back strongly into favor.

5. Language of James Hug, S.J., during the Center of Concern's 1991 summer institute.

6. For further development of this argument, see my *Shaping the Welfare Consensus* (1988, 185, n. 6).

7. Michael Novak, "The American Debate," transcript provided by Roosevelt Center for American Studies in Washington, D.C.

8. Pastoral Message paragraph 16. The Pastoral Message is an independent section (paragraphs 1–29) introducing the pastoral letter (paragraphs 30–363).

Chapter 6

1. The encyclical was written in Italian and translated into Latin for its official promulgation.

2. I was in Rome at the time and recall that the reason given for translating the Italian text's *socializzazione* into *relationum incrementum socialium* was that the Vatican Latinists knew no Latin word for the Italian word. They would not corrupt the Latin language by coining a new word.

3. In another article, I took up another problem of love and justice which is relevant to our subject. I wrote: "If one shifts perspective from motive-force to acts, love finds expression in acts of charity. It is recognized that there can well be charitable acts congenial to, if not absolutely required by, social living that go beyond the call of justice. That creates no problem. What is problematic for Christian faith is the equating of charitable works to work of counsel or supererogation. This device serves to narrow the field of obligation. Thus, what is of obligation is only what results from what is contracted. All else is charitable work and not of obligation. If one pays a worker the contracted wage on a free market, one's obligation to the worker is dissolved. Yet pope after pope has warned that the charitable works undertaken to cover needs not met by the market wage must be considered no more than provisional. Social justice will call on the employer and others to create the institutions that will provide the worker with a socially just wage or income. The Catholic tradition will never hold that deeds of free giving are nobler than giving what is owed in justice."

Chapter 7

1. Gilleman's work also forced me to give more place to the role of the historical in the natural law system as well as to comprehend Christ as exemplar of the human.
2. As Marechal influenced Gilleman, so he did Rahner. He did this by showing Rahner the way out of idealism through "turning to the subject," which is present in all reflection.
3. He adds, "and is a fundamental point of the philosophy of value."
4. Much of the rest of this chapter relies heavily on Karl Rahner. I have consulted several articles in his *Theological Investigations* and reflected on his remarkable *Foundations of the Christian Faith* (1978), especially the opening chapters. I have also been immensely aided by two studies of Rahner's moral system, by James Bresnahan, S.J., 1980; and Ronald Modras 1985. On Rahner's influence upon moral theology Richard McCormick has said: "Rahner's historicity impacts moral theology today."
5. In my time in Rome the rising of the scirocco, a wind off the Sahara which carries very low barometric pressure, was a factor that courts would take into consideration for a murder committed during its spell.
6. In Rahner, language such as "how do we sense the appropriateness of a particular act within conscious experience of global moral instinct" suggests that act of moral making which Aquinas calls the prudential judgment. Whether this is true or not, that

Aquinas's prudential judgment is of the order of historicity suggests that Aquinas's conception of natural law in moral making was far closer to the modern conception than was that of the intervening Scholastics and especially neo-scholastics.

7. Rahner has explored this theme exhaustively (1963a, 217–35).

8. Rahner (1974, 231–49) presents his most celebrated treatment of this theme.

9. In another interview reported in *Faith in a Wintry Season,* this question was posed to Rahner: "According to von Balthasar, your integration of love of God and love of human beings, according to which the primary act of God's love is the categorically explicit love of neighbor, is such that this primary act of God's love remains rather secondary over against what he [Rahner] calls the 'thematic religious act'" (Imhof and Biallowons 1990, 13–38).

10. With this, Rahner appears to concede a point to von Balthasar.

11. Rahner adds: And is reached "in no other way."

12. I found the essay by John Galvin, "The Invitation of Grace" (O'Donovan 1980), very helpful on the theme of salvation as a constituent of the human. See also the article "Grace" in Rahner and Vorgrimler 1965.

13. For the Church fathers, the human was in the image and likeness of God, and therefore spirit that would become the further likeness of God through the vision of God's glory. De Lubac, according to Komochak, shows that neither Aquinas nor the fathers ever dreamt of a natural destiny of the human, something short of the beatific vision. There is only one order—as in Rahner—in which God creates us for God's self, and we are intelligible only in view of this gift of divine destiny. Says de Lubac (1946): "For the Fathers there is no *nous* without an anticipatory participation, ever gratuitous and ever precarious, in the one *pneuma.*"

14. Chirico rejects the idea that there can be elements of natural law that are not in revelation. He bases himself on such texts of *Dei Verbum* as Christ is "the fullness of Revelation" and "Jesus perfected Revelation by fulfilling it through his whole work of making himself present and manifesting himself. . . ." Christ, then, in his risen humanity is the fullness of revelation and transcends in meaning any proposition that can be formulated about him.

Chirico concludes that the propositional notion of revelation must be rejected. Consequently, it is not just those propositions of natural law which are also propositions of revelation (for example, murder is condemned in the Ten Commandments) that may be said to be also in revelation through Christ. But see Sullivan 1991.

Working from a different perspective, Charles E. Curran (1991, 73–87) argues that moral norms set forth as being Christian norms beyond those binding as natural law are only statements of universally binding natural law. But are "turning the other cheek," "giving also your cloak," and "carrying your cross" not really specifically Christian?

15. This section follows Bresnahan (1980, 81). Bresnahan understands Rahner's natural law as a reflection of the human's actual (that is, graced) being, which necessarily leads to a Christian natural law.

16. A more difficult question is whether Jesus Christ is exemplar and source of the moral ideal for all humankind. This question brings us to Rahner's theology of the 'anonymous Christian' and to the universally salvific will of God. Rahner treats these two concepts in a section already cited in his *Foundations of the Christian Faith*. He treats it more simply in *Faith in a Wintry Season* (Imhof and Biallowons 1990, 166–67 and 181–82; see also 132–33).

Bresnahan (1980, 181) gives this interpretation of Rahner: "Any human person who is in fact living out this moral ideal at the level of fundamental option, however inadequately the person may express this basic love in acts, is actually empowered to do so by grace, the grace of Christ, shaping the person in the likeness of Christ."

17. Liberation theology has made us familiar with this concept. See also the very helpful treatment by Henriot (1989).

18. Clarke (1974) warns against becoming so preoccupied with societal revelation and grace that inadequate attention is paid to societal sin, the powers and principalities, the world for which Jesus did not pray.

Chapter 8

1. Congar (1969, 212) cites as evidence the pastoral constitution (*GS* 22, 26, 38, 41, and 57). There is much more in paragraphs 40–44. Because this is not a commentary on the pastoral constitution I have cited only what pertains to my theme.

2. In a companion piece to Alfaro's noted above, the eminent moralist Josef Fuchs, S.J. (1989, 488), shifts the ethical emphasis of the council away from the world's salvation to that of the individual person. He seems not to deny the thrust of Alfaro and many others, but rather to remind us that salvation is to be had by individuals, especially for the good lives they live. This does not seem to me to preclude the communal aspect.

3. Another expression of the pastoral: "In the incarnation the Word took the whole of humanity and the cosmos, its being, history and development as his body; all realities, all values, all are thus joined in him. It is this interconnectedness that constitutes the ontological condition making it possible for the Lord's death and resurrection to become the saving events they are."

4. All ideas and quotations are drawn from Rahner (1963b, 38–74).

5. This was a project of the Woodstock Theological Center of Washington, D.C.

6. Pope Paul VI in *Octogesima Adveniens* speaks of such creativity.

7. My own essay in Walsh 1980, "The Earth is the Lord's: Thoughts on the Economic System," sought to show what a utopian imagination, drawing on biblical sources, could contribute to bettering the economic order. As the rest of the essays, it emphasized the political character of faith.

Chapter 9

1. Since Catholic social theology and Catholic social ethics are familiar in our context, at this moment I merely want to give them at least provisional status within this body of *praxis* theologies. They can both be fitted into Catholic social teaching. Hollenbach (1990, 154–55) illustrates the fit. Hollenbach first applauds the new catechism for the "attention given to the social dimensions of Christian life." He refers to these dimensions as social morality, or social ethics. He also describes the same phenomena under the rubric of Catholic social teaching. Thus Hollenbach notes the catechism's use of the Decalogue "to present an overview of some of the major themes of recent church social teaching." He then lists some ten of these themes and affirms them as "standard Catholic social theory."

   Though we have noted dissent in the preceding chapter, Catholic social theology is widely differentiated from Catholic social ethics. The former is seen as embracing revelation, while social ethics relies only on reason. In practice the two are virtually treated as one; indeed the two are often viewed as somehow equivalent to Catholic social teaching. Speaking about social morality, Hollenbach describes ten social principles and comments that they are all standard Catholic social theory.

2. For instance, chapter 1 is entitled "The Church's Evolving Social Teaching."

3. Therefore many liberation theologians have been dismayed and baffled at the same pope's applause for the market in his latest encyclical, *Centesimus Annus.*

4. In the language of my present discourse that would read as insertion into a history of suffering and of declining culture as well as a loving insertion of solidarity, which Lamb refers to as agapeic *praxis.*

5. Others return the charge of exclusivity upon liberation theology for ignoring women's liberation and the emancipation of the earth from domination by humans.

6. I hope it is not too fanciful to suggest in this connection that a major document of Catholic social teaching, *Octogesima Adveniens,* encourages the Church to read the signs of the times and to discover where God is calling us in analysis of our own situations (*OA* 4). It implicitly invites the faithful to discover the precise sufferers to whom they should address their inquiry.

7. In his encyclical *Populorum Progressio* Paul VI calls repeatedly for harmonization and dialogue between classes. He does admit the possibility of conflict and even violent conflict, although with strong reservations. "We know that a revolutionary uprising— save where there is manifest, long-standing tyranny which would do great damage to the common good of the country— produces new injustices. . ." (*PP* 31). Pope Paul subsequently withdrew from this qualified support of conflict.

8. Lamb (1982 and 1987, 772–79) have been very helpful in guiding me through Metz. Also helpful was Rebecca S. Chopp (1988). Finally John Coleman's *An American Stratregic Theology* (1982a), to which I recently returned after a long absence, strongly confirmed me in my "hermeneutic suspicions" that Metz, however compelling, is not the whole story.

9. Narrative has certainly not been the bread and butter of Catholic social teaching. But neither had it been imbedded in Catholic theology before the time of Vatican II. That it can be introduced into Catholic social teaching is manifested most emphatically by the biblical narratives in the U.S. Catholic bishops' economic pastoral.

10. Adding this material was suggested by Suzanne de Crane, an intern working with the Center of Concern in the summer of 1992 who was finishing her doctorate in Catholic social teaching at Toronto School of Theology. Suzanne also composed paragraphs to guide me.

11. From another perspective one also distinguishes conservative, socialist, and radical feminism. In addition, a strong movement links feminism to environmentalism in interpretations which are considerably at odds.

12. In the Center of Concern's July 1992 *Center Focus,* she reports a conference which Center of Concern cosponsored with the

College of St. Catherine in St. Paul, Minnesota (third conference in four—the rest were international), colloquies the center sponsored on "The Future of Catholic Social Thought" to celebrate the hundredth anniversary of Leo XIII's *Rerum Novarum*. With Nancy Sylvester, I.H.M., then director of NETWORK (a national Catholic social justice lobby), she wrote *Trouble and Beauty: Women Encounter Catholic Social Teaching* (Riley and Sylvester 1991). The Leadership Conference of Women Religious cosponsored the book with NETWORK and the Center of Concern. Maria Riley (with Jo Marie Griesgraber and James Hug., S.J.) was a major hand in preparing the Center of Concern's *Commentary on the Occasion of the Third Draft of the NCCB Pastoral Letter "Called to Be One in Christ Jesus"* (May 1992). Themes of *Trouble and Beauty*—patriarchy and the inability of the official Church to condemn in itself the sexism which it rightly condemns in civil society—reappear there.

13. See note 12.

Chapter 10

1. Hollenbach (1990, 162) notes, although on different grounds than Metz, that the new catechism is excessively cautious about identifying the *eschaton* with accomplishments in this world. Hollenbach adds that the catechism's exposition of these eschatological themes is notably different from that of *Gaudium et Spes*. To suggest that messianic hope has nothing to do with hope for justice in history is contrary to a central emphasis of the Second Vatican Council.

2. Social thinkers in Vienna, Paris, and Berlin were pleased at seeing the papacy open up its purview of the social problems they were experiencing, such as inadequate housing, urbanization, and pollution. But it remains nevertheless true that the purview until that time was limited to the developed industrial nations.

3. John Coleman (1982a, 63) presents a thoughtful criticism grounded in a full understanding of political theology. For him, political theology's introduction of other theological themes such as social sin; salvation as liberation; the paradigmatic nature of the entire way of Christ, not just his way of suffering and resurrection; and the reign of God all remain inadequate. These theological categories, as several chapters of this book show, have their place in our retrieval of Catholic social teaching.

   Coleman adds this stricture: "There is a legitimate sense, for example, despite its possible ideological misuse, to the doctrines of orders of creation—fragile structures of civility, community, relatively undistorted communication, solidarity,—which deserve nurturance, preservation and support rather than rejection or denouncement" (ibid., 287).

4. For one thoughtful analysis of dependency theory, which raises the issue briefly mentioned here, see "The Radical Political Economy" in Weaver and Jameson 1991.

5. My comments draw also upon personal conversations with Sobrino. This Basque Jesuit, among other publications, produced in 1978 (original Spanish in 1976) one of the most formative studies in Christology, *Christology at the Crossroads* (Sobrino 1978).

6. But it is not a lie that God *created* us to be equal. Catholic social teaching makes no claim beyond that, except that it does call in the name of justice and love for implementation of that God-given equality. At least, as such, the principle does constitute a prod for conscience.

Chapter 11

1. Intrinsicism focuses on the intrinsic or essential rightness or correctness of the act, independently of intention, circumstances, and so on. Proportionalism finds the rightness or correctness of behavior through weighing the action, intention, circumstances, relationships, and consequences.

2. Some of these can be foreseen, but others cannot. In the former case, these must be taken into account. In the latter, one must be prepared to recognize the provisional character of what some would presume is intrinsically moral.

3. Yoder (1991) offers a very thoughtful piece on questions about just war.

4. Klubertanz, then dean of philosophy at the Jesuit Scholasticate in St. Louis, was editor of *The Modern Schoolman.*

5. Fuchs (1989, 485) is referring to *Gaudium et Spes* paragraph 5, which reads: "The human race has passed from a rather static concept of reality to a more dynamic, evolutionary one." Fuchs translates the word *reality* as "nature": "dynamic and . . . evolutionary concept of nature."

Kenneth Himes, O.F.M. (1990, 56), writes that a favorite phrase of Richard McCormick, S.J., taken from the official commentary on *Gaudium et Spes* is "the standard for judging human activity is the human person integrally and adequately considered." Himes (ibid., 71) cites *Gaudium et Spes* paragraphs 37–38 for that expression: *"Schema constitutionis pastoralis de Ecclesia in mundo huius temporis: Expensio modorum partis secundae."*

6. Fuchs also cites *Gaudium et Spes* paragraphs 35, 53, 55, 56, 57, and 74 to confirm the attention the council gives to the human being as criterion for correctness of behavior "in the world of humanity."

7. Fuchs makes several other observations about the council's understanding of moral making. Although we cannot discuss them all, I would like to mention several. First, *Dignitatis Humanae* (Religious freedom) speaks of the divine law as "eternal, objective and universal," that is, God knows the correctness of each thing. Furthermore, it is objective, that is, it is the correct or right answer for a person according to its total reality (*DH* 3). Fuchs suggests that some of the fathers may have believed that God decides and establishes everything from eternity. But that would oppose the natural law, which deals with essential being, not something that God might have arbitrarily (if God can be described that way) imposed on the human.

Fuchs maintains that the council uses the phrase "objective moral order" as an alternative but equivalent term for the divine moral law. Both formulae are about something objectively existing (*DH* 36, 39). Conscience is the tribunal that recognizes the law of God written in the heart; it teaches correct behavior and finds right solutions to the ethical problems of society.

In a concrete search, conscience takes into account the principles which spring from human nature and then proceeds autonomously to find concrete norms of moral behavior, which are discovered actively in human society and not already made for passive acceptance. The objective moral law arrived at is neither absolute nor arbitrary and purely relative.

Fuchs (1989, 493) amplifies the preceding with his description of the objective moral law in achieving correctness from council documents: "The objective moral law in practical terms is a considerable body of already recognized norms of behavior which, in the search for correctness of human behavior, must not be directly infringed and which are to aid the person seeking right behavior as guide to objective moral law."

8. We develop this point later.

9. In this section I draw principally upon Rahner's *Foundations of the Christian Faith* (1978), cited earlier, and his work in *Sacramentum Mundi,* especially the article "Church and the World" in volume 1. Perhaps most important is "On the Question of a Formal Existential Ethics" (1963a). Although well-known in German-speaking countries, this article was not available in English until the early years of Vatican II.

"The Experiment with Man" in *Theological Investigations* (Rahner 1972) takes up some of the same themes. "On the Existence of a Formal Individual Ethics" (Rahner 1977) sums up Rahner's ideas on historicity. He has a double intent in this article: first, to explain the existential, historical, and ethical fact; and second, to posit the need for a science of that ethical moment, hence the title. Rahner is clear that there can be no science of the individual act as such, for no two acts can be identical. What there can be is a scientific treatment to probe all the principles bearing upon understanding of historicity. He offers his considerations as a sort of trailblazing. Other Rahner material of relevance here has already been noted.

10. A consideration that seems to me linked to this point is Aquinas's claim that there is no knowledge that was not first in the senses: *"Nihil est in intellectu quod non fuit prius in sensibus."* Other language is *conversio ad phantasma.*

11. In concentrating on this article on existence, I have to caution that Rahner emphasizes individual acts of morality. But Rahner's morality is much more that of living out the fundamental option for the ground of our being, which we earlier reflected on. It is not an act-centered ethic, but a living out of the fundamental option which focuses on the fundamental normative, namely the united love of God and of neighbor. The choices we make about specific options—exercising freedom of choice—are within the life focus of fundamental being in God. The same is true of our social life. Especially for a people of redemption that social life is life-centered.

   Our earlier treatment of the role of attitudes in moral making alongside the normative is equally relevant here, as one tries to discover the correctness or the rightness of moral activity. Our decisions about social life will be misguided unless they are regulated by love, commitment to justice, sharing with the poor, and seeing reality through the lens of class, race, and sex. This seems to be what Rahner means by his "global moral instinct."

12. In the following, I draw on much of Rahner from an earlier chapter as well as extensively on James F. Bresnahan, S.J., one of the contributors to one of the best commentaries on Rahner available, Leo J. O'Donovan, *A World of Grace* (1980).

13. This has ramifications for the physicalness-of-the-act approach which pervades so much of one type of Catholic moral theology. *Humanae Vitae's* universal prohibition of any artificial birth control is the stellar example. Rahner questions it. Bresnahan would subject the encyclical's physicalness to the test of whether creativity could not—this is the position of many moralists today—enlarge a person's moral freedom.

14. Says Bresnahan (1980, 176): "The creative potential of freedom taking the form of love is for Rahner the primary subject matter of a revised natural law ethics."

15. This volume has not taken up the nature of official papal writing of different types and degrees of authority in the social field. Encyclical writing, the most authoritative of these, is of ordinary

magisterium unless a pope intended to define or solemnly declare. The Vocational Order was declared by Pius XI in *Quadragesimo Anno* to be, if not natural law, as if it were of natural law. As events turned out, that was rash, to say the least. The same can be said of John XXIII's ill-starred encyclical *Veterum Sapientia,* which required absolutely all teaching of sacred sciences in seminaries to be conducted in Latin. This requirement lasted five days—a clear case of *doctrina non recepta* (teaching not received by the Church).

    The Church tries to formulate what in this book I call "objective norms" and "calls to action." These are said to be drawn from the natural law and the Gospels. In substance, they represent the effort of conscience we have been considering.

16. Josef Fuchs, S.J., my colleague for twenty years at the Gregorian University of Rome, is one of the most formative moralists of our day. He has addressed conscience in several essays and, in particular, the problem of conscience instructed by the magisterium.

17. In the next chapter, I argue that this objectivity was of the substance of the proto-Scholastic natural law of Aquinas, which was corrupted by neo-scholasticism.

18. It is my consistent contention in this work that reality has spirit and meaning in the presence of the Creator beyond the reality which it has in itself; the surrounding cosmic reality draws further reality from its relationship to the human (as human reality draws enhanced meaning from the surrounding cosmos). That human reality has its supernatural component. This note, elaborated elsewhere, is introduced here only to complete the elements that conscience addresses.

19. Premoral values are described as conditioned goods pursued for human and nonhuman well-being, such as life, health, and procreation. Human finiteness (temporality and spatiality) imbues all acts with ambiguity, especially in conflicts in which a premoral disvalue is an integral part (effect or cause) of the action that promotes a premoral value. The *pre-* in a premoral value means that it exists independently of our will. The *moral* in that premoral value or disvalue must be considered as relevant to our moral activity. While we must avoid a premoral disvalue, in conflicts we can permit it for a proportionate reason. For example, failing to keep an appointment could be excused if one were aiding an accident victim (Walter 1990, 129).

20. This does not preclude any and all intrinsic evil. Once proportionalism has done its work of weighing the reasonableness in light of the manifold relations and consequences, the human action, thus dictated by *recta ratio* and affirmed by the will, will have its intrinsic goodness or badness.

21. How one arrives at a proportionate reason is much more complex. Rahner's moral instinct of faith is close to Aquinas's *naturaliter nota*. Connatural knowledge is the nudging of the intellect by natural inclinations. Without reflection, one intuits the morally possible action. One more typically resorts to analysis and to weighing, that is, to discursive reason. Although weighing does not have to be quantitative, does the proportionate reason hinge on declaring one premoral value to be of a higher order than another? This and other questions of proportional reasoning are extensively reviewed by Walter (1990, 139ff.; see also Vacek 1985).

22. *"Propter diversas hominum conditiones contingit quod aliqui actus sunt aliquibus virtuosi, tamquam eis proportionati et convenientes, qui tamen sunt aliis vitiosi, tamquam eis non proportionati"* (*ST* I–II q. 94, a. 3, ad. 3).

Chapter 12

1. The Vocational Order was the subject of my Ph.D. dissertation. It is that type of socioeconomic organization proposed by Pius XI in his 1931 commemoration of *Rerum Novarum,* his encyclical *Quadragesimo Anno.* I have discussed Vocational Order in chapter 1. Conversations with Klubertanz about practical reason and prudence in Aquinas led to this collaboration.

2. This contingency appears also insofar as the data of experience enter into practical reasoning (*Eth* IV lect. 9, 1253–54).

3. The preceding chapter commented on how that word with Aquinas's *quod convenit* anticipates post–Vatican proportionalism.

4. Moorhouse F. X. Millar, S.J., a revered teacher of mine from whom I learned so much, has said: "It is not too much to say that this idea of relation is the central one in the common law."

5. The Austrian social thinker Johannes Messner (1949, 171; see also 151–53, 156ff.), whose *Social Ethics* (1949) was highly esteemed in the fifties, says "law is order relative to social life" as "the outer reflection of the inner order of things."

6. *"Oportet in regimine civitatis diversam regionem ordinis observari secundum diversas conditiones eorum qui subiciuntur regimini et secundum diversa ad quae ordinatur"* (*CG* III 3).

7. Goodwill is also involved, for a "perverse reason is not reason, and so the rule of human acts is not just any reason" (*SL* 24, 1.3, ad. 3).

8. Informed: "exercised in the customs of human life." The whole sentence is worth quoting in Latin: *"Oportet illum qui sufficiens auditor vult esse moralis scientiae quod sit manu ductus et exercitatus in consuetudinibus humanae vitae."*

9. In his doctoral dissertation, prepared for Chicago Divinity School, Fr. James Hug, S.J. (1980), now director of the Center of Concern, provides us with an exhaustive exploration of the moral judgment according to Maritain.

10. Does appetite have primacy over intellect in the exercise of this practical wisdom? One could argue that appetite does have such primacy on the grounds that it is concerned with the good and the bad. But favoring the primacy of reason, on the contrary, is that this appetite or desire for the good has to be guided by a reasoning that discovers the best means or the best course (*NE* IV lect. 2).

11. The commentary on Aquinas's virtue of prudence I have most relied upon is Deman 1949. Among several others, one that covers the ground very thoroughly and insightfully is Gerhard 1945.

12. The last phrase reads: *"oportet quod prudens habeat utramque notitiam . . . vel si alteram contingat ipsum habere, magis debet habere hanc, scilicet, notitiam particularium, propinquiorum operantioni."*

13. Here is the very abtruse but insightful language of Aquinas's most notable commentator, John of St. Thomas: "In speculative knowledge the object impresses its intelligibility on the mind which is undetermined until then. [In practical knowledge it is the reverse.] The object is not determined but rather undetermined and awaits the impression of the form. That is why it was said that the matter about which the practical intellect concerns itself is capable of modifications, of being fashioned. The matter which is object of prudence is contingent and stands in need of impression of form by the knowing subject. . . . The formal and determining principle must be sought in the judgment of the practical intellect which the subsequent operation of the agent seeks to impress upon the indeterminate matter" (*Disp.* 16, a. 4).

14. We can fail in practical wisdom. Thomas (*DV* 245, a. 8) notes a first failure: "The judgment of reason is to some degree bound by concupiscence." Past indulgence prepares one in a new situation to act according to one's habit. Sense appetite blocks out such a universal as "I must control my appetites" and replaces this with the perverse generalization of seeking pleasure. Indeed, the drive to pleasure may close off any recourse to cogitation resting upon a major premise (the universal) and simply drive blindly to the object of desire.

A second failure brings us to a moral idealism. Here, the defect is to allow a universal, for example, "lust is to be avoided," to reign without permitting instinctive knowledge to enter into the final judgment. In this case, the instinct, born of experience, might suggest that, while lust is to be avoided, all carnal intercourse in marriage is not lustful. Moral idealism is more prominent in social moral life. It fends off entry into the life, it does not accept juggling with the lesser of two evils as morally good. In general, moral idealism precludes that essential act of prudence which is instinctive knowledge.

15. Though all these rules are found in Thomas, my schematic presentation may make them look excessively complicated, but some are simply refinements of other rules.

16. There are other hypermoralists. One thinks of those who cannot brook cooperation of Christians with secularists. Unless they are believers, men and women cannot, so these claim, build the good city. While it is one thing for the Christian to recognize that the basis of his or her cooperation is his or her belief in God, it is another to say that no bond of cooperation with the secularist exists. But the secularist may well understand—our U.S. bishops have noted this in their economic pastoral—rights based on human nature, if not also on the common good, and commonweal in a sense of true public good and civic friendship (Bellah et al., 1985). Catholic social teaching has long insisted that the natural law is a bond we Christians share with all others.

✠ References

Abbott, Walter M., S.J., ed. 1966. *The Documents of Vatican II.* New York: America.

Alfaro, Juan, S.J. 1989. "Reflections on the Eschatology of *Vatican II.*" In *Vatican II: Assessments and Perspectives,* edited by Rene Latourelle. New York: Paulist.

Auer, Alfons. 1969. "Man's Activity Throughout the World." Pt. I, Chap. 3 of *Commentary on the Documents of Vatican II.* Vol. 5. Edited by Herbert Vorgrimler. New York: Herder and Herder.

Baum, Gregory. 1982. *The Priority of Labor.* New York: Paulist.

—————. 1987. *Theology and Society.* New York: Paulist.

Baum, Gregory, and Duncan Cameron. 1984. *Ethics and Economics: Canadian Catholic Bishops on the Economic Crisis.* Toronto: Lorimer.

Bellah, Robert N., Richard Madsen, William M. Sullivan, Ann Swidler, and Steven M. Tipton. 1985. *Habits of the Heart.* Berkeley: University of California Press.

Berger, Peter L., and Thomas Luckmann. 1966. *The Social Construction of Reality.* New York: Doubleday.

Bonino, Jose Miguez. 1991. *Ecumenical Review* 43 (October): 392–400.

Bresnahan, James, S.J. 1980. "An Ethic of Faith." In *A World of Grace: An Introduction to the Themes and Foundations of Karl Rahner's Theology,* edited by Leo O'Donovan. New York: Seabury/Crossroad.

Brogan, D. W. 1945. "The Case for Politics." In *The Free State.* New York: Knopf.

Brown, Robert McAfee, ed. 1990. *Kairos: Three Prophetic Challenges to the Churches*. Grand Rapids, Mich.: Eerdmans.

Burke, Mary. 1980. *Reaching for Justice*. Washington, D.C.: Center for Concern.

Calvez, John-Yves, and Jacques Perrin. 1961. *The Church's Social Thought from Leo XIII to Pius XII*. Chicago: Regnery.

Carlen, Claudia, IHM, ed. 1981. *The Papal Encyclicals 1740–1981*. 5 vols. Raleigh: McGrath.

Castro, Emilio. 1991. *Ecumenical Review* 43 (October): 389.

Chirico, Peter, S.S. 1991. *Theological Studies* 52 (3 September): 539–40.

Chopp, Rebecca S. 1986. *The Praxis of Suffering: An Interpretation of Liberation and Political Theologies*. Maryknoll, N.Y.: Orbis.

Christiansen, Drew, S.J. 1989. "The Common Good and the Politics of Self-Interest: A Catholic Contribution to the Practice of Citizenship." In *Beyond Individualism,* edited by Donald L. Gelpi, S.J. New York: Paulist.

Churches' Role in Development, The. 1970. New York: Corpus.

Clarke, Thomas E., S.J. 1974. "Social Grace for a New Pastoral Strategy." In *Soundings*. Washington, D.C.: Center of Concern.

———. 1980. *Above Every Name: The Lordship of Christ and Social Systems*. New York: Paulist.

Coleman, John. 1982a. *An American Strategic Theology*. New York: Paulist.

———. 1982b. "On Political and Liberation Theology." In *An American Strategic Theology*. New York: Paulist.

Congar, Yves. 1969. Chap. 4 in *Commentary on the Documents of Vatican II,* edited by Herbert Vorgrimler. New York: Herder and Herder.

Cort, John. 1989. *Christian Socialism*. Maryknoll, N.Y.: Orbis.

Costello, Gerald. 1984. *Without Fear or Favor*. Mystic, Conn.: Twenty-Third Publications.

Cronin, John. 1959. *Socal Principles and Economic Life*. Milwaukee: Bruce.

Curran, Charles E. 1991. "Catholic Social Teaching and Human Morality." In *One Hundred Years Of Catholic Social Thought: Celebration and Challenge,* edited by John Coleman, S.J. Maryknoll, N.Y.: Orbis.

Deman, Thomas P., O.P., tr. and ed. 1949. *Somme Thèologique S. Thomas d'Aquin: Prudence II–II*. 2nd. ed. Paris: Desclèe, Sociètè Saint Jean Evangeliste.

Deploige, Simon. 1923. *Le Conflit de la Morale et de la Sociologie*. 3rd ed. Paris: Nouvelle Librairie Nationale.

Dorr, Donal. 1983. *Option for the Poor: A Hundred Years of Vatican Social Thought*. London: Gill and Macmillan; Maryknoll, N.Y.: Orbis.

Duncan, Greg. J. 1984. *Years of Poverty, Years of Plenty: The Changing Economic Fortunes of American Workers and Their Families*. Ann Arbor: Institute for Social Research, University of Michigan.

Dunne, George. 1990. *King's Pawn*. Chicago: Loyola University Press.

Dwyer, John C. 1987. *Foundations of Christian Ethics*. New York: Paulist.

Elliot, Charles. 1970. In *Search of a Theology of Development*. Geneva: SODEPAX.

Frisbie, Margery. 1991. *An Alley in Chicago*. Kansas City, Mo.: Sheed and Ward.

Fuchs, Joseph, S.J. 1989. "A Harmonization of the Conciliar Statements on Christian Moral Theology." In *Vatican II Assessment and Perspectives: Twenty-Five Years After (1962–1987),* edited by Renè Latourelle, S.J. Vol. 2. New York: Paulist.

————. 1990. "Conscience and Conscious Fidelity." In *Moral Theology: Challenge for the Future,* edited by Charles Curran. New York: Paulist.

Gerhard, William. 1945. "The Intellectual Virtue of Prudence." *Thomist* 8 (January).

Gilkey, Langdon. 1976. *Reaping the Whirlwind.* New York: Seabury.

————. 1981. *Society and the Sacred: Toward a Theology of Culture in Decline.* New York: Crossroad.

Gilleman, Gerard. 1959. *The Primacy of Charity in Moral Theology.* Translated by William Ryan, S.J., and Andre Vachon, S.J. Westminster, Md.: Newman.

Greeley, Andrew. 1985. *America* 153 (November 9): 292–95.

Gremillion, Joseph. 1976. *The Gospel of Peace and Justice: Catholic Social Thought Since Pope John.* New York: Orbis.

Gutierrez, Gustavo. 1973. *Theology of Liberation.* Maryknoll, N.Y.: Orbis.

Hellwig, Monika. 1980. "Christology and Attitudes Toward Social Structures." In *Above Every Name: The Lordship of Christ and Social Structures,* edited by Thomas Clarke. New York: Paulist.

Henriot, Peter, S.J. 1989. "Social Sin and Conversion: A Theology of the Church's Social Involvement." In *Introduction to Christian Ethics: A Reader,* edited by Ronald Hamel and Kenneth Himes, O.F.M. New York: Paulist.

Henriot, Peter J., Edward P. De Berri, and Michael J. Schultheis. 1992. *Catholic Social Teaching: Our Best Kept Secret.* Centenary edition. Maryknoll, N.Y.: Orbis; Washington, D.C.: Center of Concern.

Hentz, Otto, S.J. 1980. "Embodying Love." In *Above Every Name: The Lordship of Christ and Social Systems,* edited by Thomas Clarke. New York: Paulist.

Himes, Kenneth, O.F.M. 1990. "The Contributions of Theology to Catholic Moral Theology." In *Moral Theology: Challenges for the Future,* edited by Charles Curran. New York: Paulist.

Holland, Joe, and Peter Henriot, S.J. 1983. *Social Analysis: Linking Faith and Justice.* Maryknoll, N.Y.: Orbis.

Hollenbach, David. 1990. "Social Morality in the Catechism." In *The Universal Catechism Reader: Reflections and Responses,* edited by Thomas J. Reese, S.J. San Francisco: HarperCollins.

Hooper, J. Leon, S.J. 1986. *The Ethics of Discourse: The Social Philosophy of John Courtney Murray.* Washington, D.C.: Georgetown University Press.

Hug, James E., S.J. 1980. "Moral Judgment: The Theory and the Practice in the Thought of Jacques Maritian." Ph.D. disseration, University of Chicago Divinity School.

———, ed. 1983. *Tracing the Spirit: Communities, Social Action and Theological Reflection.* New York: Paulist.

Imhof, Paul, and Hubert Biallowons, eds. 1990. *Faith in a Wintry Season: Conversations and Interviews with Karl Rahner in the Last Years of His Life.* Translated by Harvey Egan, S.J. New York: Crossroad.

Komonchak, Joseph. 1990. "Theology and Culture at Mid-Century: The Example of Henri de Lubac." *Theological Studies* 51 (4/December).

Lamb, Matthew. 1982. *Solidarity with the Victims: Toward a Theology of Social Transformation.* New York: Crossroad.

———. 1987. "Political Theology." In *The New Dictionary of Theology,* edited by Joseph Komonchak, Mary Collins, and Dermot A. Lane. Wilmington, Del.: Glazier.

Land, Philip S., S.J. 1962. "Sull'esistenza d'una Dottrina Sociale Cristina," *Civilta Cattolica* 4: 430–38, 546–55.

———. 1976. *Studies in the International Apostolate of the Jesuits* 45 (June): 1–62.

———. 1987. "Justice." In *The New Dictionary of Theology,* edited by Joseph Komonchak, Mary Collins, and Dermot A. Lane. Wilmington, Del.: Glazier.

———. 1988. *Shaping the Welfare Consensus: The U.S. Catholic Bishops' Contribution.* Washington, D.C.: Center of Concern.

Land, Philip S., S.J., and Peter Henriot, S.J. 1989. "Toward a New Methodology in Catholic Social Teaching." In *The Logic of Solidarity*, edited by Gregory Baum and Robert Ellsberg. Maryknoll, N.Y.: Orbis.

Land, Philip S., S.J., and George Klubertanz, S.J. 1951. "Practical Reason, Social Fact, and the Vocational Order." *Modern Schoolman* 28 (4/May).

Lane, Dermot A. 1984. *Foundations for a Social Theology: Praxis, Process, and Salvation*. New York: Paulist.

Lubac, Henri de. 1938. *Les aspects sociaux du dogme*. Paris: Cerf. (Translated as *Catholicism: A Study of Dogma in Relation to the Corporate Destiny of Mankind*, New York, Sheed and Ward, 1958.)

————. 1946. *Surnaturel: Études historiques*. Paris: Aubier.

Messner, Johannes. 1949. *Social Ethics: Natural Law in the Modern World*. Translated by J. J. Doherty. New York: Herder.

Metz, Johann Baptist. 1980. *Faith in History and Society: Toward a Practical Fundamental Theology*. New York: Seabury/Crossroad.

Millar, Moorhouse F. X. 1940. "Labor and the Common Good." In *Labor Law, an Instrument of Social Peace and Progress*. New York: Fordham University Press.

Modras, Ronald. 1985. "Implications of Rahner's Anthropology for Moral Theology." *Horizons* 12 (1): 70–90.

Moeller, Charles. 1969. "History of the Constitution." In *Commentary on the Documents of Vatican II*. Vol. 5 of *Pastoral Constitution on the Church in the Modern World*. New York: Herder and Herder.

Moody, Joseph N. and Justin George Lawler, eds. 1963. *The Challenge of Mater et Magistra*. New York: Herder and Herder.

Mueller, Franz H. 1984. *The Church and the Social Question*. Washington, D.C.: American Enterprise Institute.

Murray, John Courtney. 1960. *We Hold These Truths: Catholic Reflection on the American Proposition*. New York: Sheed and Ward.

National Conference of Catholic Bishops. 1986. *Economic Justice for All: Pastoral Letter on Catholic Social Teaching and the U.S. Economy.* Washington: USNCCB.

Nell-Breuning, Oswald von. 1936. *Reorganization of Social Economy: The Social Encyclical Developed and Explained.* Milwaukee: Bruce.

Novak, Michael. 1985. "Economic Rights: The Servile State." *Catholicism in Crisis* 3 (10/October): 8–15.

O'Donovan, Leo J. 1980. *A World of Grace: An Introduction to the Themes and Foundations of Karl Rahner's Theology.* New York: Seabury/Crossroad.

Pobee, John S. 1991. "Decision-making with Regard to Social Issues." *Ecumenical Review* 43 (October): 411–19.

Rahner, Karl. 1963a. "On the Question of a Formal Existential Ethics." In *Theological Investigations.* Vol. 2. London: Darton, Longman and Todd.

———. 1963b. "The Order of Redemption within the Order of Creation." In *The Christian Commitment.* Kansas City: Sheed and Ward.

———. 1963c. "The Theology of Symbol." In *Theological Investigations.* Vol. 4. London: Darton, Longman and Todd.

———. 1972. "The Experiment with Man." In *Theological Investigations.* Vol. 9. New York: Herder and Herder.

———. 1974. "Reflections on the Unity of the Love of Neighbor and the Love of God." In *Theological Reflections Concerning Vatican Council II.* London: Darton, Longman and Todd; New York: Seabury.

———. 1977. "On the Existence of a Formal Individual Ethics." In *Meditation on Freedom and Spirit.* New York: Seabury.

———. 1978. *Foundations of the Christian Faith.* Translated by William Dych, S.J. New York: Seabury/Crossroad.

Rahner, Karl, and Herbert Vorgrimler, eds. 1965. *Theological Dictionary*. New York: Herder and Herder.

Riley, Maria, O.P., and Nancy Sylvester, I.H.M. 1991. *Trouble and Beauty: Women Encounter Catholic Social Teaching*. Washington, D.C.: Center of Concern.

Ryan, John A. 1908. *A Living Wage: Its Ethical and Economic Aspects*. New York: Macmillan.

————. 1935. *A Better Economic Order*. New York: Harper.

Sacramentum Mundi: An Encyclopedia of Theology. 1968–70. 6 vols. New York: Herder and Herder.

Schumacher, E. F. 1989. *Small Is Beautiful: Economics As if People Mattered*. New York: HarperCollins.

Sobrino, Jon. 1978. *Christology at the Crossroads*. Maryknoll, N.Y.: Orbis.

————. 1991. "Awakening from the Sleep of Inhumanity." *Christian Century* (April 3).

Sullivan, Francis A., S.J. "The Theologian's Ecclesial Vocation and the 1990 CDF Instruction." *Theological Studies* 52 (March).

Synod of Bishops' Second General Assembly. 1971. *Justitia in Mundo*. Washington: US NCCB.

Vacek, Edward, S.J. 1985. "Proportionalism: One View of the Debate." *Theological Studies* 46 (2/June): 287–314.

Villain, Jean. 1953. *L'Enseignement de Sociale l'Eglise Introduction, Capitalisme, Socialisme*. Paris: Spes.

Vorgrimler, Herbert. 1986. *Understanding Karl Rahner: An Introduction to His Life and Thought*. New York: Crossroad.

Walsh, J. P. M., S.J. 1980. "Lordship of Yahweh, Lordship of Christ." In *Above Every Name: The Lordship of Christ and Social Systems*, edited by Thomas Clarke. New York: Paulist.

Walter, James J. 1990. "The Foundation and Formulation of Norms." In *Moral Theology: Challenge for the Future,* edited by Charles Curran. New York: Paulist.

Weakland, Archbishop Rembert. 1985. "The Economic Pastoral: Draft Two." *America* 153 (21 September): 129–132.

Weaver, James, and Kenneth Jameson. 1991. *Economic Development: Competing Paradigms.* Washington, D.C.: University Press of America.

Yoder, John Howard. 1991. "Just War Tradition: Is It Credible?" *Christian Century* 108 (13 March): 295–98.

Index